ADVANCE PRAISE FOR *INNER ENTREPRENEUR*

"Jammed with difficult questions and powerful truths, this is a useful touchstone for entrepreneurs seeking to make a difference."
—Seth Godin, author of *This Is Strategy*

"A blueprint for anyone who wants the freedom that comes from building a business they love."
—Gino Wickman, author of *Traction* and *Shine*, creator of EOS®

"This book is an absolute masterpiece! It's destined to become an entrepreneurial classic."
—Bob Burg, coauthor of the international bestseller *The Go-Giver*

"This isn't just a book about profit margins—it's about creating a sustainable life through business. Grant takes you on a journey that feels personal and motivational, making entrepreneurship less daunting and more doable."
—Sam Parr, founder of Hampton and The Hustle, host of the *My First Million* podcast

"Grant Sabatier is a master entrepreneur. He has a bright mind and a nose for opportunity. He has the capacity to work hard, grow an enterprise, and then let go. His soul is on fire, on a quest for meaning and truth. You'll do well to plumb his knowledge and let his creativity and drive inform your life. It has mine."
—Vicki Robin, author of *Your Money or Your Life* and *Coming of Aging* on Substack, host of the *What Could Possibly Go Right?* podcast

"Starting a business and using it to build a life you love can be richly rewarding. But too often people wind up working for it. In these pages, Grant teaches you how to start and operate a business that works for you. A critical difference!"

—JL Collins, author of *The Simple Path to Wealth, How I Lost Money in Real Estate Before It Was Fashionable*, and *Pathfinders*

"Halfway through reading *Inner Entrepreneur* I was not only fixing my businesses, but coming up with a few new ones. Brimming with tactical details and advice, not a single word is wasted. Every aspiring or experienced entrepreneur should read this book."

—Jordan Grumet, author of *Taking Stock* and *The Purpose Code*, host of the *Earn & Invest* podcast

INNER
ENTREPRENEUR

INNER ENTREPRENEUR

A PROVEN PATH TO PROFIT AND PEACE

How to Start, Build, Buy, Scale,
and Sell Your Business

GRANT SABATIER

Avery
an imprint of Penguin Random House
New York

AVERY

an imprint of Penguin Random House LLC
1745 Broadway, New York, NY 10019
penguinrandomhouse.com

Library of Congress Cataloging-in-Publication Data has been applied for.
ISBN (hardcover) 9780593543573
ISBN (e-book) 9780593543597

Printed in the United States of America
1st Printing

Book design by Angie Boutin

The authorized representative in the EU for product safety and compliance is Penguin
Random House Ireland, Morrison Chambers, 32 Nassau Street, Dublin D02 YH68, Ireland,
https://eu-contact.penguin.ie.

To my little lady
and to anyone who has the courage
to start a business

"The amount of happiness that you have depends on the amount of freedom you have in your heart."

—THICH NHAT HANH

CONTENTS

LEVEL 4
The Empire Entrepreneur

INNER
ENTREPRENEUR

CHAPTER 1

IT'S NEVER BEEN EASIER OR MORE ESSENTIAL TO BECOME AN ENTREPRENEUR

"Opportunities multiply as they are seized."

—Sun Tzu

It's 7:00 a.m. on a quiet summer morning and my daughter is strumming my guitar on the floor. She's the spitting image of my wife, with her bright blue eyes and sweet smile, but she has my hands. I've spent the past hour with her, leisurely making coffee, feeding her breakfast, and trying to hold on to the moment as it flows across the morning. I think about how nice it is not to have to rush into an office or to a Zoom meeting.

How I don't have to answer to a boss. How I don't have to work for money and am able to choose the way I spend my time. I've experienced nothing greater than the freedom of these mornings.

When I finally look at my phone, the stock market's open, and the Dow is up almost 2 percent. I do some quick mental math; I've made over $250,000 in investment gains in the past month. The fact that I made this money without having to trade any of my time for it still blows my mind. When I log into my email, my assistant, Emily, has already spent a few hours reading and organizing it. This saves me about twenty-five hours a week. I open the revenue-tracking system for my company, MMG Media Group, and see that our websites have already made almost $10,000 in revenue today. Next year I will turn forty, and this is the seventh company I've started.

I've spent fifteen years building businesses, saving, and investing.

While stock market growth has helped me make millions of dollars in investment gains, I earned most of the money I initially invested by creating, running, and growing my businesses. In other words, none of this would have been possible if I hadn't become an entrepreneur.

I didn't get an MBA and never took a business class. I'm not a professor, business consultant, or journalist writing a book about starting and scaling a business. I'm an entrepreneur. I'm in the trenches, doing the work that needs to be done and making the decisions that need to be made to keep my businesses thriving. I'm also a bootstrapped entrepreneur—meaning I've never had any investors. I've funded all my growth through revenue, and I've focused on making my businesses profitable as quickly as possible.

The primary goal of this book is to help you do the same: to build a business that gives you more money, freedom, and peace in your life. I share everything I've learned in my fifteen years as an entrepreneur that has had the biggest impact on my entrepreneurial journey—what's made me the most money and what's brought me the most peace. There are no lofty theories in this book.

Everything I'm about to encourage you to do is something I've done or am currently doing. These strategies apply whether you're just starting to build a side hustle, working part-time as an entrepreneur, or running multiple businesses simultaneously. It's never easy to start or grow a business, but there are many things you can do to give yourself an advantage.

THIS BOOK IS CAREFULLY DESIGNED TO INCREASE YOUR CHANCES OF SUCCESS

I've designed the book to save you time by focusing on the strategies, tactics, and metrics that will increase your chances of success and reduce your risk of failure. Fair warning: you *will* fail; all entrepreneurs do. But the more you experiment and learn, the faster you'll fail and the more chances you'll have for something to work. Most people will give up or never do anything. This is your advantage. The longer you stay in the game, the more the odds shift in your favor.

Most business books and "experts" focus on one idea: how to

build a great team, increase profit, scale your marketing, sell your business, etc. But this limited view makes it impossible to understand the full scope of what's possible and what you must do to make it possible. Focusing solely on one aspect or type of business doesn't convey the many opportunities available or the many ways you can be an entrepreneur.

This book presents an *expansive view* of entrepreneurship—from coming up with an idea to selling your business, from acquiring other businesses to creating a holding company to pass down to your heirs.

By laying out all the possible paths to entrepreneurship, explaining exactly what each one requires, and providing practical information to help you make decisions, this book will help you pick the best path for you. You'll better understand the choices and trade-offs you can make on your journey. I'm confident the book will help you. But remember, I'm just a guy on the same human journey as you, and I want you to experience the same freedom, joy, and fulfillment that being an entrepreneur has given me. I'm not here to tell you what type of business you should build, what to spend your money on, or how to live your life. It's your life. Not mine.

Thankfully, you can choose what being an entrepreneur means to you.

You can also choose how you build your business and the trade-offs you're willing to make at each stage of the journey. Throughout this book, I'll encourage you to consistently examine and adapt your relationship to money so you don't get caught up in the pressure, hype, and growth-at-all-costs mentality that often drives conversations around business. This book is not about becoming a billionaire, getting rich quick, or making as much money as possible; it's about using entrepreneurship to build opportunities, resilience, and a life you love, no matter what's happening in the world.

Traditional entrepreneurship and business books focus solely on maximizing growth, profit, and efficiency, rarely acknowledging every decision's impact on your life. Any risk, complexity, or investment you take on for your business will impact your life in some way—financially, emotionally, physically, or spiritually, or some combination of all four. The question is whether the impact is positive or negative, significant or insignificant. Will it expand your life or constrict it?

While you are not your business, your business and life are inextricably linked. To run your business without acknowledging this sets you up to take unnecessary and foolish risks and limits your potential for freedom. If you give yourself over to your business, you might as well be working for someone else. You want your business to support and amplify your life, not your life to support your business.

In this book, we'll cover all of it—including how you can use your business to not only create more opportunities for you but also to help create more peace in your life. When you build a dependable business that funds your life and dreams, you can sleep better at night, be less stressed, and free up more of your mind for new things and things you love.

BUILDING A BUSINESS IS THE FASTEST PATH TO WEALTH

I'll get right to the point. W-2 jobs are the slowest path to wealth because someone else decides your salary and earning potential, and your income is taxed at the highest rates. As a W-2 employee, you have very little leverage. The average raise is 1 to 3 percent per year. You can save a percentage of your income to help grow your wealth over time, but there are limits to how much you can save in your 401(k) and other tax-advantaged investing accounts. You get a limited number of vacation days and other time off. Your job is "at will," so you can get fired anytime for any reason. You're making your boss and the owner and shareholders of your company more money, but you don't get to participate in the upside. Even if you have equity or stock in your company, most equity plans end up being worthless unless your company sells for billions of dollars—and even then, it rarely works out for anyone but the founders.

The further I get away from the traditional nine-to-five corporate world, the more inhumane the entire thing feels. I watch friends who still stress over jobs they hate, hoping to max out their annual bonus or to take home $100,000 a year. I hate that so many hardworking people get exploited, and on top of that, the vast majority of people still don't like their jobs. If you love your job and your life, you're one of the lucky ones. According to Gallup's report *State of the Global Workplace: 2023,* 77 percent of people say they are disengaged at work, 51 percent are actively looking for new jobs, and work stress is at an all-time high.

This doesn't surprise me, since most jobs are crappy jobs. Crappy jobs are jobs you don't care about. Jobs you just do for a paycheck. The jobs where you hope the day passes as quickly as possible. The jobs where you live for the weekend. Crappy jobs have consequences. They make people sad. They're easy to get, but once you've got one, you'll spend most of your time trying not to lose it. It's comfortable in life to tread water and coast. It's even easier to disengage in a large company where layers and layers of people support layers and layers of other people.

Unfortunately, increased consolidation, market instability, globalization, and other forces have made traditional nine-to-five jobs incredibly risky for the long term. As I write this, Amazon, Meta, and Google—three of the top companies with jobs viewed as extremely secure just a few years ago—have laid off a combined total of more than 75,000 employees in the past few months. Earlier this month, IBM announced it would pause hiring for roughly 7,800 jobs that executives predict could be performed by AI within the next few years. Meanwhile, the World Economic Forum estimates that approximately 25 percent of all jobs could be replaced by AI within just five years. No job is secure. Why put your future in someone else's hands?

As a business owner, you're in control and get to share in your company's profits each year. Instead of increasing your personal income, which is taxed at regular income tax rates, smart entrepreneurs focus on growing their businesses' revenue, profit, and value. As your business grows, the value of your equity ownership in the business increases, and your personal net worth grows. The best part is that you get taxed only on your equity in the future when you sell it or sell your business, so the value of your equity can grow tax-free as your business grows, until the day you sell.

You also get immense tax advantages because the U.S. tax code benefits entrepreneurs and job creators. You can grow your company's value and then reap the profits when you sell it—all at capital gains tax rates, which are lower than those of a W-2 job. The best part? There's no limit to how much money you can make. It took me five years to build Millennial Money, and selling my company increased my net worth sevenfold.

ENTREPRENEURS ARE HAPPIER BECAUSE THEY HAVE MORE CONTROL OVER THEIR TIME

Research shows that despite all the pressures inherent in running a business, entrepreneurs are less likely to suffer from burnout and more likely to report being happy than those who work for an employer. It's harder to burn out doing something you love with people you love.

The freedom and flexibility to do what you want when and how you want—even if you might be working more hours than you would at a W-2 job—means that you can derive so much more than money from starting and growing your business; you can increase your fulfillment, energy, and sense of purpose without having to look outside your day-to-day activities to find it.

There is no one-size-fits-all approach to entrepreneurship, and what works for one person may not work for you. We all have different goals, aspirations, skills, and ideas, and if you don't keep these in mind when starting your business, you may very well end up building a profitable business that depletes your soul. After all, the real goal of becoming an entrepreneur isn't just to make money; it's to give you the freedom to live your own life and become the fullest expression of a human that you can be.

ENTREPRENEURSHIP ADDS DEPTH AND RICHNESS TO YOUR LIFE

Of course, entrepreneurship has always come with risks. But as I'm writing this, it's never been easier to make money on your own terms, often with little to no start-up costs, overhead, or even needing to leave your home. We are living in the golden age of capitalism. Just imagine life fifty years ago: unless you inherited wealth or were extremely lucky, you picked a career and were stuck. Yes, you got a pension, but you had to work thirty or forty years to earn it, and in the meantime, you had no freedom and no options for how you spent a considerable part of your waking hours.

Meanwhile, thanks to remote work and technology, most full-time jobs require less time than ever, giving us more flexibility to build a business in our spare time. All you need is an internet connection, a good idea, and the will to do the work. The opportunity is huge, but not without risk. The exponential rate of change and innovation means that new opportunities rise and fall quickly, often with limited time to take advantage of them.

Influencers catapult to overnight fame, making millions, only to fall just as rapidly with an algorithm update. Even the markets that we've been able to rely on historically, like stocks and real estate, are facing more significant risk, making our reliance on a forever-growing U.S. economy and the appreciation of our homes uncertain.

Given this reality, it is now critical that everyone—even those with seemingly stable full-time jobs—take charge of building and owning their wealth by becoming entrepreneurs. The shifting trends in work and the economy have already forced us to tap into our inner entrepreneurs by becoming more creative and adaptable.

Now's the time to make the most of it.

ENTREPRENEURSHIP IS FOR EVERYONE

Most business books start with some cliché about how entrepreneurs are born, not made. Or how entrepreneurs are different. Or that they have a huge appetite for risk. Or how they are geniuses like Steve Jobs or Elon Musk—single-minded individuals with huge ambitions who took chances on untested business models, technologies, and products and became billionaires. Don't believe any of it.

You're already an entrepreneur. You are the creator of your life. You are already selling yourself and your time, but are you the one benefiting? You already have the skills of an entrepreneur; why not make the most of them?

Research shows that most entrepreneurs are just as risk averse as the rest of us. They're not once-in-a-generation visionaries; they're everyday people who want something more than a corporation or a job can promise. They're creative and passionate. They want to create value for themselves and their communities. They're normal human beings who want what we all want: to have enough to survive and to put something worthwhile out into the world.

There are many ways to become an entrepreneur, but I'd argue that the best way to start is to come up with an idea and build a business from scratch. The tactics and lessons you'll learn by starting from nothing and bootstrapping will be invaluable as you progress on the entrepreneurship path.

You can also build a business from a blueprint someone else created. I'm a big fan of this approach because you don't have to reinvent the wheel. The model has already been successful and you get to run with it. Back in the day, you'd have to go to business school or hunt down a successful entrepreneur to mentor you to learn how to build a business. Thankfully, an increasing number of successful entrepreneurs are sharing their blueprints online for free.

Take Mitchell Sorkin, who is *building in public* by going into great detail on X (formerly Twitter) about how he's growing his ATM business by acquiring smaller ATM operators, expanding into new locations, and forming more valuable partnerships with the owners of the stores in which he places his ATMs. Or Kyle Nolan, who is building his finance-tracking tool, ProjectionLab, out in the open, sharing his monthly revenue numbers online and crowdsourcing feedback on new ideas and features to improve his product. The build-in-public movement has expanded rapidly beyond just software developers to all types of entrepreneurs. You can learn how to build a business in many sectors by simply following and connecting with others ahead of you.

Another way to become an entrepreneur is to acquire and run a successful business. Right now, there's a whole movement of acquisition entrepreneurs who argue that starting a business from scratch is too risky, since most businesses fail and take too much time. They prefer to acquire companies that are already profitable and have strong cash flow. You don't need much money to acquire these businesses, but you do need to be smart, because the types of loans you typically need to buy them require you to use your personal assets as collateral.

Still, incredible deals can be found if you're willing to look. As I write this, we're in the early to middle stages of the so-called silver tsunami as baby boomer business owners on the verge of retirement are looking to sell their businesses. A savvy entrepreneur could buy one or more of these businesses, all with a proven track record of profitability.

Not convinced that entrepreneurship is right for you or worth the effort? I get it. My guess is you're worried about one or several of the following:

1. **You don't have time.** You make time for things that are important to you.

2. **You don't have the money.** You don't need any. You can start making money without spending a cent.

3. **You don't have any skills.** Yes, you do. You just need to figure out how to leverage them.

4. **You didn't go to business school.** I didn't either. This makes you see things differently.

5. **You don't have an idea.** I'll help you find one. Ideas are easy to find once you know how to look.

6. **You don't know where to find customers.** It's easy to reach customers when you have something they genuinely want.

7. **You're afraid of failing.** Everyone is. Fear means you care. You reduce fear by learning more, controlling the variables you can, and engineering more predictability into your business. Experience creates confidence.

These are mental barriers you've inherited or have been made to believe. They're the status quo. Instead of accepting something you got from somewhere else, you can learn what's in this book, try it, and then decide for yourself. You can rewire your brain and open up another path. You can start seeing opportunities you've never seen before.

Being an entrepreneur and making money are both skills you can learn.

All you need to be an entrepreneur is a product or service people want to buy or use and a business model that allows you to make money. Then, you need to make enough cash to stay in business. That's it. Thankfully, you don't need much time, money, or skills or have anything to sell to get started. You don't need a business plan or investors, and I'll argue that both restrict your freedom. You also don't need to figure everything out on your own. There are many guides, tools, technologies, and strategies you can leverage to do more with less.

SUCCESS IS A MINDSET, NOT A METRIC

This is not a book about just making money; it's about giving yourself the freedom to create a life you love. There are infinite ways to keep score in business and life, but true fulfillment, joy, happiness, gratitude, love—all the good stuff—comes from within. Having a successful business and all the money in the world matters very little if you don't love what you do or the life you've created. If you're chasing the next dollar, constantly comparing yourself to others, or stressed because you aren't as far along as you think you should be, then you are missing out on the true promise of entrepreneurship.

The happiest and most successful entrepreneurs I know measure their fulfillment with an inner scorecard. While some are motivated by money, it's never *just* about their net worth. They all have a deeper sense of purpose and love what they do. You can make money doing pretty much anything, but if you do something you love, you'll be—and *feel*—more successful in the ways that matter most. It will also be easier for you to cultivate more peace in your life, because *peace arises when you're in alignment with what you love.*

Building a business you love requires you to take the time to look within and think hard about what you really want. How do you want to spend your life? What are your deepest aspirations? How much money would it cost to realize those dreams? How can your business help you get there?

Consider these questions and keep them in mind as you start and grow your business. This will help you manage uncertainty, make better decisions, and, ultimately, build a business that anchors and expands what's possible in your life. I'm excited to be on this journey with you.

JUST BECAUSE YOU CAN DOESN'T MEAN YOU SHOULD

As you ascend the various levels of entrepreneurship and make more money, more opportunities will open up. Only some opportunities are good ones, and only some good opportunities are the right ones for you. Just because you can do something doesn't mean you should. At some point in your business life, you'll have to say no a lot more than you say yes, simply because the time you'd have to invest is no longer worth the money.

For example, I learned early in my career that I hated traveling for work unless it was to somewhere I loved or was very excited to explore. Since then, I have consistently turned down lucrative opportunities because they would require me to travel and spend time away from my family. I'm done serving clients and living out of hotels. You can't hire me for anything, no matter how much money you have. The time-money trade-off is not worth it to me.

TAKE ADVANTAGE OF THE FREEDOM
YOU ALREADY HAVE

As you become more successful in business, you will have more freedom to spend your time as you wish. But don't be afraid to take advantage of the freedom you already have. So many of us go through life doing things because we're expected to, because we're comfortable, or because we've always done things that way and don't see a different approach. Even if we aren't content living this way—even if we know the trade-offs we're making aren't worth the results—we continue as we always have because we're afraid of what might happen when we stop. We get stuck between the fear of failure and the fear of regret.

What you spend your time doing and who you spend your time with make up your life. I'm always struck by how many unhappy entrepreneurs I meet. They feel stressed, stuck, and hopeless. The reason is usually pretty clear: they are building a business they think they should build or doing things they see others doing, but they aren't building *their* business or life. Or they are trying to grow rapidly because they think that's the sign of a successful business. As a result, they hire too many people and take on overhead and expenses that reduce their cash flow and freedom. They add complexity where it's unnecessary. They're disorganized and spend their time putting out fires all day or trying to make investors happy, instead of doing work that fulfills them. They may look successful on paper, but they're miserable. If you're making lots of money but feel unfulfilled doing it, you're missing out on so much. You may be the boss, but you're still trading your limited time for money. You're still letting outside forces control your life.

Thankfully, you can always choose to do something different. Building a business you love will take time, but it's not complicated. You have to do the inner work of figuring out what you really want and need, while doing the outer work of building your business.

You can only run away from yourself for so long.

THE 4 LEVELS OF ENTREPRENEURSHIP

Throughout my journey, I have identified four levels of entrepreneurship, and this book is organized around each one. In each section, I will detail the main decisions, tasks, systems, and people you should consider at that level. I will share stories from my experience and the experiences of other entrepreneurs I have met and admired. I will provide step-by-step instructions on how to build at each level, examine the trade-offs you will face at each stage, and offer information to help you determine if those trade-offs are worth making.

Here is a brief overview of each level.

Level 1: The Experimental Entrepreneur

The best way to figure out what type of entrepreneur you want to be is to start small and experiment. The goal of this level is to find a business idea, launch it, and start generating profit as quickly as possible. This is the incubation and adaptation level, where you're trying many things, taking chances, and learning how to run a business by actually running a business. During this stage, you'll experiment with several ideas simultaneously and rapidly learn what works, what doesn't, and what you love.

You'll save money by doing everything in this phase yourself while building a foundation that will make it easier to outsource over time. You'll generate lists of ideas, analyze other businesses' products and services, set up a website, test selling strategies, manage cash flow, and more.

Experimentation will also help you build resilience. Markets, demand, technologies, and customers constantly change. The better you are at iterating and experimenting, the better equipped you'll be to adapt to the world's increasing uncertainty.

Level 2: The Solopreneur

Solopreneurs are entrepreneurs who operate alone. They have no full-time employees and keep their expenses low to maximize profit. The Solopreneur level is when your business grows from a side gig into a real, sustainable business. Here, you start generating more consistent revenue but must still trade a fair amount of your time for money.

If you keep at it, however, you can start building systems that allow you to free up your time so you can focus on bigger-picture strategy and living your life. This level is all about building sustainability: sustainable cash flow, a sustainable and growing customer base, and sustainable systems powered by processes and people so you can free up more of your time.

Level 3: The Growth Entrepreneur

You become a growth entrepreneur when you start hiring people to help you scale and are no longer trading your time for money. This level is about accelerating your growth by taking advantage of and doubling down on the systems you've put in place. It's about reinvesting money back into your business to increase sales and profit.

Growth entrepreneurship is not about growth hacking or growing at all costs. It's about learning to manage growth in a way that supports your life. You might have to say no to good opportunities to grow the way you want. It takes time to find your limits and figure out what "enough" means for you. At this level you can hire people to run most, if not all, of the day-to-day of your business. This level also unlocks deeper business and personal growth opportunities, as your business starts to expand your life by giving you more resources and time.

Level 4: The Empire Entrepreneur

Once you start making more cash than you can reasonably invest back into your business, you can start building your empire. While you might think of an empire as being massive, size does not matter here. Empire Entrepreneurship is about making the most of your money and expanding your investment holdings beyond one business to maximize your income, returns, and impact. It's also about diversification.

While many business owners in this position take extra money as a profit distribution, pay tax on it, and then invest it in another asset class like stocks as part of their portfolio, it can be more effective to keep that money in the business and invest it in different asset classes on behalf of the business or your holding company. By doing this, you can save on taxes and keep growing your net worth as an owner/shareholder within the tax-efficient structure and legal protection of a business.

You can also diversify your holdings across many asset classes such as real estate, stocks, and alternative assets, or directly in other companies, through investments, acquisition, or building a new company from scratch. The empire level is all about optimizing your time, money, effort, and joy. With the right alignment, your business or businesses will open opportunities you've never imagined.

EXPAND YOUR LIFE INTO THE SPACE AND FREEDOM YOU CREATE

Being an entrepreneur can be challenging and lonely sometimes, but it's helped me grow and expand my life in ways I never could have dreamed. Not only do I have more money than I ever thought I would and the ability to control my time, but I also have a business constantly opening new opportunities to experience life. I've built a community of hundreds of thousands of people from all over the world who derive value from what I create and from whom I'm able to learn.

And the best part is that I can choose what I want or don't want to do. As my life changes, I find myself saying no to things that I would have said yes to only a few years ago, so I can spend time with my family. But I'm also saying yes to connecting more with others—expanding my community and mind. I recently opened Clintonville Books, a brick-and-mortar bookstore—a notoriously low-margin business—in Columbus, Ohio, because I want my community to have a bookstore and I love books.

Money rarely comes first in my decision-making. Instead, I focus on: How does this benefit my family? How happy will this make us? How much impact can this have? How much fun will this be? Will this make me feel alive? That's how I make choices.

When you're stressed about money or your business, it's often all you can think about. I estimate that 80 to 90 percent of most people's thinking time is dominated by money, work, or business stress. There is often little room for anything else. Thankfully, your relationship with money will change as you make, save, and invest your money and build your business to amplify your life.

You'll start reclaiming more space in your mind. As you make more money and acquire the freedom that develops as your business grows, you'll have more time to expand into the new space you've created. You'll have more options and peace of mind. You can move toward what feels right. There is so little we can control in life, but our relationship with money is something we can control. It takes time and practice to figure out what works for you, but this is the path to a fulfilling life.

As you read this book, I hope you will free yourself to imagine the possibilities without clinging too tightly to them. I hope you take control of your life while embracing uncertainty. That you can fully embrace the beginner's mindset and let go of any beliefs that have been holding you back. That you can see how expanding your life is a process of subtraction, not addition. That you get comfortable with not knowing and recognize that everything you seek is already within you. I hope this book helps you expand your experience of freedom.

CHAPTER 2

THE 7 TRUTHS OF SUCCESSFUL ENTREPRENEURS

*"Peace isn't an experience free of challenges, free of rough and smooth,
it's an experience that's expansive enough to include all that arises
without feeling threatened."*

—Pema Chödrön

The doctor looked me in the eyes and got straight to the point: "Grant, if you keep going this way . . . I don't know how long you're going to last." I was in my early thirties, and my blood pressure was through the roof; I wasn't sleeping well, and I'd gained over fifty pounds during my pursuit of becoming a millionaire.

For five years, I pursued money like an addict. I naively thought it would solve all my problems, make me happy, and bring more peace. So I chased it at the expense of everything else. But it only magnified my problems. If you don't take the time to do the inner work to figure out what you *really* want and need, chasing more money becomes an aimless pursuit. Leaving the doctor's office that day, I was ready for a change.

Thankfully, the money I had earned to that point gave me space and time to breathe and figure out who I was and what I wanted. When I was twenty-five, I had set out to become a millionaire by age thirty so I would never have to work for money again. Only a few years into a career in corporate America, I realized that the time and life energy I was spending doing a job I hated in exchange for a steady paycheck wasn't worth it. So I set out to learn everything I could about money and started experimenting with entrepreneurship to increase my net worth.

Eventually, I cofounded a digital marketing agency and consulting firm that helped me reach my goal of becoming a millionaire by thirty. However, it came with a cost; the work was time-consuming and stressful, and I didn't care about it. Fortunately, the wake-up call at my doctor's office made me realize that I didn't have to do it anymore. I had already reached financial independence, but it was only then that I decided to take advantage of it.

As a passion project, I had started Millennial Money, a website and community where I shared my story to help others achieve financial independence. By the time I left the consulting world, the site was getting a few hundred visitors a month, but it wasn't a business. I hadn't set out to make it a business. Using the new space I had created in my life by leaving my job, I decided to lean into Millennial Money while working to regain my health.

It took me a while to fully detox from the corporate grind and stop relentlessly focusing on money. But slowly, I started opening up to the world and feeling a more profound peace settle into my life. I was calmer. My blood pressure came down without medicine. I started sleeping better. I wasn't stressed all the time. Most days, I was happy. I was growing my mind, and my life was starting to look how I wanted it to look. I was starting to flow into a life that I loved.

The following chapters will show you exactly how to start, build, and grow a business. But before we dive into the *how*, I want you to take a moment to explore the *why*—the reason you want to start a business in the first place. I often see new entrepreneurs rush from idea to idea or opportunity to opportunity without having a way to filter what's best for them. Doing this inner work up front will make it easier for you to make choices and trade-offs that move you toward a business and life you love.

Most books about business and finance assume that the reader's ultimate goal is to make more money. But a singular focus on acquiring more money limits money's potential to expand our lives. Money is not merely an object. Money is energy. How you direct this energy determines how much impact it can have on your life. Like money, energy can be either spent or invested. Are you making money doing something you love or something that makes you miserable? Do you spend it or compound it? Do you use it to create or destroy? Do you have enough, not enough? Or more than you need?

When you expend energy, you use it up and then have to expend additional energy to make more. When you invest energy, it compounds and grows exponentially. Certain activities, like working at a job you hate, waiting in traffic, attending boring events, or spending time with people you don't care about, deplete your energy. This has detrimental long-term effects on your health and happiness.

The most successful and happiest entrepreneurs can use and align this energy to enrich their lives significantly. They ride it like a wave. They understand that you can want more while simultaneously having enough. There's an effortlessness and lightness to their business that feels right. That doesn't mean it's easy. But it's challenging, fun, and deeply satisfying. Most important, it makes them feel alive.

I encourage you to think for a second: Why do you want more money? What do you intend to do with this extra energy? Is it more money that you want or something else? I call this *money masking*. It's easy to think we want more money when what we really want is more time, less stress, more peace, more companionship, more time with our families, and more options.

While doing this work, you might realize you already have what you seek. Maybe you've already won the game.

MONEY IS EASY TO CHASE— WHICH IS WHY MOST PEOPLE DO IT

It's easier to chase money than to do the deeper work of going inside to uncover what you really want, not what you've been conditioned to want. This can be tough work, but there's no path to true fulfillment that doesn't require this introspection. If you're not honest with yourself, there will always be a lack in your life.

If you can figure out what you want from your business, you can use that reason as a powerful filter for every opportunity and trade-off you face down the line. Entrepreneurship requires trade-offs, especially in the beginning. You must trade your time and energy to get the business up and running and to a place of sustainability. The question is, are these trade-offs worth it? For example, if you want to spend more time with your kids, you should build your business to help you do that. Kids are only kids for so long.

But I often see people saying they want to spend more time with their family, and then they work sixty-hour weeks for years when they don't have to. They're racked with guilt and get stuck just chasing more money. What trade-offs you're willing to make are up to you, but make sure you're building a business that aligns with and supports the type of life you want.

To help guide you, I've identified seven truths about entrepreneurship that I've uncovered in my journey or seen in the journeys of others who have built profitable businesses while staying clear on their larger priorities and principles, and cultivating peaceful lives. I will refer back to these truths throughout the book as a way for you to check in with yourself. Think of them as a lens you can look through when evaluating a business or opportunity.

TRUTH #1: FREEDOM COMES FROM LIMITS, NOT UNLIMITED CHOICES

I remember the first time my mom said I could ride my bike past the end of the street and into the woods alone. For the first seven years of my life, the edge of my block was as far as I could go, my boundary, the limits of my world, set by my parents. But on this day, without notice, the limits were lifted. Suddenly, anything and everything became possible. I was no longer being watched or monitored. Instead of my parents setting the boundaries, I was free to set my own. If I wanted to ride my bike six miles into Washington, DC, I could, but I'd set a limit on not going farther than the elementary school up the hill just beyond the woods. This was uncharted territory, and I needed to feel it out.

Over the next several months, I constructed an elaborate fort deep within those woods with my neighbor Brice. We took great pride in collecting and assembling fallen limbs so the fort was sturdy and protected from intruders. We covered it with an old tarp to keep us dry.

For the first time, we had a space to call our own. And we had infinite time until the dinner bell rang from down the hill to call us home.

This was our space of freedom.

Wanting to have complete freedom and living with it are two different things. True freedom is so immense that you need boundaries to function. You need to set up your own space of freedom. If you don't create this space, set these boundaries, and build your walls, then you default to the limits that society, class, and the world place on you. You'll get stuck inside someone else's limits if you don't set your own.

If you don't make choices, the world will choose for you.

We tend to think of freedom as having unlimited choices. Research shows that having too many choices creates stress, confusion, and dissatisfaction in our lives. This is called the paradox of choice. When we limit our choices, it's easier to make decisions, and we feel more confident in them. When you have more money, you will naturally have more choices. By creating limits for yourself based on what you truly want—and what you don't want—you'll be able to make better choices and feel more fulfilled. Remember: just because you can do something doesn't mean you should.

Choices drive your business, and the limits keep you focused. The best business owners are great at making choices quickly because they've consciously and subconsciously developed filters and frameworks for their decision-making.

As more innovations hit the market, from cryptocurrency to the rise in AI, and as more entrepreneurs try to capitalize on them, protecting your time and energy becomes increasingly necessary. You need to insulate yourself from distractions so you can focus on what's important in your life. It's true that there's never been a better time to be an entrepreneur. But if you're constantly diverting your attention to the next new opportunity, you'll follow the herd off the cliff instead of walking your own path.

With the right mindset, strategy, and skills, you can do anything, but you can't do everything. As you become successful, you will open up possibilities you never imagined. The better you become at making money, the better you will be at spotting opportunities to make money. There is freedom in this state of being, but the paradox of freedom is that it exists only within limits, because we have only a limited amount of time.

Without limits, you risk always chasing the next dollar instead of taking advantage of the freedom you already have. No matter where you are on your entrepreneurial journey, I encourage you to start setting limits today. Start with what you don't like and narrow it down from there. Paring back tends to be easier than adding on because paring back means you've tested your limits, as opposed to being too cautious.

We also tend to put up too many limits without testing them because we're scared of what could happen or who we could become. We default back into safety. This is a balance. Are you setting a limit, or scared to try something new?

TRUTH #2: TRUST WHAT YOU FEEL BEFORE WHAT YOU THINK

In the Western world, we're taught to prioritize our rational mind over our bodily emotions, effectively missing out on the most powerful force we have in our lives—our intuition. We're taught we need to come up and lead with data-based arguments for all our decisions when, in reality, our intuition likely already has the answer. Our intuition is connected to a deeper level of consciousness that is always working for us and beyond our rational comprehension. It is our pathway to the universe. The more you open this pathway through meditation, nature walks, music, mantras, prayer, or any form of pure reflection, the clearer things become.

Emotions are signals. They tell you what you need to hear and allow you to sense information that may not be practically conveyed. If you feel stressed or conflicted, there's a reason. If you feel stuck, it's because you are. If you feel you shouldn't do something, you probably shouldn't. If you feel like you *should* do something, you probably should, but you should try to back it up with what your rational mind tells you.

The entrepreneur's mind is driven by intuitive feeling and counter-intuitive thinking.

Intuition leads. Rational thinking supports.

Humans aren't machines, and when we ignore how we're feeling, we ignore the deepest part of our subconscious designed to help us make the best decisions—even if they don't make sense on paper or to anyone else. For example, when I decided to leave my first company, most people thought I was crazy for leaving money on the table. But I knew I would never be happy, no matter how successful the business was. Since then, every time I've trusted my intuition over my mind, I've made the right call.

The more you trust your intuition, the stronger it becomes. It will start to feel easier, then easy, and eventually effortless. Your intuition will help you define success for yourself and to grow at your own pace. Find the balance between something challenging, engaging, and effortless at the same time. Easy gets boring quickly. I find that I'm happiest when I'm growing—when I'm challenged—when there's a balance between the unfamiliar and the familiar.

By simply paying attention to what stirs inside you and how things make you feel, following your intuition will lead you toward a life that aligns with your most authentic self and help you thrive. Surrendering to the unknown is the path to knowing. You already know what you need.

TRUTH #3: DOUBLE DOWN ON YOUR STRENGTHS INSTEAD OF FIXING YOUR WEAKNESSES

In America, we are obsessed with self-reliance—the idea that we can do anything we want on our own as long as we put our minds to it and work hard. This is the myth of the "self-made individual" and the crux of the American Dream. Popular self-help culture makes us feel we must constantly improve ourselves to succeed. But trying to become better at things you're not naturally good at or interested in takes a tremendous amount of time and energy that could be directed at much more impactful things. Recognize your strengths and what excites you, and build a business that caters to those. I don't like managing people and am not good at it. So, instead of hiring full-time employees, I build businesses with partners who manage themselves, or I outsource any work I'm not good at to contractors.

That said, I'm a big advocate of doing things on your own when you're starting as an entrepreneur. There's an immense amount of value in teaching yourself the basics of how business works: how cash flows in and out, how you attract customers and keep them coming back, what your biggest expenses are, how to reduce your tax liability, and how to maximize the use of each dollar. But any successful entrepreneur knows you can't do everything by yourself forever if you want to scale. The bigger your business gets, the more complex it becomes. When that happens, you need to double down on your strengths and outsource for your weaknesses.

Outsourcing is more effective if you've already learned to do something yourself. While you don't need to become an expert in everything, knowing the basics makes it easier to find an expert and judge whether they're doing what you need them to do. Far too many entrepreneurs waste money hiring experts they don't know how to evaluate because they don't understand the basics of the task they're outsourcing. You can't provide oversight if you don't understand how something works.

When you have a problem, think about who you can hire instead of how to solve it yourself. One advantage of being older and further along in your career is that you can usually command a higher income than you did when you were younger. Think about ways you could spend money to buy back your time so you can focus your energy on things that bring the most rewards. If you can buy back even a few hours a week, you can turn the energy you save into massive returns over time.

Can you outsource specific household or administrative tasks? I pay a college student $20 an hour to wash our dishes and do all our laundry, saving me and my wife almost twenty hours per week. It's a no-brainer for $400. Can you hire an assistant or purchase tools or software to save time?

TRUTH #4: INCENTIVES DRIVE EVERYTHING

As I write this, I know that my business partners in MMG Media Group are working on building our company. I don't have to monitor their actions because I trust them. Why? Because I've worked with them before, we respect each other, we have complementary skill sets, and our incentives are aligned. While I'm the majority shareholder, we all own the business. While feeling valued, fitting in with a company's culture, and believing in the core mission are essential for hiring, re-taining, and keeping your team happy, incentives are arguably more important than anything else.

Incentives motivate people to work hard, add value to your company, and build your business. But your incentives need to actually incentivize. People need to want what you're offering them—whether it's a salary, more flexibility, opportunities to learn, a growth path for their career, connection, or all of the above. Everyone wants to know: "What's in it for me?" The better you understand what your employees want, the more you can use the business to meet their needs. We all want to feel valued. For some, that means more money. For others, it means more flexibility or a way to work with incredible people on cool projects.

The best way to align incentives is to personalize them to each person. While most people want more money, to be a part of a team, to feel valued, to have flexibility, and to have a clearly defined growth trajectory, the ratio for everyone is a bit different, depending on who and where they are. A young twentysomething with few commitments might be willing to invest more time in your business, require less flex-ibility, and be motivated more by money than someone in their forties with three kids and many commitments.

If one thing has made me a successful entrepreneur, it's figuring out what people want and then doing everything I can to give it to them. If you can align the incentive structure in your business with what your team wants, you'll be able to keep your team happy and you'll be able to retain great talent. It costs the average company 40 to 60 percent of an employee's first-year salary to replace them—and that's just the monetary trade-off. It doesn't account for all the lost company knowledge, experience, and potential compounding impact that team member could have had on your business over time.

The next time you negotiate, ask yourself: What's in it for them? Put yourself in their shoes and work hard to give them exactly what they want. Aligned incentives are the key to motivation, loyalty, and the foundation of a strong business.

TRUTH #5: MASTER ONE THING, THEN DIVERSIFY FOR RESILIENCE

Many entrepreneurs try to offer too many products before they've figured out what their customers want. They also try to launch too many businesses at once and don't give any idea enough focus. Or they overthink things and never get started. Successful entrepreneurs stay focused on one product and continue to make it better. Only once they succeed with one product do they start to diversify.

While writing this book, I spoke about this idea to Travis Hornsby, a fellow entrepreneur I admire and the founder of Student Loan Planner. He said something that stuck with me: "You should pick a business where you can be one of the top twenty people in the world at it." Travis founded his student-loan consulting company after helping his wife and her friends refinance their six-figure student loans. In the process, he discovered that he had a deep passion for this work. Travis has since diversified his business into insurance, loans, and other financial products. But for the first several years, he focused solely on mastering his proprietary student-loan refinancing spreadsheet and helping hundreds of clients reduce and pay off their debt. By first tapping into his passion to master his core product, Travis could learn more about what his customers needed before diversifying. This strategy helped him be successful.

Most entrepreneurs have shiny-object syndrome and are easily distracted by new ideas or opportunities. But building a business requires focusing on the one thing that you're selling and trying to be the best at it. The nice thing is that because the bar is often so low for most industries because people are just in it for the money or they get complacent, by showing up and working to continually improve your product, marketing, and customer experience, you'll be doing far more than most of your competitors. The more you put into improving your business, the more success you'll have. People and customers can tell when you care. It's that simple.

TRUTH #6: COOPERATION IS MORE POWERFUL THAN COMPETITION

Most business books argue that the only way to be a successful entrepreneur is to constantly outsmart your competition. But when you see your competition as the enemy, you enter into a zero-sum game where only one party can win. You don't succeed at business by "winning"; you succeed by building something sustainable. Most markets and opportunities are large enough for many companies to thrive.

When you cooperate with your competition instead of competing with them, you benefit from one another's skills and knowledge. This creates greater value for yourselves and your customers. You can also work together to grow the market, increasing your opportunities. Community is a valuable currency.

Since 2018, I've belonged to a group of about twenty other personal finance website owners who have helped me rapidly accelerate my learning. All these creators are my direct competitors in some way, but they each recognize that there is more than enough opportunity for all of us to succeed. We're also all competing with some huge media companies that are trying to dominate our market. Working together helps us thrive within a very competitive industry.

One benefit to this group is that many members have different skills, and almost everyone is an expert in something that someone else is not. I was invited to join because I'm good at getting exposure in traditional media and had a book deal with a major publisher. Since joining, I've learned a lot about optimizing web pages, affiliate marketing, tracking tools, managing a network of writers, and much more. When questions arise or someone is looking for advice, we actively help each other in a private message group.

Another benefit of cooperation is the camaraderie that comes from it. Entrepreneurship can get lonely, especially if you're working alone. This is even truer if you do most of your work virtually. When I first started Millennial Money, I wrote and built the website alone. As I expanded my network and began collaborating with my competitors, I built a community that kept me sane and motivated throughout even the most stressful moments. These collaborations have been instrumental to my success, and there's no way I could have accomplished so much alone.

TRUTH #7: MOMENTUM IS THE MOST POWERFUL FORCE IN BUSINESS

Business requires and generates momentum. If the momentum dies, your business will die. As its creator, you're responsible for injecting life into your business. This is why caring about what you're building is essential. You can't fake this—your customers, employees, and partners can tell if your heart is in it. Yes, your energy will fluctuate from day to day. There are times to push and build and times for rest. Successful entrepreneurs learn to manage this energy flow. If you don't, it will stagnate, your business will feel heavy, and you'll burn out.

Simple strategies like working in sprints, regular rest, exercise, general movement, eating well, and taking time with your family keep your energy in balance. When you manage your energy, your business will feel lighter. I've managed a cumbersome, stressful, life-energy-draining business (a higher-education marketing agency). I now run two light, life-energy-generating businesses that enrich my life. The most significant differences are the people I work with and the passion I have for the work we're doing.

Most new entrepreneurs I've worked with are paralyzed by choice: they're afraid of making the wrong one, so they make no choice at all. The most financially successful people on the planet are the ones who make the most choices every day. A choice could be as consequential as whether to buy another company or as small as whether to cancel a meeting to free up an hour, but all choices push energy into the world and will, when compounded, make an impact.

Choice leads to action. Action breeds momentum. Momentum produces results.

The world is always going to be full of risk and uncertainty. Unproductive people try to manage this uncertainty by trying to optimize each choice. Productive people deliberate to a point, but prioritize action. The most successful people I know make decisions quickly. They respond to emails quickly. They move quickly. Speed is an advantage. Over time, the smaller, more consistent actions they take, the more information they gather and the better they get at managing uncertainty. If something doesn't work, learn to let go and keep moving. Small failures are inevitable; don't let them turn into momentum killers.

It starts with small things. When I first decided to pursue financial independence, I had no idea how I would do it. It was such a huge goal, and I was starting from zero. I set out to become a millionaire, but I didn't map out a plan because I didn't have the necessary knowledge. Instead, I took small actions every day that would, at best, bring me a step closer to reaching my goal and, at worst, teach me something valuable.

Eventually, these small actions compounded into noticeable results and gave me the information I needed to make better decisions. Because the world is changing rapidly and time is valuable, the less time you spend contemplating a decision and the more decisions you make, the closer you will get toward what you want.

Making decisions trains your intuition to make decisions for you. Before long, you can start making decisions almost unconsciously. Next time you feel stuck or like you're not seeing the results you want, ask yourself these questions:

- What am I holding on to that I should be letting go of?
- Which action brings me closer to what I want to accomplish?
- What choices can I make *today* that will lead me closer to my goal?
- What actions have I been putting off?
- What stops me from making choices and how can I remove those barriers?
- What do I value? What action is in line with those values?

- How much information do I need to make a decision that is good enough?
- What is the opportunity cost of acting versus *not* acting?

Remember, time is scarce, and uncertainty is inevitable. Any action involves risk, but inaction leads to stagnation, and you'll never get ahead if you stay in the same place. Practice taking action and being open to the results. See how it makes you feel. The more momentum you build up, the more it carries you.

LEVEL 1
EXPERIMENTAL ENTREPRENEUR

Entrepreneurs never stop experimenting, but everything is an experiment when you're first starting. There's no escaping this—it's a phase every successful entrepreneur goes through, so you need to be ready to act, assess, and keep going. Most businesses fail, so don't expect your first idea or attempt to be the one that makes you a millionaire. Expect the process to be messy and long. If you remain open, curious, and put in the work, I promise that you'll get where you want to go.

In the next four chapters, I'll show you how to use this time to figure out what you need to create a business that empowers the life you want to live. We'll explore the different types of businesses you can start, how to spot market opportunities and assess your competitive advantage, and how to price your offerings to make the most money.

Experimentation helps you build resilience. The better you are at iterating and experimenting, the better equipped you'll be to adapt when, inevitably, challenges arise or forces outside your control compel you to change. To save money early on, you will be spending more time than money to get things done. But by learning how to do as many things as possible on your own, you'll be more knowledgeable when it comes time to outsource the things you don't want to or aren't great at. Experimenting with limited resources trains your mind to get creative and think differently.

This stage is not just about experimenting with ideas to make money. This is also about experimenting with your life. Throughout this level, you should ask yourself what kind of business owner you want to be. What trade-offs are you willing to make to save time or earn money? What do you want to spend your limited time on earth doing? What brings you energy and what drains it? The better you get at answering these questions, the easier it will become to make the decisions that will help you build a business you love.

CHAPTER 3

ALIGN YOUR PASSIONS AND SKILLS WITH A MISSION TO FIND THE PERFECT IDEA

"If you're not passionate enough from the start, you'll never stick it out."
—Steve Jobs

This was it. The coffee made me more tired and my flight home to Chicago was delayed three hours. I wasn't just tired. I was dead, numb, and catatonic. I'd spent the past three weeks working on client deliverables, developing new business pitches, and traveling to present an end-of-year performance review. I was over it.

It was November 2015. Earlier that year, I had reached my goal of becoming a millionaire by thirty, thanks in no small part to my job as a partner at a consulting firm where I led the digital marketing campaigns for some of the top MBA programs in the world. I had joined four years prior, and using the skills I had acquired earlier in my career, I was now generating a substantial amount of the firm's revenue.

And yet, I knew this wasn't what I wanted to spend the rest of my life doing. I was proud of my accomplishments, but I hated the day-to-day routine. I hated the travel. I hated managing a team with an unnecessarily heightened level of drama for a group of twenty- and thirtysomethings. I hated telling clients the same things week after week. While I could smile and deliver great results for my clients, I wasn't passionate about growing MBA programs. I had all the money I needed. Now I needed something more.

Sure, I could quit. The whole point of reaching financial independence was so I wouldn't have to work anymore if I didn't want to. But ever since I'd started my financial independence journey, I had become so excited about all the opportunities to create businesses and build wealth that I couldn't stop. Just because I didn't *have* to work doesn't mean I didn't *want* to work. Crappy jobs suck joy and energy from your life, but worthwhile work provides meaning and creates energy. Plus, I was still only thirty. I wanted to create something great and have an impact.

Which is why, on that miserable winter night in Chicago, when most people would have been trying to squeeze in a nap or zoning out in front of their phones, I was typing away on a blog post about how to diversify your income streams for my new website, Millennial Money.

I didn't know it then, but this website—which I started as a passion project and would sell in 2020 and reacquire in 2022—would become my most successful business venture. Not only has it earned way more money than the marketing agency ever did, but it has also helped millions of people worldwide and unlocked experiences I could have never imagined in my wildest dreams.

From my marketing career, I already knew how to design and build websites, write engaging content, and optimize websites for Google search. But unlike the higher-education business, Millennial Money allowed me to channel my passion for personal finance and investing into my work. The combination of these two elements— skills and passion—compounded to create something that brought immense satisfaction and joy to my life while simultaneously providing inspiration and information to others on their own quests for financial independence.

Millennial Money was the perfect business for me, but it was possible only because of my years of experimentation and trial and error before I wrote my first blog post. Even before I set out to become a millionaire, I started acquiring the skills and discovering the passions I would later use to create Millennial Money. While in the throes of my entrepreneurial journey, I experimented with several other business ideas, all of which taught me valuable lessons about making money. Along the way, I also learned invaluable lessons about myself and my limits that would allow me to grow Millennial Money in the way that best suited me—even as everyone around me was doing something different.

THE PERFECT BUSINESS FORMULA

You can start a business selling anything, but for a business to be successful *and* fulfilling, you need to find an opportunity, dedicate enough time to work on it, leverage your existing skills, and do something you're passionate about.

Then, if you really want to get the most out of your business, amplify it with a mission or purpose bigger than yourself.

**The Perfect Business =
(Time + Skills + Passion+ Market Opportunity) x Mission**

Anyone can start a business with some amount of time, money, skills, and a market opportunity. If you can solve someone's problem, make their life easier, make them happier, make them more money, or entertain them, and you're willing to put in the time, you'll be able to make money. Business isn't some abstract thing. It's a skill you can learn, and there are an infinite number of business ideas available to you right now.

When I first started writing online, there was a lot I didn't know about creating a content business. When I got stuck, I'd google an answer or watch a how-to video on YouTube to figure it out. You can fill any necessary skills gaps if you have the time to learn or the money to outsource. It doesn't take a lot to launch something and start generating revenue.

But this book is about something more than starting a random business to make money. This is a book about using entrepreneurship to expand your life. If I had wanted to make a lot of money relatively quickly, I could have continued scaling my consulting firm and tried to sell it once it got big enough. I had the resources and there was plenty of market opportunity.

Unfortunately, despite the opportunity, it wasn't big enough for me. Consulting businesses are typically valued at only one to two times their annual revenue because they rely so much on their owners and a select group of clients. It also didn't fulfill me. I was going through the motions. It was a good business, but it wasn't a business I loved. I was making money, but wasn't getting the most joy from my time.

Life is too short to not do something you love.

TIME IS YOUR MOST VALUABLE RESOURCE

You don't need any money to start a business. Yes, certain types of businesses, especially brick-and-mortar ones and those that sell physical goods, require some investment up front. But plenty of businesses allow you to start earning money without first spending any money. Think of services like babysitting, tutoring, or consulting. If a customer is willing to pay you for these services or skills, you can start earning cash immediately. If you're running an online business, you may need to shell out some money up front to create a website, but the barrier to entry is low and it's often no more than a couple hundred dollars.

The main resource every entrepreneur needs is time. If you're unwilling to invest enough time in your idea, it will remain just an idea. If you have the capital, you could hire people to do most of the work for you, but you will still have to manage the operations, oversee them, and ensure everything is working—otherwise, it's not your business.

We're all pressed for time, and some of us are busier than others. But if you can set aside just five hours of productive time each week to work on your idea, you can and will make progress—especially if you know what to focus on and keep building momentum. When you're really into your idea, you'll find the time, because it becomes a priority and you're willing to make the trade-off. Instead of watching Netflix or scrolling on your phone, you're building your future.

Having a child has decreased my available time but increased my productivity. I'm naturally more focused because I know I have less available time. Getting older has also reduced my available time, since I don't have as much energy as I did in my twenties and can't work until 2:00 a.m. every night. The constraint of less time makes it easier for me to focus, so I'm actually more productive.

Look over your calendar from the past few months to see how you use your time and when you can realistically work on your business. Are you a morning person or an evening person? When do you focus best or have the most energy? Do you have any time on the weekends? What nights are you free to work on your business? When I was starting, I worked on Saturday mornings (when I wasn't distracted by my day job) and two mornings and nights each week.

Don't wait for "the right time" or to "be motivated." Life gets messy, but you need to keep moving. Remember Truth #7: Momentum is the most powerful force in business. Many companies run out of oxygen because the business owner loses momentum. As an entrepreneur, especially in the early stages, it's essential to cultivate this energy and keep the momentum going. Once you start building and feeding this momentum, you can feel it. There's a lightness and effortlessness to it. It just feels right—like you're doing what you were meant to do.

If you don't see any obvious blocks of available time, consider creative ways to reclaim your time. One way is to buy it back. As your business grows, you'll be able to grow it by paying other people to do certain work for you, but you can start doing this in smaller ways now. For example, outsource chores or tasks you don't enjoy. Yes, these things cost money, and if you're working your way to financial independence, you want to keep expenses low. However, the value you can create by spending a little money to save time can potentially make up tenfold for the money you spend.

One of the best investments I made as an Experimental Entrepreneur was hiring a bookkeeper to set up and optimize my QuickBooks account. This allowed me easily to see where I was making and spending money. I had learned how to set up and manage QuickBooks on my own when I started one of my earlier businesses, but it took a lot of my time and I knew I was probably making mistakes. I was right. Later on, when I started my website development agency, I spent about $300 a month hiring someone else, which saved an incredible amount of time. A more efficient QuickBooks system helped me make more money and optimize my taxes. I also learned a lot about accounting by watching how someone with experience managed my books.

Once you start being strategic, you'll be surprised by how much time you can save. Increasingly, I see hourly employees who slowly reduce their full-time-job commitment from five to four days a week to dedicate more time to their side business. If you're a salaried employee, brainstorm ways to automate or systematize parts of your job so you can do more in less time. Many jobs are now remote, but even if you still have to go into an office, you probably don't need to dedicate the full forty hours you sit at your desk to do your job. Your new business idea is the perfect motivation to complete your work faster.

If it doesn't jeopardize or compete with your full-time job, try to find all the time you can to work on a side business. Just be smart about it. The time will add up and you need enough time to experiment. If you can't dedicate a few hours of productive time to the project each week, you need to rethink the idea. When you enjoy doing something, you spend time doing it. If you're not consistently carving out time, that's a sign you're not invested and need to find something else you're more passionate about.

WHAT SKILLS DO YOU HAVE (OR CAN YOU DEVELOP)?

When first starting, it's essential to do something you have the skills to do. Yes, you can always acquire new skills, and the more you grow your business, the more skills you will acquire naturally. However, the point of the experimental entrepreneur phase is to start making money so you can iterate and learn quickly. It's a lot easier to do this when you can capitalize on something you already know how to do.

The first company I got excited about starting was an app I tried building in late 2010 and early 2011 called digthevibe. The idea was to create a way for users to search for bars and restaurants that matched the vibe they were looking for. It could tell you how packed a bar was or if people were having a good time there by asking people at the location what the vibe was like. It was a big idea and I was passionate about it at the time.

I was still early in my financial independence journey, but had already started saving 80 percent of my income. So, I spent $5,000 of my savings to build the app while trying to learn everything I could about the process. Unfortunately, the technology barrier was too great. I lacked the tech skills to get it to function as needed, and because I had limited resources, I couldn't afford all the development work required to make it work. I probably could have raised the money from outside investors, but I didn't want to be accountable to any third parties, especially early in my entrepreneurial career.

I tried to make digthevibe happen for about eighteen months on the side. I worked hard on it, but it gradually lost momentum and my interest. Thankfully, it wasn't the only business I was pursuing, and my marketing agency business was starting to grow. It was easy to turn my full attention to the other business. If you experiment with a few different business ideas simultaneously, you can pivot to the one you most enjoy, which works best.

When digthevibe failed, I realized I needed to start smaller and honor Truth #3: Double down on your strengths instead of fixing your weaknesses. I needed to build on what I was already good at (building websites and attracting customers through digital marketing campaigns). This experimentation and the success of the marketing agency would eventually allow me to combine my skills and passions into one successful business.

WHAT'S YOUR PASSION?

One of the biggest reasons businesses fail is that owners aren't passionate about their businesses. They try to build a business they saw someone succeed with, or they try to get rich by jumping on a trend they don't understand or care about. Entrepreneurship is about building *your* life, not trying to copy someone else's.

What works for someone else may not work for you—even if it is a great idea. And while you don't need to know every single thing about your chosen industry or business to get started, if you try to enter an area where you're entirely out of your depth, you'll spend so long getting up to speed that you'll either miss out on the opportunity, get frustrated and give up, or fail.

There's a lively debate among entrepreneurs about whether you should pick a profitable idea to test or whether you should pick something you're passionate about. I've made a lot of money doing both. For me and for the entrepreneurs I know who are happiest, we are always more fulfilled working on something we're passionate about. Not only does doing so make it easier to spot opportunities, since you know the market, but it's also a lot more fun and energizing to do work you love.

A big part of using a business to build a life you love is building a business you love.

I didn't find my passion until I was thirty. If you don't have a passion or don't feel compelled to build a business around your passion right now, no worries. The most important thing is to start a business and start experimenting. This is the only way you can learn how to build a business and do enough experimenting to move you toward a business you love.

WHAT'S YOUR MISSION?

While it's not essential, embedding your venture with a mission or sense of larger purpose can help compound the effort you put in so it can have an even greater impact on your life. In the beginning, you might not know what your mission is. Or you may have a mission but don't yet know how to work toward it as an entrepreneur. That's okay. Trust what you feel and all will become clear.

When I first started writing for Millennial Money, I wanted to show people everything I had learned about creating wealth because it had helped me and I thought it would help others. My mission is simple: to help people save and invest money for more freedom. All my work maps back to that.

Unlike my passion, which was more about personal fulfillment and the satisfaction I got from writing about money, this mission extends far beyond me. It also motivates me to keep doing what I do every day. It's bigger than my business. This mission and my work connect me to people all over the world. It also adds a level of deep fulfillment and purpose to my life. I can feel the love and energy I put into my work coming back to me magnified through every reader's email and conversation.

Having a mission also makes it easier to make decisions because I can filter every opportunity through it. It's a limit I set in my life. I always think, "How does this opportunity support the mission?" If it doesn't, then I don't do it. I get invited to speak regularly, which I don't like to do, but if it supports the mission and is for a university, a nonprofit, or a place where I know my message is needed, then I'm much more likely to say yes.

Ashley Hamilton, a single mom who was making $20,000 a year as a waitress, started investing her tax refunds in real estate on the side with the mission to offer affordable, high-quality rentals to low-income families in Detroit, Michigan. Ashley's grown it into a multimillion-dollar real estate business that does just that. Having such a defined mission makes it easier for her to make decisions that grow her business to have the biggest impact.

There's nothing wrong with building a business to make money for yourself and your family, but when your business is built to make a difference in people's lives outside your immediate circle, it will bring you more fulfillment. Humans are hardwired to give to and help others, so when we do, it unlocks a level of joy we can't otherwise access. I've found the popular adage "The more you give, the more you get" to be true. The universe rewards you for helping others in profound and immeasurable ways.

Your mission doesn't have to be huge or change the world. It can be as simple as building a company that improves your employees' lives and your community. Or maybe you have a bigger mission to change millions of lives. There is no mission too big or too small—the important thing is that it's bigger than you, and the joy of helping others will add a richness to your life that you can't get on your own. In a world where so many are hurting and need help, you have a real opportunity as an entrepreneur to have an impact through your business.

Exercise: Finding Overlap

The following exercise provides a simple way to align your passions and skills to determine what type of business you should build. I know this works because I wrote about it in my first book and thousands of people have told me they used it to find a business they were passionate about.

Get a piece of paper and fold it in half. On the left, write *passions* at the top; on the right, write *skills* at the top. You can also do this on your phone or a computer; just ensure you've created two lists. Under *passions*, write down everything you love to do, which could also include things you do for work. For me, it's playing guitar, writing, investing, collecting books, riding my bike, kayaking, caving, hiking, traveling, collecting art, and meditation. Put down everything you can think of, even if you think there's no way you could make money doing it.

Next, list all your skills in the *skills* column. List both "hard" skills that require specific training or accreditation (e.g., back-end web development, copywriting, SEO optimization, graphic design, electrical repair, etc.) and "soft" skills or talents (e.g., public speaking, mediation, negotiation, etc.).

PASSIONS	SKILLS

Need help? Ask friends, family members, and coworkers what you're good at. Consider the feedback you've received in job assessments or other performance reviews. What do people constantly ask you to help them with? What validation have you received for your work? Don't limit yourself to things you've used to make money in the past. You never know where a good idea can come from.

For example, I will use a recent chat with my friend Nick. Nick loves golf, and at the age of thirty-nine, he's interested in experimenting with entrepreneurship. He has a full-time job that he likes, but he's looking to diversify his income by doing something he enjoys. He needed an idea. Here's what Nick's list looks like:

PASSIONS	SKILLS
Golf	Excel
Traveling	Strong Writer
Hiking	Project Management
Basketball	Conflict Resolution
Thai Food	Teaching Others
Weight Lifting	Physically Strong
Gardening	Optimistic

After a round of golf in Palm Springs, where he demolished me by twenty strokes, Nick shared with me that he would like to teach others how to play golf. But Nick isn't a certified golf professional or interested in getting certified. While this limits who he can teach, we both concluded that Nick should work with seniors who used to play golf but wanted to get back into the game to socialize, stay mentally engaged, and stay flexible and in shape. Nick lives in Seattle, where many aging baby boomers also have money to spend.

We quickly picked a business idea, a growing market to target, and a sales pitch. While Nick doesn't want to trade his time for money as a golf instructor, he will start charging hourly and get a few seniors on board to test his idea and refine his offering. Over time, he's optimistic this could turn into a business where he hires other people to train clients in addition to doing it himself and diversify the business into events, a membership, and more.

Look for overlaps between the left and right sides. Are any of your passions also one of your skills or strengths? For me, that's writing. I love writing and think I'm good at it. That's why I started a media company. If you find any clear overlaps, that's very likely something you should be doing or building into your business. Don't worry if it's not that clear yet.

Here are some other questions that can be helpful in finding an idea:

1. What is something that you're great at?

2. What do you know a lot about?

3. How do you spend your free time?

4. What do you love today that you know you'll still love in five years?

5. What is a challenge you've overcome in life?

6. What do other people ask you for help with?

7. What problems or pain points do you encounter daily or at work?

8. What skills or expertise do you have that others might find valuable?

9. Are there any new emerging trends or technologies that you know more about than most people?

10. What products or services do you wish existed but can't find in the market?

11. What industries are you passionate about, and how can you innovate within them?

12. What common complaints or feedback do you hear from friends, family, or colleagues?

13. How can you improve or simplify existing products or services?

14. What do you want to learn that could be turned into a business?

15. Are there underserved markets or customer segments that need attention?

16. What changes in regulations or laws could create new business opportunities?

17. What existing networks do you already have access to?

18. What resources do you have access to that others might not?

19. What gaps do you see in your local community or region that you could fill?

20. How can you combine existing ideas or concepts in a new and innovative way?

Another benefit of experimenting is testing how monetizing your passion or hobbies feels. Not all hobbies or passions need to be or should be monetized. But they are great places to experiment with finding a business you love.

Maybe one of your strengths is that you're incredibly detail-oriented, good at Excel, and passionate about social media. You could be like Kat Norton, aka Miss Excel, and leverage social media and YouTube to sell courses that teach others how to use Excel effectively. Kat's passion for Excel and organizing information inspired her to get certified by Microsoft to train others in how to use Excel. She's so good at it that Microsoft paid her to do workshops. She saw an opportunity to scale this training through her social media and YouTube channels, using entertaining dances and humor to help young professionals learn how to use Excel in their jobs.

Maybe you're a great team leader, busy climbing the corporate ladder, but you're really into fitness. You can be like Tanvi Shah, the British-Indian former professional athlete who showcased her experience working as an accounting consultant at a Big Four accounting firm on LinkedIn, Instagram, and TikTok to build an audience, and then left accounting to pursue her passion for increasing representation of South Asian women in sports. She used her experience and skills to build a following she could leverage for her passion. She then ditched the corporate grind to build her own business and now regularly appears in ad campaigns with large global brands like Samsung.

Maybe you're passionate about helping small-business owners, love using social media, and have a specialized degree. You can be like Eric Pacifici, a mergers and acquisitions attorney who left his large, reputable law firm to build his shop entirely through referrals he received through his X network. His company, SMB Law Group, is the first social-media-driven law firm. He saw an opportunity to distance himself from the old-school Big Law grind-at-all-cost culture to build a fully remote, different type of law firm that helps small-business owners and entrepreneurs buy and sell businesses.

Just as important as the things you like to do, consider things you *don't want* to do. Add this to the back side of the paper. You're trying to design a business that supports your life—not vice versa. If you aren't clear on what you do and don't want, you can quickly build a business you hate.

Remember Truth #1: Freedom comes from limits, not unlimited choices. These are the trade-offs you're willing to make—and not make. While these trade-offs will inevitably change as you change, start thinking about and setting the limits of your business before you even start it. Write these down. Revisit them often. Choosing not to do the things you don't like to do will inevitably get you to where you want to go faster than trying to do everything.

For example, I didn't want to travel all the time or deal with clients to make money, so I focused on building an online business where I didn't have to do either unless I wanted to. I don't have to travel to clients, but I like traveling to a few conferences each year, especially if they're in cities I love visiting. I also don't like managing people, which limits the types and scale of businesses I can launch. I don't like dealing with contracts, so I have a good business attorney. I also don't like focusing on one project at a time, since I'm inspired when I'm building multiple things at once. So, instead of having one company that sells one product, I'm much more an Empire Entrepreneur (which I'll dive deeper into in Level IV).

SOLVE A PROBLEM TO MAKE MONEY FROM YOUR IDEA

Businesses don't make money by selling a product or a service; they make money by selling a solution to a problem.

People don't want to hear about your product or service, how it works, or why it's the best. They want you to identify their problem, explain why other products haven't sufficiently solved it, and show them why your product can finally solve it. You need to make a clear promise that you can deliver on.

The product promise equation is simple:

Promise =
What (is the problem?) + Why (will this help you?) + How (will you do it?)

Here's how it looks using Travis Hornsby at Student Loan Planner as an example:

> **What (The Problem):** How can individuals reduce student-loan debt?

Next, consider the *benefit* the customer will derive from using your product. What are you promising that the customer will gain from doing business with you?

> **Why (The Benefits):** The tool will help you save money on—and reduce the stress associated with—your loans.

Next, how are you going to deliver on this promise? What is your product or service offering? This is why whatever you are selling needs to actually provide value.

> **How (The Offer):** A custom student-loan payment plan that details how you should pay your student loans and connections to private lenders who can help you refinance your debt at a lower rate. We guarantee it will save you more money than our fee. If it doesn't, we'll refund your fee.

Let's dive into how to deliver your solution through a product, a service, or a productized service. There are pros and cons to each.

PRODUCT BUSINESS

A product is an object someone can buy, like a dog leash, digital book, or an apple pie. The biggest pro of a product business is that they are relatively easy to scale. Once you have a product that people want to buy, you can sell as many of them as you want without having to design and market a new edition every time.

The biggest con of a product business is that you typically must create a product before you know how well it will sell. And if you're selling a physical good, you need to spend money up front to produce and store it. I like digital goods, e-books, online courses, printables, or other things people can download. Once you invest the resources to produce the initial digital product, you can sell as many as the market will buy without spending additional time or money. You also don't need to spend resources warehousing or shipping any physical products, since everything lives online.

DIGITAL PRODUCTS: EASY TO TEST AND SCALE, BUT MARKET IS COMPETITIVE

Digital products include software, digital downloads, e-books, online courses, premium podcasts, paid membership communities, marketplaces, and more. One of the primary reasons digital products are a great place for entrepreneurs to start experimenting is that they don't require much money or time to create, you can easily update them, and you can start selling them right away. They offer infinite scalability and flexibility.

Unlike physical products, which require manufacturing, shipping, and storage, digital products can be instantly accessed and downloaded with just a few clicks. Back in the day, it was easy for me to sell my side-hustle e-book for $9.99 and then use the e-book to sell my side-hustle starter course for $49 and membership to my side-hustle community for $49 a month, all from my email list. Then, I was able to sell $500-per-hour coaching calls, followed by a $397 course. But it all started by giving away a ton of value for free and selling small products first.

While selling digital products has become more challenging over the past few years due to increased competition and more discerning consumers, it's the easiest and best place for a digital entrepreneur to start if you have a great niche audience, product, and unique perspective.

Cody Berman and Julie Berlinger are great examples of entrepreneurs capitalizing on the digital goods market. Through their respective Etsy stores, each sells printables (digital files that people pay to download) that customers can buy, download, and use for their creative purposes. Cody's store sells seasonal printables (like Halloween party invites, valentine love coupons, and letters to Santa). In contrast, Julie's store, the Swag Elephant, sells bachelorette party game templates, themed gift-card holders, and goal planners, among many other things.

Each item takes a few hours to design and upload, but can then be sold an infinite number of times with little to no effort on Cody's and Julie's part. This is passive income at its finest. Based on their success with printables, Cody and Julie cofounded Gold City Ventures, another digital products business offering courses, and a membership community to help other would-be entrepreneurs start their printable businesses from scratch. The duo earns more than $2 million a year in revenue between the three businesses.

Not a designer? That's fine. If you have a specialized skill or have developed a template you use in your own life, you might be able to make money—even a lot of money—selling a version of it online. I made more than $30,000 selling the Excel template I used to track my net worth on Millennial Money.

Not sure what kind of digital products to sell? Here are seven tips to come up with and optimize your ideas:

1. Start Small to Test the Market

One of the things I like about printables and e-books is that you can create them quickly to test market demand. If you can get your audience to buy something for $9.99 or $19.99 on a particular topic, there might be an opportunity to sell a higher-priced course or create a membership community. It's challenging to go from selling nothing at a lower price point and then trying to sell a $197 course. When you start small, it allows you to test new product ideas quickly, iterate quickly, and start generating sales. Then, you can use this momentum to ladder up to more expensive digital products, expand your reach, and improve your products.

2. Sell What You Know

You can create a digital product about anything, but the more you know about the topic and niche, the easier it will be for you to find an idea. If you have a certain professional background, research the most successful digital products in that niche with over 1,000 sales, the most successful courses being sold in your niche, and who's running the most successful Facebook groups or membership communities. If there are other popular products, that is a good indicator that the niche could be profitable.

For example, in 2019, Rob Phelan, a high school teacher, started selling printables on TeachersPayTeachers.com, an online marketplace where educators can create worksheets and other classroom resources for other teachers. Rob got the idea after starting his quest to reach financial independence and realizing he could offer educators resources on how to teach personal finance in their classrooms. As of this writing, Rob has created about ninety printables that generate roughly $1,300 per month in near-passive income for him and his family. For Rob, who still works full-time as a teacher, this is very much just a side hustle, but he's met other teacher-entrepreneurs on the platform who have been able to earn six figures and turn printables into a full-time business.

3. See What Buyers Are Searching For on Each Marketplace

One of the best ways to make sure there's demand for your product is to use data. Websites and software are available to analyze search data and see what's popular and trending. For example, you might notice that the phrase "water intake tracker" or "editable 1st birthday party invitation" is getting a lot of monthly searches. Another lesser-known trick to finding in-demand products is to start typing into the search bar on Etsy, Google, Pinterest, etc., and seeing what auto-completes. This will show you exactly what the most popular searches are on those platforms. It takes some time to understand search data, but it's one of the most helpful skills for selling digital products. We'll dive deeper into search data later in the book.

4. Sell What You Want to Buy

Is there something you really want to know or learn? Learn it and then build your own digital product for it. Take other digital courses and then create your own based on what you've learned, sharing your unique perspective. Would a workout tracker help you toward your fitness goals? Do you need to send out invitations for your friend's birthday party coming up? Could you use a spreadsheet to help track income and expenses for your side business? After you create the digital product for yourself, listing it on a marketplace like Etsy is not much extra work.

5. Customers Want Something Unique

The digital product market is competitive, so you need to offer something unique to stand out. You don't need to reinvent the wheel, but you need to do something different. This is why leaning into your authentic story and experience is so important. For example, there are an infinite number of "How to Start Investing" courses, e-books, and printables, but the most successful creators are able to put their own spin on it that resonates with consumers. Some use humor or have a unique perspective because of their race, gender, or where they live. Lean into what makes you unique so you can stand out from the crowd.

6. Understand Seasonality

Customers follow a seasonal schedule; they buy certain products at certain times of the year. For example, customers look for personal finance and fitness advice in January, gardening advice in the spring, and Advent calendars in late November. Research seasonality trends for your product ideas and make sure you start building your product months in advance of when everyone is searching for a product like yours.

7. Keep Experimenting

You might need to create and try out a number of different digital products before you create a successful product. Expect this going in and understand it's just part of the process. It took me many tries before I had a hit, but I kept searching for the perfect product for my audience. It will take some time, but the more you test, the more you learn and the better your products will become. Selling digital products is not a get-rich-quick scheme, but it can be a legitimate source of passive income and is a great place to start experimenting with entrepreneurship.

PHYSICAL PRODUCTS: HIGHER UP-FRONT INVESTMENT, BUT OPPORTUNITIES ABOUND

Selling physical products online is a big opportunity for anyone willing to put in the time to create a good product and build a brand. According to eMarketer and *Business Insider*, U.S. retail e-commerce sales will reach $1.720 trillion by 2027, growing 10 percent per year from 2024 to 2027 and hitting a milestone of more than 20 percent of overall retail sales.

One of the easiest and most popular ways to start selling physical goods online is through Amazon's Fulfillment by Amazon (FBA) program. While competitive, FBA gives you access to Amazon's massive platform, so you don't have to build one and find your audience on your own. Logan Leckie currently sells several successful products on Amazon. As of this writing, his products generate more than $5,000 a month in profit, which covers Logan's living expenses and allows him to spend his time pursuing bigger entrepreneurial ventures.

After overspending on one night out with his friends, Logan came up with his first product idea: the secret flask. He wondered if there was a simple way to sneak his alcohol into bars and events to save money. A quick search on Amazon revealed a few sellers selling flasks concealed inside umbrellas and sunscreen bottles, but there weren't many sellers. Using Helium 10 (a tool that analyzes Amazon product sales), he saw how many were being sold by each seller. There was low competition but high sales volume, so he launched a competitor product. He regularly looks for products that generate at least $2,000 a month in revenue and have fewer than six sellers on Amazon.

Once he's identified a potential product based on these criteria, he digs deeper to look at who the sellers are, how strong a brand they have, and ways he could outcompete them. There can be a real opportunity for U.S. sellers because so many product sellers are based in China and aren't great at building attractive brands for the U.S. They have weird names, poor logos, incorrect grammar, and other indicators of weak branding in their listings. But they do have low prices because they have access to low-cost manufacturers. This is why I almost always recommend trying to build a high-end brand with high-quality products and design. Even though your manufacturing costs will be higher, you can charge more and make more money. Competing on price alone isn't a sustainable strategy.

After analyzing his competitors, Logan saw how much demand there was for the flasks and what he could do differently. Logan took advantage of one of the two core product strategies you can pursue when launching an Amazon FBA or any physical product. He found an unsaturated market and emulated an existing product, making small improvements to the brand and features.

There was high demand, low competition, and clear marketing and branding angles for Logan to play. However, because the product was not unique or novel, Logan could easily find a manufacturer on Alibaba and place a low-cost order. While many people think of Alibaba as an Amazon competitor, you can use it to find manufacturers for pretty much anything.

If a manufacturer already produces a product, it's easy for them to make another version of it, and therefore they usually require a relatively low minimum-order quantity. Logan ordered a few samples of the umbrella flask through Alibaba. After testing the prototype and reading negative reviews of competitor products on Amazon, he requested a few improvements from the manufacturer.

For example, he read many competitor reviews about the flasks leaking and had a similar experience with his own initial product. So he asked the manufacturer to make a tighter seal and make it leakproof. He also noticed how cleaning the flask after use was difficult because the nozzle was too small (something others noted in competitor reviews), so he requested a larger nozzle and evaluated including a small cleaning brush with each flask.

Once the product was ready, he listed it and had it shipped directly from the manufacturer to Amazon to sell. Then he googled "how to get alcohol into a music festival," "how to hide alcohol," and many other keywords. He then contacted the website owners who ranked in the first five results for each query, offering them money to include a link to his product. This worked incredibly well, and these unique links to his Amazon product pages skyrocketed his product into the top Amazon search results. Amazon prioritizes products with high conversion rates, as these generate revenue for the platform. Additionally, products that draw customers from external websites and convert them into sales are ranked even higher, capitalizing on their potential to enhance Amazon's customer base.

Another approach to creating a physical product is to create something entirely new. This is what Logan did with his Prismic Knives business. After visiting a small market in London, he noticed all the knives for sale were black and dull. He wondered if there was an opportunity to create colorful knives with more personality. After searching on Amazon, he found no knives he thought looked cool or colorful enough, so he decided to test and create a new product.

Logan was confident that there were more people out in the world like him who would be interested in having colorful knives in their kitchen, so he started designing the product himself and contacting manufacturers to make a prototype. To manufacture a unique product like this takes longer and costs more, since the manufacturer has to create custom machinery, designs, etc. However, doing so has a huge potential upside. Logan has the first-mover advantage in harvesting profits and cementing himself at the top of Amazon for specific keywords related to his new product.

Like anything else online, once you have a successful product, it's easy for someone to copy you, so it's essential to build a strong brand and diversify your sales outside of Amazon through your own website. For this reason, Logan also sells directly to customers through a Shopify store integrated with his website and regularly adds new, similar products. He has also built a robust social media presence, notably on TikTok, engaging a growing audience. Many Amazon FBA sellers make the mistake of relying solely on one product and distribution channel. They don't diversify their traffic sources, sell outside of Amazon, diversify their product mix, or focus enough on building a brand. This limits their potential and makes them beholden to Amazon's algorithm and platform.

I've seen several top sellers removed from Amazon and their businesses destroyed overnight without explanation. This is why it's so beneficial to build your own website to sell direct to consumers (DTC) and build traffic from Google, social media, and affiliates (a lot more on this later). This is the difference between creating a product and building a brand. With a product, you must fight to distinguish yourself from thousands of other products. With a brand, you build consumer trust by offering several quality products and excellent customer service. We'll discuss this more later in the book. This is where the real opportunity is because most products sold through Amazon's marketplace aren't strong brands—they are just international sellers exploiting niche, high-demand opportunities.

If you have some capital you're looking to invest, you can buy an established, already profitable FBA business through a reputable broker or online platform rather than trying to launch your own. Two good places to look are EmpireFlippers.com and Flippa.com, although competition for strong-performing Amazon FBA businesses is high. One nice thing about FBA businesses is that they are typically easy to buy and sell once profitable. There is a lot of buyer demand for FBA and other e-commerce businesses.

If you're looking to buy an established business, focus on one that is cash-flow positive, has positive revenue growth over the past twelve months with limited volatility, and has at least 70 percent gross margins (defined as revenue minus the cost of goods sold). Also, focus on products that aren't fads, have high recession resilience, are difficult to replicate, and address a clear customer need. Even better—look for businesses that serve typically underserved markets.

As I write this, well-branded e-commerce products for typically stigmatized medical conditions are growing in popularity, but there is always a new or emerging market to uncover when you pay attention. I'll dive further into how to evaluate a business for sale when we get into the buying and selling section of the book.

While there are infinite product categories with which you could experiment, I encourage you to consider products that are always in demand year after year. Seasonal businesses can be great diversifiers, but I wouldn't make them your core business because of the limited earning potential for the rest of the year. Of course, if you want to be the Christmas tree seller down the street in Chicago and then use your cash to live in Miami for the rest of the year, that's up to you—and it does sound like a pretty nice life! Here are some product categories that are worth considering or potentially avoiding. Just because I put a category in the Potentially Avoid column doesn't mean you should avoid it if you have a great idea. These categories are just more challenging because of the reasons noted.

PRODUCT CATEGORIES

WORTH CONSIDERING	POTENTIALLY AVOID
Pet Products and Accessories— Pets are part of the family, and owners spend a lot on them.	**Grocery and Food—**High start-up costs, very high competition, low margins
Baby Products, Toys, and Accessories—Parents typically spend as much as they can on their children, and the types of things that small kids are interested in don't change much over time.	**Consumer Electronics—**Get outdated quickly and have high development costs
Health, Beauty, Medical, and Personal Care—High margins, low storage and shipping costs, high repeat customer value	**Software and Digital Games—**Get outdated quickly and have high development costs. Increasingly vulnerable to disruption with the advent of AI
Travel—People love to travel and will spend as part of their trip planning. This includes trip planning guides, advisers, products, and accessories.	**Clothing and Accessories—**Tend to be fads, high competition, little differentiation, brand driven. Require a lot of marketing spend and high customer acquisition costs.
Home, Kitchen, and Garden—Most people invest a lot of time and money in their homes.	**Hobby and Collectibles—**Tend to be very niche, limiting market opportunity
Sports and Outdoor Equipment— Competitive but popular category with a lot of opportunity for innovation	**Tools and Automotive—**Extremely competitive

SERVICE BUSINESS: BROKER OTHER PEOPLE'S TIME INSTEAD OF SELLING YOUR OWN

In a service business, customers pay you to perform some action for them. Service providers include dog groomers, business coaches, Realtors, life coaches, personal trainers, tutors, plumbers, car mechanics, graphic designers, and more. The higher the quality of service and the more in demand it is within a particular market, the more the provider can charge.

The biggest advantage of a service business is that you can start with basically nothing because you're selling something you already have—your skills and time. You don't have to warehouse anything and can pivot quickly if your service needs to be changed or expanded. The biggest problem with service businesses is that they can be challenging to scale because you're trading your time (or someone else's time) for money. You're limited by how much you and your team can work, and you must keep working consistently to keep your momentum going.

One of the first ways many people experiment with entrepreneurship is through consulting. A consultant has expertise in a topic and sells that expertise to someone who needs it. Consultants work in every industry—home-decorating consultants, business consultants, marketing consultants, landscape consultants . . . if you need help doing something, you can find a consultant to help you. Just google "[anything] + consultant," and you'll likely find someone who offers consulting for that exact thing.

Consultants can charge by the hour or by the project. When I owned a consulting practice, I always charged a project fee because my clients were paying me to produce something specific. If I was efficient with my time, charging for a result was far more lucrative than charging per hour. I started my side-hustle journey by branching out as a marketing consultant in addition to my day job. Once I learned how to run Google Ad campaigns in my full-time job at a digital marketing agency, I looked for clients I could work with on my own time. After a year, I left my full-time job and started consulting full-time.

However, I quickly encountered many of the limitations of being a consultant. The first is that, even though I could charge as much as my clients were willing to pay, and I was able to move from selling $500 websites to $50,000 websites in less than six months, I was still trading my time for money. The business was still great, but I was doing all the work. Second, I still had to spend time hunting for the next client. In the beginning, I would take on any client because I was trying to build my pipeline and learn the ropes.

Over time, I narrowed my focus to building websites and marketing campaigns for MBA programs. Within a year, I became highly specialized and one of the top three consultants in my field. And because MBA programs are expensive, my work had high monetary value for my clients. My work made my clients a lot of money, so I could charge more for my services than a general marketing agency. If you're trading your time for money, you should maximize how much you can charge per hour by finding the right customer base or niche to serve. Typically, the more specialized you are within a market, the more you can charge for that expertise, with the caveat that your market has to have money to spend.

As a highly specialized expert, I was getting more money for my time, but I still had to trade all my time for money. I also had hired a team to do most of the day-to-day work of managing the marketing campaigns, but I was unsuccessful at removing myself from the business. The business didn't work unless I put in the hours. I also didn't love working with clients, so I eventually determined consulting was not right for me. Finally, as I noted earlier, valuation multiples for consulting businesses tend to be low because they often depend on the founder or a select group of consultants. This limits the amount of money you can make from selling a consulting firm compared to other types of businesses.

There is nothing wrong with being a consultant, and it can be a great way to learn the ropes of building a business and figuring out the value of your time and skills. Many of my friends who are consultants love what they do. That said, if your passions + skills assessment points you toward a consulting or service business, you should consider the limitations of this business model when first starting.

However, many other service-based business professionals also trade their time for money. A service-based business needing a license or certification can be more lucrative and scalable, even if you sell your time for money. If you're an electrician or a plumber, and you need a license and certification, that's typically more lucrative than being a deck power washer or exterminator, which have comparatively low barriers to entry.

The profitability of service businesses is driven by supply and demand. There's a large supply of Realtors in the U.S., for example, so it's difficult to be a successful Realtor. But there's a massive shortage of plumbers, so it's lucrative to be a plumber.

As the population grows and more homes get built across the United States, the demand for all home-service businesses will increase. This is a massive opportunity if you're willing to get into one of these recession-resistant and climate-resistant service businesses. There's a reason why private equity firms are buying up home-service companies—because they're always in demand and very profitable. My friend Mike is thirty-nine and an electrician in Columbus, Ohio. He started his company in 2016 and sold it in 2021 for $18 million. His noncompete recently expired, and he's doing the same thing again, following the same exact blueprint.

Here's a list of service-based business ideas to consider:

Service-Based Business Ideas

B2B (BUSINESS TO BUSINESS)	
Many of these can be built entirely online, are essential support services for online entrepreneurs, and have immense scalability potential.	
Accountant and Bookkeeper	Graphic Designer
Writer and Editor	Payroll and Benefits Specialist
Virtual Assistant	Researcher
Proofreader and Copy Editor	Customer Support

Mobile Notary Public	Website Designer
Social Media Consultant	Copywriter
Rental Property Manager	Ad Campaign Manager
IT Consultant	Business Coach
Data Analyst	Contract Drafter and Reviewer
Video or Podcast Editor or Producer	Public Relations Representative
SEO Strategist	Lawyer
Affiliate Manager	Presentation Designer

HOME-SERVICE BUSINESSES

Many of these are climate-change and recession-resistant businesses. When demand is high and supply is low, all of these can become extremely profitable and cash-flow-rich businesses. This is why, as I write this, private equity firms are rapidly acquiring HVAC companies.

Handyman	Electrician
House Cleaner	Plumber
Mobile Car Washing and Detailing	Lawn Care (Mowing, Planting, Leaf Removal, etc.)
Window Washer	Landscaper
Power Washer	Roof Repair
Floor Refinisher	Driveway Repair
Tree Removal and Arborist	Fence Builder and Repair
Solar-Panel Installer	Pool and Hot Tub Maintenance

Lighting Consultant	House Sitter
Home Decorator	Organization Consultant
Locksmith	Irrigation Consultant
HVAC Tech	Furniture Assembler
Exterminator and Pest Removal	Mosquito and Tick Spraying

PERSONAL-SERVICE BUSINESSES

These tend to be luxuries and could do well as wealth and people's focus on personal health and wellness increase. But they could suffer amid climate and recession pressures if not viewed as essential.

Personal Trainer	Personal Chef
Caterer	House Manager
Financial Adviser	Massage Therapist
Nutrition Consultant	Hairdresser
Meditation Teacher	Private Driver
Yoga Teacher	Acupuncturist
Event/Wedding Planner	Senior and Eldercare/Home Health Aide
Makeup Artist	Family Photographer or Videographer
Personal Stylist or Shopper	Physical Therapist
Travel Planner	Dating Consultant
Personal Assistant	Tour Guide

CHILD- AND PET-CARE BUSINESSES We spend money on our kids and our pets. These are likely climate-change and recession resistant.	
Doula or Birthing Consultant	Dog Walker
Nanny	Pet Groomer (Mobile or In-Person)
Babysitter	Pet Sitter and Boarder
Lactation Consultant	Pet Trainer
Baby Sleep Consultant	Private Sports Instructor
Day-Care Provider	Tutor
Private Music/Art/Language Teacher	College Test Prep
Baby Item Rental Company in Vacation Locations	Pet Portrait Artist

PRODUCTIZED SERVICE BUSINESS: THE HOLY GRAIL OF SCALABILITY AND PROFITABILITY

The biggest reason some service businesses struggle or fail is because they let too many variables or uncertainty into their business. Since everything is customized, unpredictable, and built on pleasing a diverse client base, owners must deal with an unnecessary amount of complexity that makes it difficult to manage clients, cash flow, and employees. Many service businesses will offer anything to help them get customers and grow, but the lack of specialization makes it difficult to run the business because they can't focus or streamline their operations.

Marketing agencies are notorious for this. They often don't specialize in any industry or particular type of service, so they end up trying to sell different services to various industries. This makes their agency highly inefficient because nothing is standardized and there are no economies of scale. In trying to be everything to every potential client, there's nothing unique or distinctive about their offering, so they end up selling a commodity.

An excellent way to solve this is to do what's known as "productizing" your service. When you do this, you define a clear set of deliverables with a specific price and timeline for a defined market. This makes it easier to control all the variables and keep things simple. You can more easily calculate how many hours it will take to deliver the service, how much it costs you to deliver it, and what the profit margin will be. It also makes teaching other people how to provide the service easier, so you don't have to constantly trade your time for money. Productized services can be sold for a one-time fee or through a subscription.

To set up a productized service business, you begin by testing the idea and learning the ropes by delivering the service yourself. Then, based on customer feedback, you systematize the service offering into a product. The product is then delivered the same way for every client. This makes it easier for you to market the product because its outcome is defined—the customer knows exactly what they will get and for what price. Standardization also makes it easier for you to hire someone else to deliver your particular service.

This is why, when I started my first digital marketing business, I built websites only for law firms and Realtors. Instead of taking on any client in any industry, I identified two industries with specific needs (and typically decent marketing budgets) and then developed a standardized offering I could use for every client within those industries. A few years later, I shifted industries and starting working with MBA programs to help them grow their enrollments. This included offering all types of services—including building websites and marketing campaigns. But as I grew, the business grew, and when I got to know my market better, I stopped building websites altogether and only ran Google Ad campaigns for MBA programs because I was best at it and it was the most profitable product to offer because it was heavily automated.

Our productized service was a Google Ad strategy and campaign management that included an annual strategy presentation, monthly campaign management, and a monthly performance report with a team call. It started at $30,000 and went up to $250,000, depending on the institution's size, the number of degree programs offered, and my client's monthly advertising budget. That one product generated 70 to 80 percent of my firm's revenue. We could sell it easily because we used the same proposal template for every client, and my team could deliver the service easily because I created standard operating procedures (SOPs) that outlined exactly how my team should perform the service without my having to oversee all their work.

This is precisely how Travis Hornsby built his business at Student Loan Planner. When some family members asked him for help paying off their student loans, Travis took the financial-planning and data-crunching skills he'd developed in his day job as a bond trader to figure out various formulas to help them reduce their debt. At the time, no other company provided this service, so he decided to sell the service he'd used so successfully with his family.

At first, Travis did all the work himself. However, he soon turned his consulting service into a product by developing a standardized procedure he taught others to deliver. This allowed him to hire additional consultants to take on the clients he couldn't handle himself, while still maintaining the quality of the service. Travis paid these consultants a percentage of the fee he charged clients, and the business took the rest.

Productizing his business allowed Travis to grow Student Loan Planner into a multimillion-dollar-a-year company. We'll talk more about how to productize your business in chapter 8, but it's worth thinking about how to productize your service to make it easier to offer, sell, and scale from the beginning.

EXAMPLES OF PRODUCTIZED SERVICES

You can productize almost any service, but here are some popular examples.

Home-Cleaning Subscription—Provide regular home-cleaning services on a weekly or monthly subscription basis, with set cleaning tasks and pricing.

Personal Fitness Plan—Provide personalized fitness plans with predefined durations, workout routines, and nutrition guidance.

Baby Photo Packages—Photograph a growing baby every three months and offer a set number of edited photos with a set annual price.

SEO Audit and Optimization—Provide a comprehensive website SEO audit and optimization package with a fixed fee, including keyword research, on-page optimization, and reporting.

Virtual-Assistant Services—Provide virtual-assistant services on a monthly retainer, with a specific number of hours for tasks like email management, scheduling, and data entry.

Bookkeeping and Accounting—Offer monthly bookkeeping and accounting services with a fixed fee based on the complexity of the client's financial needs, instead of an hourly fee. Price your fixed fee to have dependable revenue and a higher profit margin than you could earn by the hour.

Content-Writing Packages—Offer content-creation services with packages for blog posts, articles, or website copy, each with a set word count and turnaround time.

SAAS BUSINESS

A Software as a Service (SaaS) business sells software that customers access over the internet through a subscription. Popular SaaS businesses include Dropbox, Slack, Salesforce, and many others. As with any subscription business, a SaaS business can generate significant recurring revenue if you find product-market fit and add value to users. It's also an asset-light business that you can continue to work on and update from anywhere in the world.

Some SaaS businesses have achieved remarkable success. For instance, Salesforce excels in helping companies manage their customer relationships, boosting their efficiency and profitability. During the pandemic, Zoom gained fame for its user-friendly online meeting platform, which was in high demand. Slack became a go-to tool for teams to communicate and collaborate effectively. Adobe Creative Cloud provides cloud-based access to popular software like Photoshop and Illustrator, streamlining the work of creative professionals.

After discovering the financial independence movement, Kyle Nolan, a software engineer from Boston, decided to build a financial-modeling SaaS company to help others reach financial independence. As of this writing, he's been running ProjectionLab for two and a half years and generating $24,000 in monthly recurring revenue (MRR). He recently left his full-time job to dive into the business full-time.

To build the software, Kyle worked almost forty hours a week on nights and weekends outside his day job, often working every night from 8:00 p.m. to midnight and about ten hours a day on Saturday and Sunday. It took Kyle fourteen months to reach five hundred customers, and now he gets five hundred new customers every two months. "Try to find a problem you understand deeply and truly care about solving," he advises new entrepreneurs. "And build something that you'll actually be a user of."

Unless you're a skilled developer, building high-quality software requires substantial time and financial investment. However, AI is making it easier for those without development skills to build SaaS products, which lowers the entry barrier for new entrepreneurs and makes it easier for SaaS companies to be copied and potentially more difficult for new and existing SaaS companies to compete. As these skills become more commoditized and their functionality easier to copy, a strong brand and story become even more essential.

Like any subscription business, retaining customers while adding new ones is challenging. SaaS businesses can also require a lot of money and be stressful to operate, especially if you take on venture capital funding. If you aspire to launch the next groundbreaking SaaS venture, focus on delivering software that genuinely enhances people's lives and consistently meets their evolving needs.

AFFILIATE OR ADVERTISING BUSINESS: MAKING MONEY ON CLICKS AND REFERRALS

With an affiliate or ad-based business, you produce free or low-priced content and earn most of your revenue from affiliates or advertisers, who pay you for referrals or access to your audience. Through this model, you earn a commission every time a visitor to your website clicks on an ad or link or buys a product from one of your affiliates.

You make money, your affiliate partner makes money, and your users get access to high-quality content, even if only a few purchase anything.

Millennial Money started, and remains in large part, an affiliate business. Readers get free access to all my content, but I make money if they sign up for one of the third-party products or services I mention on the site. I don't make any money if they don't sign up. So I need to write great content that adds value to readers and keeps them coming back, while working with affiliates my readers will find valuable.

My company gets paid anywhere from $5 for a mobile app download to $1,000+ when someone signs up for a business credit card. What I love most about affiliate marketing is that there's no limit to how much money you can make as your audience grows. As your traffic and conversions increase, many brands will pay you even more money to further incentivize you. This scale compounds over time, so you're making more money for even less of your time.

A 2023 survey on the state of the affiliate industry published on Authority Hacker highlighted the largest single commission by affiliate niche. This is for one sale, so you can do the math to see how revenue could scale rapidly over time.

Another huge pro of these types of businesses is that they're a way to monetize a creative pursuit that might otherwise be hard to sell directly, especially when you're just starting and trying to build your brand. People are so used to getting content for free that you typically need a built-in audience or a huge differentiating factor to get people to pay you directly for content. By courting advertisers and brand partners who want to reach your audience, you can make more money by attracting more visitors and focusing on creating content you love and serving your audience. I've made millions of dollars this way, as have many of my fellow entrepreneurs.

Take Harry Campbell, aka the Rideshare Guy. Harry started writing about his experience as an Uber driver on his blog. He also partnered with Uber to become an affiliate so that whenever someone signed up to be an Uber driver through a link on one of his YouTube videos or blog posts, Uber paid him a commission. As his reputation

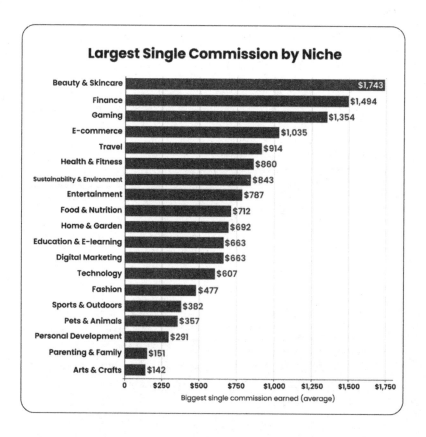

Largest Single Commission by Niche

Niche	Biggest single commission earned (average)
Beauty & Skincare	$1,743
Finance	$1,494
Gaming	$1,354
E-commerce	$1,035
Travel	$914
Health & Fitness	$860
Sustainability & Environment	$843
Entertainment	$787
Food & Nutrition	$712
Home & Garden	$692
Education & E-learning	$663
Digital Marketing	$663
Technology	$607
Fashion	$477
Sports & Outdoors	$382
Pets & Animals	$357
Personal Development	$291
Parenting & Family	$151
Arts & Crafts	$142

and traffic grew, so did the amount of money Uber was willing to pay him every time a new driver signed up. Harry has over 2,000 posts, many containing affiliate links and generating over a million dollars annually.

One of the significant challenges with building an affiliate business is that it takes a lot of time to create content and a fair bit of marketing skill to build an audience that you can monetize through affiliate relationships. Most brands with affiliate programs will work with you no matter your audience size because it's all upside for them. All you need to do is add a link to their product or service on your website, which costs them nothing and can potentially lead to more sales. But you won't make much money if you don't have enough traffic.

This is fine starting out, but typically, you need at least 5,000 visitors a month to make at least $100 a month. This is because only a small percentage of your visitors will buy or sign up for your recommended product or service.

Conversion rates vary widely, but fall between 1 percent and 10 percent for most products. The better the product aligns with your core audience, the higher your conversion rate. However, revenue can scale quickly as traffic grows and you focus on conversion rate optimization (CRO). You can optimize conversion rates through improved website design, creating more prominent offer placements, and more, once you've reached about 10,000 monthly visitors.

Before that point, CRO doesn't work because you don't have enough traffic. But no matter how much traffic you have, you should invest in good link tracking to see exactly how much money you're making and where it's coming from.

The most critical factors for selecting a solid affiliate niche are:

1. How much experience do you have with the topic?

2. How interested are you in the subject?

3. How popular is the subject?

4. How competitive is the subject?

5. How profitable can this niche be?

The profitability of affiliate niches can vary depending on various factors, including the level of competition, the quality of products or services offered, and the target audience. Here are some affiliate niches that have historically been profitable, although it's important to remember that market dynamics can change over time.

15 MOST PROFITABLE AFFILIATE NICHES

The more profitable the affiliate niche, the more competitive it is, but I still encourage you to get into a niche you're passionate about, even if it's competitive. You can also arbitrage niches, which means you can take advantage of smaller niches with little competition quickly when you uncover them.

1. Health and Wellness—Niches related to health and wellness, such as weight loss, fitness, nutrition, supplements, and mental health, often have high profit potential. People are willing to invest in products and services that improve their health and well-being.

2. Finance and Investing—Affiliate programs related to personal finance, investing, credit cards, and insurance can be lucrative. Financial products also often have high commissions.

3. Travel—The travel industry offers many lucrative opportunities for affiliate marketers, including commissions on hotel bookings, flight reservations, car rentals, and travel insurance.

4. Fashion and Beauty—Affiliate programs for clothing, accessories, cosmetics, and beauty products can be profitable, particularly when targeting fashion-conscious audiences.

5. Technology and Gadgets—Promoting technology products, such as smartphones, laptops, software, and electronics, can be profitable due to the constant demand for these items and high purchase prices.

6. Home Improvement—Promoting products related to home improvement, DIY, and interior design can be lucrative, as homeowners are always looking to enhance their living spaces.

7. Online Education and e-Learning—With the growth of online education, promoting online courses, e-books, and educational platforms can be a profitable niche.

8. Web Hosting and Domain Registration—Website-related services, such as web hosting and domain registration, often offer high affiliate commissions.

9. Software and App Downloads—Promoting software applications and mobile apps can generate income, especially if the software is in high demand.

10. Gaming and Entertainment—Given the popularity of gaming, affiliate marketing in this industry can be profitable, with partners offering commissions on purchases of things like video games, gaming accessories, or streaming services.

11. Pets and Pet Care—Niches related to pet products, pet care, and pet health can be profitable, as many people consider their pets to be part of the family.

12. Green and Sustainable Living—With the growing interest in eco-friendly and sustainable products, promoting green and sustainable living products can be a profitable niche.

13. Home Office and Remote Work—As remote work grows, affiliate marketing in the home office niche, including office furniture, productivity tools, and remote-work software, can be profitable.

14. Relationships and Dating—Affiliate programs for dating websites and relationship advice can be profitable, particularly when targeting specific demographics.

15. Arts and Crafts—In 2022, the online sales for craft supplies grew to $16 billion, and this is a growing niche.

As you grow, your business may eventually become a combination of different monetization methods. For example, Student Loan Planner started as a service business. Today, Travis makes money off the core service (helping six-figure student-loan borrowers refinance and pay down their loans), products (like an online course on how to invest), and affiliate revenue (the company gets paid when a customer signs up with one of its partners for related financial products, such as small-business loans, mortgages, or insurance plans).

But when you're first starting out, select the type of business that allows you to combine your skills and passions most easily and enjoyably to make money. Speaking of making money, that brings us to the final ingredient for building a successful business: market opportunity.

CHAPTER 4

ASSESS THE OPPORTUNITY, PRICE IT RIGHT, AND START SELLING

"Don't worry about failure; you only have to be right once."
—Drew Houston, founder and CEO of Dropbox

When you're in the Experimental Entrepreneur phase, you must embed yourself in the market you want to explore. The easiest way to learn about anything is from the inside. It was easy for Phil Knight and Bill Bowerman, the founders of Nike, to spot the market demand for and create the Nike running shoe because Knight was a runner and Bowerman was a running coach. They knew what runners needed and what was already available because they were their target customers.

Before launching Millennial Money in 2015, I attended FinCon, a conference for personal finance content creators and people who create content around money. I had no website, just a deep interest in the topic. I was already a consumer and lover of personal finance content, which made me part of the market. But I didn't know anything about being a creator. While at the conference, I noticed many things I likely wouldn't have been able to uncover if I hadn't attended.

The biggest revelation was the gap between amateur bloggers and mainstream personal finance websites. The amateurs were open, vulnerable, and transparent about their finances and struggles, but their websites often looked amateurish or outdated. While the content was great, the websites provided a lackluster user experience. I could see why brands might hesitate to work with them. Then there were the big websites run by banks, investment companies, and mainstream media companies. These websites looked great, but the content was bland and uninspiring due to various corporate and legal restrictions. What they had in sophistication, they lacked in humanity.

This was my opportunity. Drawing on my digital marketing skills, I would launch my website with a great user experience and a solid brand like the big, institutional websites, but my content would be vulnerable, open, and transparent like that of the amateur bloggers. That way, I hoped, users would pay attention to my content, get value from it, and keep coming back for more. If I succeeded, brands would be open to working with me.

I knew my market because I *was* my market. I wrote about what readers cared about because I cared about it. I already knew the market opportunity was immense because the U.S. is home to more than 85 million millennials. I saw how I could use my passions and skills alongside my unique story to differentiate myself from other finance websites.

Yes, it's possible to spot a market opportunity in an area outside of one you're personally familiar with, and this becomes easier to do as you learn more about starting and running a business. If you're not already in your target market, you can build a successful business based on your skills and passions, but you will need to do more market research before you can take full advantage of the opportunity. Whether you're in the market or not, you need to answer the following questions:

1. DOES THIS PRODUCT EXIST? IF NOT, WHY? IF SO, HOW CAN I OFFER MORE?

Just because something doesn't exist yet doesn't mean there's an opportunity for it. Many things don't exist simply because no one wants them or they serve no logical purpose. Another reason something might not exist is because legal or logistical restrictions make it unviable. If nothing else like your idea exists or others have tried and failed to market it, ask yourself why.

If something similar exists, ask yourself why the market would benefit from your iteration. In my case, thousands of personal finance websites were available when I launched Millennial Money. But I knew I could differentiate myself because I had a unique story, perspective, and the writing and marketing skills to build a website people would read.

2. DO I HAVE THE ABILITY TO REACH MY CUSTOMERS?

While great products and services are essential, marketing is the most valuable skill when building a business. If people don't know your product or service exists, they can't buy it. With so many distractions today, getting people's attention is hard—but it's a lot easier if you know who your customers are, where they are, and what they want.

Even if you're not your target customer, starting a business where you already know the target customers or how to reach them is easier than launching into a completely unknown market. Think of people in your communities (geographic, demographic, and social) and industries you work within or adjacent to. What content can you create that they'd be interested in? What do they search for? Where can you distribute that content (blog, podcast, video, social media)? Where do they hang out online (Reddit groups, forums, social media groups, certain bloggers)? What events do they attend? Can you join the association they all belong to? You have to join these groups or hang out where your customers are.

Last week, I was chatting with Matt, a member of my community, who wants to offer financial and career coaching to first-year consultants and business analysts at large consulting firms. He works as a full-time consultant at Deloitte, so he knows how to reach his target customers because he works with them daily and belongs to the same social and networking groups. It's the perfect fit.

Building a business from within or inside an existing community is always easier and less expensive than building one from outside. So many new entrants and start-ups with great products and massive budgets are unsuccessful simply because they think they can pay their way into a market. Over the past decade, I've seen the vast majority of new finance and personal finance start-ups fail for this reason. They thought they could spend enough money to build a community, but the personal finance community never accepted them. You can't pay for trust or a great reputation. You have to develop it authentically.

3. HOW BIG IS THE MARKET? IS IT GROWING? ARE PEOPLE TALKING ABOUT IT?

While there are many ways to research the size of a total addressable market (TAM) and what percentage of that market you can service (SAM), the most efficient way is to follow the news, study industry reports, analyze Google Trend and search-engine-volume data, and use spy tools. Let's dig into each:

First, start with a search of the recent news for your target market, as most news stories are built around new industry studies. Just doing a simple Google search for "pickleball market size" or "pickleball market trends" and looking at the recent news stories and top results can give you a decent overview of the high-level market trends.

Next, read the industry reports linked within the articles and search for others. These reports often contain valuable data on market size, growth rates, and forecasts. Many market reports are released by industry associations or consulting firms and can be downloaded for free. You can also find reports on many markets that are compiled by research companies like Gartner, Nielsen, and IBISWorld. The U.S. government's Bureau of Labor Statistics and the Census Bureau also put out valuable market insight and trend data on consumer behaviors and patterns that can help you measure the size of a market.

Next, head back to Google to analyze Google Trend data or use one of the newer AI search engines like Perplexity for the topics related to your market. If you can access a paid tool like Ahrefs or Semrush, you can also use it to analyze search data. I recommend signing up for a one-month subscription to Ahrefs or Semrush to do this analysis, as you can spend a few weeks gathering all the search volume data you need and cancel the subscription if you aren't using it for a content business. Since 90+ percent of all consumer searches happen on Google, their trend and search data are exceptional proxies for market demand. But it's also worth searching on social media as well—since platforms like YouTube and TikTok are where people are also searching. Always try to pick a growing market; in most instances, the earlier you can predict a new and durable trend, the more opportunity you'll have.

Finally, many "spy tools" can help you analyze the size of the market, uncover who the competition is, determine how many sales a particular product generates, and uncover what products are being talked about. I already mentioned Helium 10 (for Amazon), but there's also Jungle Scout (for Amazon), EtsyHunt (for Etsy), GummySearch (for Reddit), and many other tools you can use to see what consumers are searching for and talking about on each platform, what they're buying, and how much sellers are selling of anything on the platform.

When I started writing about side hustles in 2015, there were only a few thousand searches of that term per month. Today, there are hundreds of thousands. While there was no way I could have predicted such a meteoric rise in the interest of "side hustles," I was confident that more people would be interested in diversifying their income streams using all the new ways to make money online.

It's worth mentioning that even if a market isn't growing, and sometimes even if it's in decline, there could still be incredible opportunities to make money if there's enough volume. Baseball in the U.S. is a great example—even though attendance, viewership, and online searches are declining for the sport, it's such a large market that a blog, content platform, or product built around baseball could still be popular and profitable. However, it's always best to pick a growing market.

4. DO THE PEOPLE IN THIS MARKET HAVE MONEY?

The more money people in your market have, the more money you can charge them. No matter how big a problem you solve, you'll never make any money from someone who doesn't have money to spend. Find a market that isn't price-conscious or looking for value. Sell premium products, not commodity products. Being the most expensive or at the top of the market will result in fewer but more profitable sales. It's always best to be perceived as the best or highest-value option rather than the cheapest. You'll never win by competing on price; it compresses your margins and will add unnecessary stress to your business.

When I was a partner at the higher-education consulting firm, I could charge a premium for running Google Ad campaigns because I specialized in a lucrative niche (MBA programs), the universities had money, and I was doing high-value work—recruiting the exact students they needed to fill their class. We could charge three to five times more than other providers in the market because of the value we provided. I did the same thing when I built websites for law firms. I started selling websites to small single-lawyer firms and scaled up quickly to large firms with a lot more money and a lot more potential upside for a new website. For a single lawyer, $500 is a lot of money to spend on a new website, but $50,000 is nothing for a 100-person firm.

5. IS THERE A TIME LIMIT TO THE OPPORTUNITY?

During the height of the COVID-19 pandemic, many people made quick money by selling items that people desperately needed but were in short supply. Textile companies and home-based crafters started making handsewn masks. Commercial and home-based distillers began producing hand sanitizer. Some of these entrepreneurs pivoted existing businesses to meet the needs of the current market, while others quickly set up a system to capitalize on it. But there was a precise time limit on the need for such products. Savvy entrepreneurs considered ways to keep their new customers engaged and coming back. Others lost their market as soon as the demand for their products cooled.

Yes, it's okay—and often fun—to capitalize on a trend or quickly fill market gaps. But unless you figure out how to continue serving those customers for the long term, your business cannot scale, and you risk losing your profit if you don't time your exit just right.

If you can't answer these questions with your existing knowledge, do your research. Talk to people within the market and ask for feedback on your idea. Do they see value in it? Would they buy it? How could you make it better? Have they tried something similar? If so, what did they like or dislike about it? Don't ask your mom or your friends unless they are in the market because they will tell you they like it no matter what, and their feedback won't be relevant. I've seen far too many business books and "experts" recommend asking your family and friends, but they are not likely your target market, so temper their opinions and don't let them derail you.

You don't have to learn everything there is to know about your target market to get started. But the more you understand going in—and the more you get into the habit of learning about your market—the better you'll be at spotting opportunities and making decisions in the future.

PRICE YOUR PRODUCT TO FIT YOUR MARKET

Pricing your product is equal parts art and science. The amount of money an individual will pay for something varies wildly depending on several—sometimes highly irrational—factors. That's why experimentation is vital. Below is a simple five-step process I go through when pricing any product.

Step 1: Analyze the Competition

Your most successful competitors have already figured out how to price their products* to fit the market, so use them as a baseline to determine how you should start thinking about pricing. Take some time to research your competitors online and act like a potential customer by calling or visiting them directly:

- What do they charge for comparable products and services?
- How do their offerings differ or compare to yours?
- Do they offer discounts? If so, what kind?
- How do their prices compare to others in your market?

---

* For the sake of simplicity, I will refer to all business offerings (whether they're products, services, or affiliations) as "products."

- Do they offer something (like a premium option or additional service) to justify a higher price?
- How many units are they selling, and what's the revenue? (You can use spy tools to determine this.)

Make a spreadsheet to track their prices, note what makes their products distinctive from yours, and their sales data if you can gather or estimate it.

If you have a local business, do this analysis locally, for pricing can vary widely from market to market. But also take a look at similar companies in other similar-size markets to see if there's any price flexibility or if you can learn anything and bring it to your market. Maybe a Chicago competitor offers a unique product or pricing option that might appeal to your target customers in Columbus.

If you have a national or primarily online business, search Google or any popular social media platform. Which companies are ranking in popular searches? While you can use specialized tools like Ahrefs or Semrush to analyze Google rankings, you should also spend some time searching on Google and social media. Search for keywords you would use as a customer for your product or service and see who ranks. Spend at least a few hours searching Google and social media to make and analyze your competitor list.

Pay attention to who is running ads. Most companies that consistently run Google ads have a profitable product, or they wouldn't be spending money on search advertising because it can be so competitive and expensive. In Ahrefs, you can see what companies have been running Google ads for a long time. Look at each brand's landing pages. Study their website and sales copy. What can you learn from their examples?

Keep up with market changes by analyzing your competitors at least once a quarter. I look at my competitors to see if they've changed their offerings, pricing, products, launches, messaging, and what else is different. I also analyze their search traffic rankings to see if their visibility changes and review the new type of content they're creating.

And remember Truth #6: Cooperation is more powerful than competition. Join a community, online or in-person, of people working within your market and use their resources to learn about pricing and other strategies. Reach out to competitors to connect with them. If they're smart, they will also understand that cooperation is more powerful than competition. Over time these relationships will pay dividends and you may end up being able to acquire or be acquired by one of your competitors.

Step 2: Factor in Expenses

Your business needs to make a profit to succeed, so figure out how much you'd need to charge per product in order to make more than you spend. Consider what is known as your cost of goods sold (COGS), which are the costs of materials, production, warehousing/storage, and shipping (for physical product businesses), as well as any other expenses that go into making your product or your ability to provide a service. Also factor in any transaction fees you will incur in producing and selling your product or service. For example, if you accept online payments, you'll usually have to pay a fee for taking credit cards or using any electronic payment method.

Additionally, check to see what fees any third-party platforms you use might charge per sale. For example, Etsy charges a fee for every product you list on its site and takes a 6.5 percent commission on each sale's list price, shipping, and gift-wrapping fees. One of the reasons I advocate for owning your platforms (more on this in the next chapter) is so you can avoid some of these fees, but if you're first starting and testing an idea, it can make sense to use third-party sellers to build a market. Just make sure to price your product high enough to cover those fees and still generate the profit you want to see.

The more you sell of something, the less expensive it typically becomes to produce it. This is true for physical products (since it's generally less expensive to order products or materials in higher quantities), but especially for asset-light businesses like digital products or service businesses. There may still be some up-front costs to running these—like software to design your Etsy printables or hosting fees for your website—but they are spread out over all your units.

Another way to determine how to price your product is to reverse engineer the price based on how much profit you want to earn. When still experimenting, set a reasonable goal to stay motivated without setting yourself up for failure. For example, maybe you'd like to be able to cover your rent based on your business profits each month. You have a passion for design and like the idea of starting a printables business like Cody and Julie did. You already own the design software you need (most printable creators use Canva, which is affordable), so the only fees you have to factor in are Etsy's. Assuming a 6.5 percent commission, if you charged $5 per item, you would net $4.67 profit for each sale. If your rent is $2,000, you must sell roughly 428 items each month to cover it.

Step 3: Test Your Market

In the experimental stage, your goal is to find the right price for your product or service, but this will typically require some testing. This is easier for digital products and any product or service you're selling online because most e-commerce carts have price-testing capabilities so that you can offer the product at one price to some visitors and another to others.

This is called A/B price-testing. If you're getting enough traffic to your store, the data will show you the most *profitable* price. Remember that the one who sells the most might not be the most profitable.

Say you're selling a baby bottle through your e-commerce store and are price-testing it at either $15 or $40 for a pack of five. Let's say you sell 100 packs at $15 weekly, but only 40 packs at $40. The simple math shows you that even though you sold fewer packs at $40, the higher price still generated more revenue. E.g., 100 x $15 = $1,500 vs. 40 x $40 = $1,600.

But now let's factor in the cost of goods sold to see how that impacts our overall profit.

Profit Margin = (Revenue — Cost of Goods Sold) / Revenue

Let's say it costs you $1 to manufacture, package, and ship each bottle. This means you'll spend $500 for 100 packs (500 bottles) but only $200 for 40 packs (200 bottles). When you subtract the COGS from the overall, you can see that selling at the higher price becomes even more profitable.

$1,500 − $500 = $1,000 profit on 100 packs at $15 each

vs.

$1,600 − $200 = $1,400 profit on 40 packs at $40 each

This is why it's so valuable to price-test. Also, as you build your email list, you can also survey your market to ask them what they would be willing to pay for a product before you create it. Many successful entrepreneurs take this strategy a step further and presell a product, taking money up front for something they haven't developed yet. Kickstarter is built around this concept. Crowdfunding is a great way to presale a product, even if you already have an established audience, because it allows you to prove demand before you shell out money to produce a product and use your customers' money to finance the creation of that product instead of having to dig into your own pockets.

Step 4: Determine Your Premium

Consumers are irrational. Behavioral economists have proven time and time again that people will make choices about how to spend their money based on reasons that have very little to do with its actual value. What something is worth varies widely from person to person. Knowing this can help you set prices effectively.

A big mistake new entrepreneurs make is pricing too low because they want to attract as many customers as possible. Sure, the more you charge, fewer people might buy from you, but this is not always the case. When I was selling my course for $397 instead of $97 I got far more sales at $397, because the perception of the value was higher, so more people were willing to sign up. Often the higher the price, the higher consumers value something and the more they want it.

People will pay premiums for products and services that solve for or provide the following:

Complexity

In the words of Elon Musk, "You get paid in direct proportion to the difficulty of the problems you solve." If you have a dog-walking company, there's a limit to how much you can charge because pretty much anyone can walk a dog. But if you can solve a complex legal issue that few people understand, you can likely charge a ton of money.

Convenience

There's a reason a bottle of water costs more at an outdoor concert in the middle of the summer than at a suburban gas station in the winter. If people want or need something right now, they will pay more to get it immediately.

Quality

People will pay more for things they perceive to have superior quality than a competing product. Let's look at one entrepreneur where I live, in Columbus, Ohio. His name is Dan Riesenberger, aka Dan the Baker. Dan bakes several types of sourdough bread, croissants, and pastries. He uses high-quality ingredients, and everything he bakes tastes incredible. Dan started selling his bread at local farmers markets in 2009 and opened his storefront in 2013. As of this writing, he charges $11 for a loaf of bread and $11 for a croissant. These are at least twice the price of similar products in the city, but people line up for them. Dan's bakery is open only Friday, Saturday, and Sunday. By noon each of those days, he's sold out of everything.

I don't know Dan personally, but I estimate he sells about 1,000 croissants and loaves of bread each of those three days. At an average of $11, he's making $11,000 in daily revenue or about $33,000 weekly. Multiply that by 52 weeks; conservatively, he makes $1,716,000 in annual gross revenue. This figure doesn't include any products he sells at other markets around the city or any specialty products he sells around the holidays. While his ingredients, I'm sure, are expensive, he has only one location and a few employees. I imagine Dan the Baker is netting nearly $1 million in profit yearly from his bakery—and doing it on his terms.

Dan knows his market and the perception of his product's value so that he can charge more than others. Plus, he can hire other people to make the bread for him, using his methods and recipes, allowing him to pursue his passions, like surfing around the world. While I'm sure he's at his bakery often or doing work behind the scenes, I've seen him only once in almost three years, and I've been going there almost weekly. And he wasn't even up front; I could see him in the back filling up pastries. Dan, if you're reading this, I love your bread and your business!

Uniqueness and Scarcity

What is rare or one of a kind is often valuable. This goes for high-end luxury items like art and collectibles and things that are scarce but necessary. During the early months of the COVID-19 pandemic, we saw how quickly something can go from cheap and available to expensive and scarce.

PERCEIVED VALUE

You can often charge two different people wildly disparate amounts for the same service because one of them perceives a greater value in what you're offering than the other. This largely depends on how much money each person has, since the value of money goes up or down depending on how much of it you have. For example, a millionaire might be willing to pay more for the same service as someone living paycheck to paycheck because, even though the real value of those dollars is higher, the perceived value is less than all the other money they have.

Businesses know this, so when I recently requested quotes for paint jobs for two homes I own, I got two vastly different estimates from the same company. Even though the scope of work for the paint job was relatively the same and the homes are in the same neighborhood, one of the homes is worth $1 million. The other is worth closer to $500,000—a fact any housepainter could learn just by looking up the properties on Zillow. They were looking up my address or using some program that did it to price according to the value of my home.

Similarly, customers may be willing to spend more money on something they believe will generate a lot of value for them or their business. For example, a business owner might be willing to spend a lot of money designing a new website because they know the return on the investment will pay off in higher conversion rates. However, that same person might not be willing to spend as much designing a website that catalogs their collection of vintage baseball cards because they aren't trying to make any money off it.

Step 5: Experiment with Pricing Models

Generally speaking, there are three pricing models: flat, hourly, and recurring. In a flat-fee model, you charge a specific product or service price: $11 for a croissant, $60 for a haircut. The price factors in all the costs of delivering the product (cost of goods, labor, shipping, overhead, etc.) and adds a margin on top so the owner can make a profit.

With an hourly fee, you charge someone for your time and some output: $15 an hour to babysit or $100 for an hour of personal training. You need to factor in the value of your time and expertise. The more expert or specialized you are in your field, the more you can charge. And because you have only so many hours in the day, the more in demand you are, the more you can charge.

The rise of digital and subscription-based businesses over the past decade has led to massive growth in the third type of model—recurring revenue, specifically monthly recurring revenue (MRR). MRR is precisely what it sounds like. Customers sign up for your product or service and pay a monthly fee to access it. This is nothing new. Since their inception, magazines, newspapers, utility companies, insurance companies, and landlords have depended on this model. What's different is that, thanks to how easy it is to sign up for a service or software and have it automatically renewed online, more companies can experiment with the model.

MRR has several advantages. First, you get guaranteed cash flow each month, which allows you to cover your expenses and plan better. Second, MRR makes a business more valuable from an acquisition standpoint because there is dependable revenue. Third, you can weather seasonality or adapt more quickly to shifts in the market. During the pandemic, for example, MRR businesses were more durable because they had a base of guaranteed subscription revenue.

The process of setting up an MRR-based subscription service is more obvious for some types of businesses than others—for example, if you're offering a product or service that people would typically purchase regularly. Or if you're offering access to a library of something, as Netflix, Spotify, Audible, MasterClass, and other media companies do. But even if the model is not standard in your industry, there are likely creative ways you can offer an MRR option that will appeal to certain customers.

One monthly subscription I pay for is natural mosquito spraying for my yard (don't worry, it's nontoxic cedarwood oil and doesn't kill other bugs). I pay a monthly fee of about $100 for my yard to get sprayed for mosquitoes every three weeks during the spring, summer, and fall. This is well worth it to me. I'm always offered a discount at the end of the season if I sign up for next year, which I've done twice. Every time I sign, I smile and daydream about buying a mosquito-spraying company. It's a great business, but I have seen the market get more competitive over time.

PUTTING IT ALL TOGETHER—THE ONE-PAGE BUSINESS PLAN

I am generally not a fan of business plans because they are too long and vague, and often, that's where new entrepreneurs get stuck. Every "How to Start a Business" book I've read always starts with the business plan. Sometimes entrepreneurs need them in order to secure the financing to buy a business, get a mortgage for their business, or solicit investors. But repeatedly, I see entrepreneurs spend many months and even years trying to write the perfect business plan, losing valuable time and momentum because they get stuck in the planning and theoretical stage instead of building something.

You need to start experimenting as quickly as possible. You'll learn from the doing, not the planning. If you want investors or need a business plan, you can create one after you've already started building. It will be a better plan because you've already spent so much time building and learning instead of trying to figure it all out before you start.

I have found a one-page business plan helpful because you can put it together quickly and it forces you to distill everything onto one page. Please keep it to one page and continue to refine it over time. Here is what it includes:

Target Market:
Who are you serving?

_____

Size of Market:
How big is the market?

_____

Problem:
What is the problem?

_____

Solution:
Why will this help the customer?

_____

How:
How will you deliver on your promise? What is your offer?

_____

Marketing:
How will you get your product in front of people who need it?

_____

Price:
What will you charge?

_____

Action Steps:
What are the next three actions you need to take?

_____

_____

_____

_____

START SELLING NOW

No amount of planning and strategy can make up for a lack of action. At some point, you'll need to transition from the planning stage to selling your product to customers. Many people stop here. I've seen it countless times. They have a good idea but then never do anything about it, either because they've walked through questions like the ones in this chapter and determined they don't have the time or the skills to pull it off, or they've recognized that even though they believe they have a great idea, it's not the right idea for them. They care about it, but recognize the amount of effort and passion it would take to achieve, and they're honest with themselves about how valuable their time is.

Or they stop because they're too afraid. Being scared of starting something new is natural, especially with a business. Still, it's up to you whether or not you let this fear paralyze you or leverage that energy and use it as motivation. Fear is normal. It's good. It means you care. It also protects you from doing stupid things and making bad decisions. I still have fear when I launch a new business and I've been doing this for years. This is where Truth #2 comes in: Trust what you feel before what you think. How does this idea make you feel? Does it excite or exhaust you to think about it?

Don't overthink it. If it feels right, it probably is, so now's the time to start experimenting. Remember, you're in control here. Experimenting is about taking risks, learning from what happens, and adapting. Experimenting is about building resilience, knowing your limits, and figuring out what you're made of. Nothing will help you do all three faster than trying to sell something to someone.

Selling has a bad reputation. Many people think selling is about manipulation. It brings to mind a used-car salesman or aggressive men in cheap suits trying to convince you of some dubious "opportunity." But selling is really about adding value to someone's life. It's about making someone aware of a product or service that will improve their lives and solve their problems. If you believe the product or service you have to offer will help do that, then selling it will come naturally. If you don't, it won't. The energy you put forth into the world will compound on itself. Make sure it feels right.

The only way to determine if you believe in what you're selling and if someone else believes in it enough to buy it is to try to sell it. No matter what it is, try to sell it to someone. If you are already participating in a market, sell to your friends or other people you know. If one person is willing to buy from you, someone else will be, too.

CHAPTER 5

SHARE YOUR STORY, BUILD A BRAND, AND LEVERAGE YOUR PLATFORM

"Those who tell the stories rule the world."
—Hopi proverb

It's 2:39 a.m. on a Wednesday, and the only light in my Chicago loft is coming from my laptop. I'm so nervous and my breathing is shallow. I add a title to the blog post I've been working on all night: "Money Is Freedom." This is the first post on Millennial Money, a fresh website with no readers. I've built it from scratch using the skills I've learned as a digital marketer. But this experience feels different from anything I've done before. This is *my* site. My voice. My story.

Up until now, every website I've built has been designed to make someone else money. But I have enough money. I'd become a millionaire by thirty, and if I chose to, I'd never have to work for a paycheck again. I'm not up in the middle of the night writing a blog post because I have to; I'm up because I haven't felt this energy before. I want to share something with the world and, thanks to all the tools available, I can.

I don't know for sure, but I somehow recognize that this blog will change my life. I can feel it. The post is about my journey from a broke twenty-five-year-old to a financially independent thirty-year-old—all with no formal financial training. I've held nothing back. I am sharing my story under my name, making myself vulnerable about the trade-offs I've made in pursuit of money. I'm honest about the mistakes I've made and the lessons I've learned. I tell my readers—or at least my potential readers—I want them to learn from my successes and failures.

I'm not your typical personal finance expert, so I must earn their trust.

As I hit publish, I wonder what my business partners, employees, friends, and family will think if they ever come across this post. I've never shared anything online because I've never felt I had anything to say until I reached financial independence. Now I want to share my story and how I did it with everyone I know.

I can feel the energy stirring inside me—the energy that comes when you know you're doing something meaningful and potentially life-altering. But, at the time, I had no way of knowing what was about to happen. It won't be until years later—after I've amassed millions of readers and started generating seven figures in annual revenue from this site—that I understand the advantage I have at this moment, the chemistry of combining my passions, skills, and story into a business I care so deeply about. I have everything I need to build a brand people will care about, but I have no way of knowing just how incredible my life is about to become. I hit publish, and breathe a sigh of relief and anticipation as my site goes live for the first time.

THE THREE ELEMENTS OF AN AMAZING BRAND

Once you've identified your business idea, you need to figure out the best way to share it with your potential customers.

The only sustainable way to do this is to build a *brand*.

Brands are built on stories, promises, and experience. While you can tell people what your brand is, brands are ultimately built in the interaction between your company and your customers. Everyone has access to the same brand-building tools, but when you're in the experimental stage, you likely don't have the same resources to leverage those tools to their fullest extent.

Luckily, even if you are just starting out, you have access to the three key elements every entrepreneur needs to build a successful brand and rise above the noise:

1. **Story**—a compelling story and experience that is unique to you

2. **Content**—people connect with people and brands through great content

3. **Platform**—a platform you own that allows you to reach your audience on your terms

Looking back on the early days of Millennial Money, it's clear that these things set me apart from other personal finance writers. I had a compelling story and was confident I had value to bring to my audience. I had once been in their shoes, but had since developed a unique perspective on investing and money management that I knew would resonate. Plus, I built my website from scratch, which meant I had complete control over how I communicated with my audience. These three elements are the subject of this chapter.

EVERY BUSINESS STARTS WITH A STORY

When I was twenty-five, I woke up one morning to discover I had $2.26 in my bank account. Five years later, just before I turned thirty, I had a net worth of $1.25 million. I achieved this by saving as much money as possible, investing strategically in the stock market, and side-hustling/starting businesses to increase my income. I had never taken a finance or a business course. During those five years, I spent all my time thinking about money and read over three hundred personal finance, entrepreneurship, and investing books. I put what I learned into practice and, in the process, gained a unique perspective that I knew other people could use.

I wasn't the typical personal finance expert. I had a shaggy beard, long hair, and drove a VW Westfalia camper van. And that made me unique and memorable. It wasn't an act. It was 100 percent me. "Average Joe saves more than $1 million in just five years" is a great hook. Plus, because I reached financial independence using tools that anyone with a computer has access to, people could relate to my story; it was aspirational but accessible. It was authentic, but it also helped me stand out and get attention.

Your story is your competitive advantage.

Your story makes you memorable and stand out in a crowded market, and connects you to others. Your personal experience is unique to you. It has helped shape who you are and why you do what you do. It fuels everything in your life and, therefore, in your business. People connect with people, and humans love stories.

You need to figure out what your story is. Why are you launching this product or service? What makes you different from your competitors? Why are you passionate about offering this product or service to others? Who are you? Why do you care? It doesn't matter what background you have or what business you're in; *everyone* has a story.

As you build out the platform you will use to market and sell your product or service, consider how you can use this platform to share your story with the world. You don't need to run a digital content business like I do to leverage your story.

If you look at some of the most popular product brands that have appeared in the past several years, you can see how they highlight the founder's story alongside the product. Burt's Bees, Warby Parker, Patagonia, Airbnb, and Apple are great examples of brands that effectively integrate their founders' narratives into their brand stories, making their products more relatable and memorable, while creating a strong emotional connection with their customers.

To make your story compelling, you must create a narrative that engages customers and reflects your brand's values and vision. This means showing, not just telling, your story with actions and experiences. It also means developing a long-term story arc that evolves, keeping your customers connected and engaged as you continue to build your brand. I shared all the business's wins and challenges as I was building it. Readers could come on a journey with me. I built in public.

For all entrepreneurs, it's easy for impostor syndrome to set in and undervalue your experience. Long before I started Millennial Money, I was learning information and gleaning insights that would have benefited many people. But I put off sharing them because I worried no one would care what I had to say. No matter how much experience you have, there is likely something you can teach others. Then they can keep learning with you as you learn. Everyone is looking for a leader and someone to learn from. You don't have to be the world's foremost expert on a subject to add value. The world is so large that there's an audience for you.

Consistency is also critical, so make sure your story is reflected the same way across all your platforms, communications, and engagements with your audience and customers. Authenticity is crucial—your story must be genuine and reflect the true essence of who you are. You can't fake it, at least not for long. People can tell when your heart is really in it.

This narrative doesn't change the actual brand's quality, but creates trust between the brand and its potential customers. People would rather buy from someone they know than a faceless corporation that doesn't care about them. Of course, you must also deliver a quality product or service; sharing your story gives you an edge.

Story has always been important, but it's become essential in the era of artificial intelligence. Any chatbot can write a decent ad or website copy or describe the benefits of your product or service. They can also increasingly act like real humans.

However, the more people adopt AI tools, the greater the value of genuine human connection will become. I'm hopeful that we as humans will always be able to feel what's real and connect with what's real and that this will differentiate us from AI. We need human stories to engage with our audiences and stand out.

In short, your powerful brand story needs to be authentic, consistent, and engaging.

Once you start creating, people have something to connect with, and then you have to reach them by building a platform. A platform is everything that represents you to the world—from your message to your website, newsletter, and social media.

GREAT CONTENT BUILDS GREAT BUSINESSES

All great businesses are content businesses. Great content allows you to connect with customers and establish your competitive advantage. Content marketing—offering users free, high-value content—is the most powerful form of organic marketing.

Whether you own a plumbing business or you're an in-demand influencer, people will judge you and your products based on the content you put into the world. Content allows them to determine if you're trustworthy, an expert, and worth paying attention to.

The right content strategy is equal parts art and science. The science involves researching what your target customers are searching for and creating content that speaks directly to that need. The art involves connecting with them in a way that is authentic and unique to you. This helps you distinguish your brand from your competitors, attract the customers most likely to buy from you, and create avid fans of your brand.

Content delivers value by educating or entertaining your audience. Great content does both. When I launched Millennial Money, one of the main ways I distinguished myself was by being open and vulnerable. My vibe was authentic, raw, honest, and human—the complete opposite of most of the buttoned-up, jargon-filled, overly serious personal finance content at the time.

Yes, I provided educational, well-researched, credible information about how to invest and grow wealth, but I was also candid about my struggles, fears, and desires because I knew that so many people shared them. By earning my readers' trust through my authority and authenticity, I grew an audience interested in what I had to offer as a person and Millennial Money as a brand. It kept readers coming back.

You can engage an audience through written, audio, or visual content, but in the beginning, you'll want to focus on the strategy that will deliver the most value quickly and plays to your strengths. Even though people have ever-decreasing attention spans, I'm bullish on the written word. If you want to connect with smart people, writing is the best way to do it. Also, despite the growth of video and audio content, the written word is still the most powerful converter because it allows users to click through to an offer or sales page. Writing great content is the best way to connect with people and keep them engaged. The more you write, the better you'll become at writing and communicating.

Audio—primarily podcasts—can also be a great marketing tool, but typically requires a lot of time and investment and doesn't convert customers as quickly or as powerfully as written content. I have hosted two different podcasts, and they were both useful in helping me build trust with my audience because I could tell deeper stories and have conversations with well-known writers and thinkers like Tony Robbins, James Clear, Vicki Robin, Kevin O'Leary, and others. This helped boost my credibility and generated links from authoritative websites to my website, which helped my SEO. In the beginning I edited all the episodes myself, but eventually hired an editor who could increase the production's quality considerably for only $100 an episode.

You can also monetize podcasts by selling ad space and partnering with affiliates to offer discounts to listeners who convert using a special code. Over two years, I generated more than $250,000 in revenue from advertisers while the shows were live, and I managed all the relationships with the advertisers. Like audio, video content lets you tell deeper stories and engage with your audience. It also requires less effort on the part of your users than written content and allows you to demonstrate products and offer tutorials that may be way harder to convey via text.

Video is increasingly included in search results (YouTube is the world's most popular search engine after Google), and embedding videos on your site increases the time visitors spend on your page, improving SEO. The major downside of video is that it takes work and skill to produce quality video, and poor-quality video can negatively impact your brand. Unless you're passionate about long-form video for platforms like YouTube and have the skills and technology necessary to do it well, focus on experimenting with short-form video for social media or written content.

CREATE CONTENT THAT EDUCATES, INSPIRES, AND ENTERTAINS

Every day, billions of pieces of new content are created, attention spans are getting shorter, and search engine and social media companies are making it harder to reach people, so how do you get people to pay attention to your content? Whether you're writing, creating podcasts, or making videos, all great content educates, inspires, and entertains. You can be successful by doing one or two of these, but the most impactful content does all three.

For this chapter, I will assume you're starting with written content, but the strategies presented below apply no matter what content you produce.

Identify Your Target Audience

The internet is so vast that if you're not specific about whom you're trying to reach, your message will get lost in the noise of everyone else clamoring for your customers' attention. Your brand might appeal to multiple customer groups, but you should pick the one you most want or can best serve.

Be as specific as possible. Consider the customers' location, age, education, gender, profession, political affiliations, religion, income level, hobbies, race/ethnicity—anything that will help you differentiate between ideal customers and those who won't be as well served by your product. My target audience on Millennial Money are millennials who are between twenty-five and forty years old, 50 percent male and 50 percent female, with an average net worth of $110,000. Most live in the United States, primarily in big cities like San Francisco, Los Angeles, Chicago, New York, Dallas, Seattle, and Atlanta.

They're interested in side hustles, entrepreneurship, investing, and traveling. While I've confirmed these details through surveys of my audience and many discussions with readers, I chose this as my target audience from the beginning of Millennial Money based on who *I* was and what I knew about the millennial demographic. I knew that if you were a millennial and lived in a city, on average, you'd have a higher salary and net worth and thus more opportunities to invest money.

After writing down this information, create two to five simple target-customer profiles (also known as personas or avatars). These are fictional characters who represent your ideal customers. This is a worthwhile exercise because it gives you a hypothetical audience to consider when deciding what content to produce.

They're also helpful as the business grows and can serve as a filter for decisions like how to expand a product line, where to open additional locations (if you have a brick-and-mortar business), where to market a product, etc. These profiles might change over time, but not often. There will likely be overlap between your personas, since people interested in the same products will likely have common interests or needs. Still, they should be diverse enough to represent the full demographic breadth of your target customers.

Give your personas names to distinguish and personify them and a two- or three-sentence description. Don't overcomplicate this or spend too much time on it. It should take an hour or so and come quickly, since you've already identified your market and their needs.

Here are the five personas I developed in the early days of Millennial Money:

- **Matt, 25, Chicago:**
  A marketing manager earning $70,000 annually, Matt is interested in entrepreneurship, digital marketing, and investing. He wants to make $30,000 to $50,000 a year in side income to start investing in real estate. He hopes his side income will eventually be enough to cover his full-time-job salary. Matt is moderately liberal and cares about giving back, but he is a typical self-focused mid-twentysomething.

- **Samantha, 30, Dallas:**
  This attorney is stressed and wants to make big changes in her life. She's been saving and investing diligently for eight years and has saved $200,000, but she doesn't know what's next. She's curious about leaving her job and starting her own firm or consulting business.

- **Trevor, 35, St. Louis:**
  He just had his first kid and is ready to take money seriously. He has a 401(k) and a brokerage account, but wonders if he has the right investment strategy and if it's too late to consider a side hustle. He likes his job, but doesn't want to work until he's sixty-five.

- **Ann, 40, Los Angeles:**
  She owns her bookkeeping practice with two employees and is netting $250,000 in profit per year. She has a successful, growing business and wants to learn what to do next. Can she sell her business? Maybe retire early? She increasingly believes she can reach financial independence and wants to know the steps she can take.

- **John, 38, Denver:**
  Already a millionaire and wonders if he has enough money to retire. He's also interested in what he should do next. Is he ready to retire early? Can he downshift into a less stressful job? How would he spend his time? Could he live off his investments?

As you can see, these are five different "people," but they share an interest in personal finance, entrepreneurship, and investing. Having been in their shoes, I knew the type of content and tone that would most appeal to them.

Once you've created your personas, ask yourself what content would best educate, inspire, and entertain them. The more you distinguish your content from your competitors, the more likely it is to engage readers. The more involved they are, the more likely they will remember you, share your content with others, return to your website, and sign up for your newsletter.

Educate to Build Trust

Most Google and social media queries are questions. What questions are your target customers asking and how can you answer them? Demonstrate you're an authority by comprehensively covering a wide range of topics related to your business. The more completely, accurately, and uniquely you can answer your target customers' questions, and the more helpful you are, the more impactful the content will be. Any content you post should be factually correct, but don't be afraid to share opinions or counterintuitive perspectives.

Inspire to Create Connection

Most people are stressed out, tired, anxious, depressed, and seeking inspiration. The world already has so much negativity, pessimism, and suffering. Create content that inspires and people will pay attention. Be positive, optimistic, and passionate about what you're selling. Share your story and be vulnerable. People can tell when you care. When you share your authentic self, it will inspire others.

Entertain to Be Memorable

Do you remember the most entertaining blog post or book you've ever read? Or the most entertaining video you've ever watched? I do. We remember the things that entertain and delight us. While not everything needs to be an over-the-top Mr. Beast YouTube video, entertaining content will always be more memorable and drive more engagement than forgettable content. Good writing, storytelling, podcasts, and videos can all be entertaining.

Stay Consistent

Most people quit creating content after a few weeks or months because they lose momentum. Either they weren't passionate enough about their idea, they picked a form of content they didn't want to get better at, they burned out, or they just gave up. Half the battle is staying in the game.

You must consistently create new content for a content strategy to work. This can be daunting—especially if you are not a natural writer or have little time to spare. That's okay. Come up with a strategy that honors your limits while building momentum and you'll get to where you need to go. The more the results of your efforts pay off, the more motivated you'll be to keep creating.

More is not better if it's not sustainable. One to three posts per week is a perfect target for starting, but post at least once a week to maintain momentum. Don't wait for inspiration to strike or to be "in the mood."

Set aside time on your calendar to brainstorm ideas and draft and publish posts. If you can ramp up your frequency, great. Frequent posting and fresh content have been shown to positively impact rankings, but always honor your limits. You realistically have to invest at least three to six months consistently publishing content to start building an audience and appeasing the algorithms. Then, once you start generating momentum, you need to stay consistent or momentum will dwindle.

While this might feel like a big commitment, I can assure you that just keeping with it significantly increases your opportunity for success because 95 percent of people give up after three months. The numbers are pretty staggering. As an example, 90 percent of podcasts don't publish past three episodes, and less than 1 percent of all podcasts that are started make it past twenty episodes. You gain a huge competitive advantage just from staying in the game and narrowing the competitor field.

Start Now and Keep Experimenting

The best way to get good at creating great content is to create a lot of content. The more you create, the better you'll get. And the sooner you start creating, the quicker you'll get great at it. Create the best, most valuable posts or videos you can about your topic, but don't wait. As long as you keep going, you'll improve. I was mediocre when I started writing on Millennial Money, but my readers didn't care. All the mistakes I made and the way I wrote just made me more human and relatable. Ultimately, it didn't matter if I was Shakespeare because the information and expertise I shared were solid and delivered a ton of value for my readers.

Your initial content should answer the primary questions that any searcher would have about your product or service. Let's say you're selling a new type of camping stove. Examples of the type of content you should produce include: "What Is a Camping Stove?," "Top 5 Camping Stoves," "How to Pack for a Backpacking Trip," and "Are Propane Stoves Safe?"

Pick topics that appeal to a broad swath of your target audience (something all five of your personas would want to learn about). Combine a mixture of evergreen content like "Top Food Prep Tips for

Campers" and more timely content like "Best Places to Camp This Year." You can find these topics through keyword research, and you should write about topics that showcase your expertise and appeal to your target customer base.

You Need to Own Your Platform

When I started my money journey in 2010, no one used the term *influencer* to describe those who made money by creating content on the internet. YouTube had been around for only five years, Instagram was just about to be invented, and TikTok wouldn't launch globally for another eight years. Today, influencer is one of the most popular careers on the planet. The influencer economy is worth $104 billion and over 85 million Americans (roughly a quarter of the U.S. population) post creative content online.

Setting aside the fact that most online creators don't earn enough income to live on, let alone achieve financial independence, there's another major, often overlooked issue with deciding on influencer as a career path. Most influencers make money through established third-party platforms like YouTube, TikTok, and Instagram. But as any creator will tell you, these platforms constantly change their algorithms in ways that dramatically impact who sees what. There is no way to make money without a way to reach your audience or customers. This is true of any business, but only on social media do so many people place their faith in a giant corporation (with millions of other users vying for the same followers) for access to that audience.

To succeed as an entrepreneur, you need to *own* your platforms. You can own an email list, a website, a text list, a book, a podcast, and self-hosted videos.

Social media can be an excellent tool for promotion, brand awareness, and engaging with your fans. You can also use it as your initial content-creation platform to test your ideas and build an audience before investing time and energy into building your proprietary platform. But as you grow, you don't want to worry that all your income will dry up if one of your accounts is banned or the algorithm starts hiding your content from users' feeds.

Owning your platforms—particularly a website and email newsletter—puts you in more control and guarantees your customers will always be able to find you. These tools also allow you to collect data to better understand your customers' habits and meet their needs.

Building a fully functional website and email newsletter list in the influencer era may seem old-school, but these platforms provide the most effective way to build and scale your customer base. This is true no matter what kind of business you have—physical or online, product or service. The more you experiment with building them, keeping them updated with fresh content, and optimizing for SEO, the more efficiently they will grow.

HOW TO EXPERIMENT WITH SOCIAL MEDIA

While relying exclusively on social media to market and sell your brand is never a good idea, it can be a valuable audience builder, depending on your industry. The biggest issue with social media is that there are so many platforms, and mastering one, let alone several, requires tremendous effort and consistency.

The paradox of the opportunity is that it is extremely competitive because it's so easy to start and grow quickly. This means you have to create good content, be consistent, learn the newest features and trends, and get a little lucky.

Social media platforms are also designed to keep you on them for as long as possible, so very few users will click on links in your profile or under your videos. This makes it nearly impossible to sell products or services directly from your social media accounts unless you have hundreds of thousands or millions of followers, so you have to default to selling brand partnerships (which can be tedious) or rely on getting paid a percentage of advertising dollars from the platform (which several platforms like YouTube, TikTok, and X have all decreased in the past few years).

Plus, since any platform can change its algorithm without warning, it's impossible ever to be fully in control of how your content performs. The addictive nature of social media also makes it easy to start focusing on the wrong things—like how many likes a post receives or how to ride the wave of the latest TikTok trend—instead of what will help grow your business.

Here are my best practices for using social media as an Experimental Entrepreneur:

1. *Pick One or Two Platforms and Ignore the Rest*
   Pick your platforms carefully, based on where your audience and market hang out and the ones you enjoy working with the most. If you're an attorney serving small businesses looking to acquire, you should probably engage on X and LinkedIn rather than Instagram or TikTok. By contrast, a graphic designer must focus on visual platforms, especially Instagram, TikTok, YouTube, or Pinterest, to showcase their work and process.

2. *Establish a Channel of Communication and Leverage Messaging Automation*
   Keep your DMs open so followers can reach you and you can easily connect with customers, competitors, and any brands you might want to affiliate with. An increasing number of technologies, like ManyChat, can automate your message responses to help you generate leads, sales, and other conversions through direct messaging on social media.

3. *Follow Your Competitors*
   Even if you don't post content on a particular platform, following your competitors across their biggest platforms can still be an efficient way to stay aware of what they're doing. Set aside twenty to thirty minutes every few weeks to check out their latest posts.

4. *Consider the Time-Value Trade-off*

Andrei Jikh, creator of the Magic of Finance You-Tube channel, spends twelve to fifteen hours making every ten-minute video he posts. It takes a lot of time to concept a video, write a script, film a video, edit it, create thumbnail graphics, and optimize titles and descriptions. TikTok creators I've spoken to said they can spend four to five hours making a sixty-second video. The time trade-off here is enormous, but if you love creating this type of content and are willing to put in the effort to study the platform and learn how it works—and if your target audience uses this platform—then there are real opportunities to grow an audience.

5. *Set Your Limits*

No matter what platforms you're on and how successful you are with them, I cannot overemphasize the need for you to set limits around how much time you spend on them. As you know, social media is powered by algorithms that try to keep you engaged for as long as possible. Studies consistently show that the more time you spend on social media, the bigger the negative impact on your mental and physical health.

Even the creators I know who have made social media a centerpiece of their strategy complain to me about its toll on them. If you decide to use social media, figure out how much time you want to dedicate each week and stay within those limits. As you experiment, pay attention to not only what's working but how you feel. If you start to feel unfulfilled or addicted, that's a sign to pull back and restrategize.

PAID VS. ORGANIC MARKETING

When building an audience, you can use two broad strategies: paid marketing and organic marketing.

Paid marketing is paying for better access to your target audience through advertising, affiliate links, or sponsorships. Paid marketing can be helpful to grow your business to its maximum potential, but as the name implies, it requires you to lay out cash—usually a lot of it—to see results. It's also very competitive, and it can take a lot of time to keep up with ad platforms that change often. When you're still at the experimental stage, you want to keep expenses as low as possible, which is why I love organic marketing.

Organic marketing involves tactics that build your customer base without your having to spend any money. These include search engine optimization, blogging, email marketing, word of mouth, and social media. Organic marketing works best when you lean into your story. The best organic marketing also compounds over time: you put something out into the world that resonates with people, and those people share it, so it spreads even further. People share things that are entertaining or useful. A good story is both.

USE A LANDING PAGE TO EXPERIMENT, BUT A WEBSITE TO TAKE YOU FURTHER

You don't need to build an entire website while still testing whether your idea is viable. Although you can technically set up a website in a few hours and for relatively little money, a *good* website requires some effort. Instead, set up a basic landing page that you can use to capture email addresses and generate sales quickly. Use a tool like Click-Funnels or ConvertKit, or most email management platforms now have landing-page features to create one in as little as twenty minutes. When you've started generating sales and are ready to build your platform and scale, you should build a full website.

Your website provides the foundation for a robust platform and organic marketing strategy. I'm not going to cover all the basics of creating a website from scratch because there are plenty of online tools and videos to help you. I learned by watching YouTube videos and tinkering on my own for a few weeks. That laid the groundwork for me to grow the website into the multimillion-dollar revenue generator it is today. Now it's even easier—you can use website builders at GoDaddy, Bluehost, and others to get a solid starting website up in less than an hour.

For now, I want to share some things many new business owners overlook or struggle to get right when launching their website. If you want a deeper dive into website basics, check out my free email course at https://grantsabatier.com/website.

SEARCH ENGINE OPTIMIZATION WILL GROW YOUR BUSINESS

Search engine optimization (SEO) is the process of making your website, videos, products, social media profiles, or Amazon pages relevant to users and search engines. SEO used to focus only on Google, the world's largest search engine, but now you can optimize any platform where users search. As of this writing, Google is the most popular search engine, followed by YouTube, but according to Google's data, nearly 40 percent of Gen Z are using TikTok and Instagram for searching instead of Google.

Learning SEO will transform your business by getting you in front of people who want exactly what you sell. Whether you're running a thriving baby skin care brand online or a specialized HVAC company in your neighborhood, you will generate more sales and make more money if you show up in the top five search results on Google. In some industries, the websites and businesses that rank in these top positions earn millions of dollars in monthly revenue from search traffic alone.

While you can pay to have your business show up in the top results, optimizing your website to rank there for free is far more valuable. Then you can convert free traffic from Google or social media into sales.

Websites optimized for SEO rank higher in online searches and attract more visitors. SEO attracts high-intent traffic, meaning the people who find your site are actively seeking your product, services, content, or information. If someone searches "How much do solar panels cost?" and clicks on a link for a post on your website about the price of solar panels, you can infer that they are at least somewhat interested in buying solar panels.

Imagine you're a local plumber who wrote an article on your website about the top five reasons basements smell like sewage. If someone in your area searches Google for "Why does my basement smell like sewage?" Google will rank you in this person's top search results because it identifies you as a local "expert." The searcher clicks on the link to your article and notices a call to action at the top of the page. "Need some help? We can identify why your basement smells and fix the issue within 24 hours. Give us a call." This is precisely how I recently found a plumber for my own home.

SEO also compounds—the more you optimize your website, the more people visit it because it becomes easier to find. The sooner you start paying attention to SEO, the more it will pay off. Search engines use different methods for ranking websites in search results, but Google dominates the global search market. Google processes trillions of searches every year. Interestingly, 15 percent of all Google searches are unique, meaning approximately 1.275 billion searches every day have never been searched before. Because Google tries to show relevant results for every new query, there are always new opportunities for your website to rank and get traffic.

Google has not released its proprietary algorithm for ranking search results, but we know a lot about how it works. For Google to return the most relevant search results to users, it has established specific criteria to determine what makes some sites more credible, relevant, and reputable. When a user searches for a particular term or phrase, Google crawls the entire internet, evaluates which sites best meet these criteria, and presents results based on what the user is looking for.

Among the many elements Google searches for when assessing a site are the quality of its content; the experience, expertise, authoritativeness, and trustworthiness (also known as E-E-A-T) of its brand and writers; whether other sites have linked to this website and how they talk about it; how many other visitors the site receives; and whether the site poses any security risks to the user. Google also analyzes how much time a visitor spends on the site, how fast it loads and responds to user navigation, how many pop-ups and links it has, and hundreds, if not thousands, of other things.

Considering all these factors, SEO is equal parts art and science. There are basic things you can do to make your site better for users, but there's also a ton of creativity involved, especially with things like creating content and using links. It can feel intimidating at first, but the longer you do SEO, the more you learn and the more intuitive—and lucrative—it becomes. I've turned free Google traffic to my websites into many millions of dollars in revenue. Here are some of the most important things to keep in mind.

THE POWER OF KEYWORD RESEARCH AND TARGETING SEARCHERS

Google ranks a website based on how helpful it is in answering a searcher's query and prioritizes content from people with experience and expertise in the topic they're writing about. I have experience writing about money, and that's why Millennial Money ranks high in searches for things like "how to make extra money" but not for searches for "classic French recipes" or "carpet cleaning." If you want to appear in searches for your particular product, service, or industry, you first need to know what your target customers are searching for and then make sure your content answers their questions. That's where keyword analysis and optimization come in.

Keywords are the words or phrases people type into search engines. They can range from short and broad, like "personal finance tips," to longer and more specific, like "How much money can I contribute to my 401(k) this year?" The better your website can answer these queries, the higher it will rank.

The best way to determine the most relevant keywords for your business is to analyze your competitors. Which keyword searches do the top-ranking businesses in your market rank high for? What content on their websites might show up in searches for these keywords?

The answers to these questions can help you figure out what topics you should cover with your content and if there are any gaps you can fill in the meantime.

As you perform your keyword research, keep track of the relevant topics you should cover and what keywords they use. I like to use a spreadsheet to keep all this information in one easy-to-update place. Create your topic list using the relevant keywords you see your competitors ranking for. If they are writing about a topic, consider writing about it in a way that can be more helpful and add more value to readers than your competitors. This is how you outrank them and attract high-intent searchers to your website.

Your target topic list should be comprehensive and something you can continue to add to and refine over time. As you publish content, copy the URL for the page on which that content lives next to your target keyword(s) on your topic list. For added clarity, organize all your target keywords by related categories (aka "silos"). For example, on Millennial Money, we have four primary silos (Make Money, Invest Money, Save Money, and Borrow Money).

These silos represent the core content focus areas that you want Google and users to associate with your website. They should be relevant to your topic, and you should have fewer than five, especially early on. Inexperienced entrepreneurs often make the mistake of creating too many categories and trying to write content on too many topics. This makes it difficult for users and Google to figure out what your website is about and what you have expertise in.

Stay focused on the most relevant topics your target customer is searching for and then expand over time by adding related topics. The more focused you can be and the more helpful your content is, the easier it is for users and Google to understand what you're about and evaluate the quality of your content. It is always easier to rank for longer phrases (three or more keywords) than for shorter phrases. Many websites pick keywords that are too short, competitive, and general.

It is often easiest to rank for keywords with between 500 and 3,000 monthly searches. Over time, as your website gets traction, you will have a better shot at ranking for the shorter, more competitive keywords. One caveat to this is geography: you might be able to rank for higher-search keywords in a local market, where there is less competition, by adding the location modifier to the keyword phrase (example: "best plumbers in Gulf Shores, Alabama").

There are three types of tools you can use to do keyword research:

Google (Free): Search a phrase on Google that one of your target customers would search for and see which sites appear at the top of the results. You can then click on those sites and explore the types of content that satisfy those searches.

Google Keyword Planner (Free): For more granular search-volume data, you can use Google's Keyword Planner tool within Google Ads. If you don't already have a Google Ads account, you can register for free. This allows you to analyze the search volume for any Google search query, but there are limitations on the amount of data you can get.

Paid Keyword Tools: There are many paid SEO tools that are more powerful and helpful than Google's free ones. If you're taking SEO seriously, I highly recommend investing in at least one. Among their many features, you can see the keyword rankings for any website, see who links to any website, and find topic ideas to write about. You can also use these tools to identify competitors' rankings for any search on Google. As of this writing, Semrush, Ahrefs, and Surfer SEO are popular paid tools, but new ones are being released regularly.

You can start building your website once you've done basic keyword research, but SEO is ongoing. No matter what stage your business is in, you will have to maintain and update your website. Thankfully, this will all get easier as time goes on, and at some point, you will likely outsource the bulk of your website management to other people. The goal is to build a site that functions well and will serve your target customers. Do not worry if it's not perfect or all of this feels overwhelming. Take things one step and one day at a time. All the energy you put forth at this stage will compound.

Here are some essential steps to get started.

Select a Good Domain and Brand Name

Your domain name is your brand. You want it to be clear and memorable. The shorter the domain, the better. One word is best, two words are good, and three words can be okay, but it can be challenging for people to remember anything longer than that. Make sure you choose a domain that relates to what you do and that matches your brand name. You don't want a blog called "Money Machine" living at coolmoneyguy.com. Think of the brands profiled in this book for inspiration: Millennial Money, Student Loan Planner, and the Rideshare Guy. They're short, to the point, and memorable—and they make it evident what services they offer.

Search for available domains using reputable sellers like GoDaddy or Bluehost. Most domains start at $12, but because domain flipping has become a popular investment strategy, some of the more popular keyword-rich ones will cost you a few hundred or even a couple of thousand dollars. If you can spend a little more for a high-quality domain, do it. If your business succeeds in the long term, it will be worth the investment. If it doesn't, you can always sell the domain later on.

Buy the .com version of your domain first. If that isn't available, come up with a domain name that is. Domains ending in .com rank higher in Google and are the default for many searchers. Before purchasing your domain, ensure another brand does not have a trademark for the name. If it is already trademarked and your company becomes successful, you may wind up in legal trouble and have to change the name. That would be a massive headache and could severely disrupt how your customers find you. Check out the U.S. government's free trademark search tool to verify whether your name is safe.

If you have the financial resources, it's worth trademarking your brand name at this stage if it's unique and you plan to make a longer-term investment in growing your business. You can also set a goal to trademark the brand name once you've generated $10,000 in sales or some other proof point. If your name is more descriptive than unique, you might have difficulty getting on the primary registry, which gives you the most protection.

I have a trademark for Millennial Money, but it's on the secondary registry because it is descriptive. This doesn't give me much protection; as a result, other brands have used the same term for their content or series. CNBC, with whom I have worked on and off over the years, launched a video series called *Millennial Money*. This ended up helping me because I rank #1 for Millennial Money on Google, so when searchers are looking for the CNBC series, they always find my website first.

Remember that even if you trademark your name, you're still responsible for enforcing it. It costs money to send cease-and-desist letters to those infringing on your trademark, and the whole process can be a big headache. That said, having some protection is better than none, and it's worth it if you're at that stage in your business where you're confident that you will be using this brand name for a few years or will want to sell it someday.

Use Your Website to Tell Your Story

Once you set up the back end of your site, you can start building the public-facing pages your target audience will see. Keep in mind that you're still in the experimental stage. Your site doesn't need to be perfect to be effective. You can—and should—refine and update your website frequently to showcase the most accurate and relevant information.

There are three types of content you will need to create:

1. **Evergreen content** that provides critical information on your brand and doesn't change frequently. These include your home page, About page, and Contact page.

2. **Content-marketing pages** that showcase your expertise and provide information your visitors are searching for.

This type of content is updated and added frequently and will most often appear in your target audience's search results.

3. **Conversion pages** are where visitors can take action that turns them into customers or followers.

All these pages work together to improve your SEO. Here are some examples of each:

EVERGREEN PAGES

Home Page

The basics of a good home page are simple, but they're essential to ensure you're presenting your brand well for your audience. Remember, visitors are judging you. We've all been excited by something and then gone to a company's website and been turned off. We've all also been inspired and drawn in.

Ensure that it has clear branding and navigation to make the most of your home page. If you have one, include your logo, a compelling headline, and a brief introduction explaining your offering. Use eye-catching and relevant images or graphics that resonate with your brand and message. Also, optimize any image's file size for faster page loading, and include alt tags that describe each image for accessibility and SEO.

Provide a well-structured navigation menu that makes it easy for visitors to navigate your site. The navigation should include roughly five to eight items representing your site's primary focus. Include your About and Contact pages and three to six other keyword-rich items in your navigation. For example, Student Loan Planner's site navigation includes "Refinance," "Get Help," and "Calculators." Millennial Money has "Make," "Invest," "Save," "Borrow," and "Life You Love."

On the home page, you should also showcase your most important or popular content, products, or services in a visually appealing way. Use images, brief descriptions, and links to direct visitors to relevant pages. If you have a specific action you want a user to take, like signing up for your email list, exploring products, or starting a free trial, include a prominent call-to-action button that makes it easy for visitors to do so.

If you have them, include customer testimonials, reviews, awards, or anything that conveys social proof to your visitors. On my website, I have "As Seen in the *New York Times*, CNBC, and NPR." If you have a blog, news, or events section, include links to "Featured Blog Posts," "Popular Blog Posts," "Latest News," or "Upcoming Events." You should also showcase your featured products or most popular services.

Finally, you want to ensure visitors have an easy way to contact you, so include a contact form, email, and phone number, depending on your primary contact method.

About Page

Your About page is the most important page on your website because it helps visitors connect with your brand, understand your story, get a sense of your experience, and build trust.

To make the most of this page, introduce yourself and explain why you've started your business. This is the most obvious place to tell your story. Use your personal voice and try to humanize your brand as much as possible. Share photos of yourself and any images that support or add emotional weight to your story. If you're selling a new ultra-lightweight camping tent, show yourself using it somewhere beautiful. Did your dad inspire your love of camping? Include a photo of you and your dad enjoying nature together when you were younger.

Include your mission statement and brand values if you have them. You should also use your About page to establish your brand's expertise and credibility. Include links to any media mentions about you or your business, links to your business profiles, links to any associations with which you are affiliated, and links to your Wikipedia page if you have one. If you have any certifications, licenses, or awards relevant to your industry, note those on the page.

If and when you decide to add new members to your team, add their bios to your About page. If your team becomes very large (say, more than five to ten people), you'll want to set up a separate Team page.

Contact Page

A good, easy-to-find Contact page indicates to users that your business is legitimate, with a real person behind it, and gives them an easy way to get in touch if needed. Google rewards sites that make this easy. At the very least, include an email address or a contact form linked to an email address that you check often so customers or potential customers can reach you easily and on their own time.

Google wants to verify a physical location behind your business, so include a mailing address, even if it's a P.O. box you set up at your local post office. If you include a phone number, that would be even better. I use a free Google Voice number, so my personal number is unavailable online. If you have a physical address for your business—like a storefront or public office—embed a Google map on your Contact page. This will help elevate your local search rankings.

CONTENT MARKETING PAGES

As I explained, a consistent, relevant, and engaging content marketing strategy helps build trust, recognition, and credibility among your target customers. Even if you're not a content-first business like a blog or YouTube channel, you will benefit from creating and sharing quality content online, especially if you optimize that content for search. Here are my best SEO practices for your content marketing pages.

Select a Keyword-Rich Title and URL

The more relevant your title to your target reader, the more likely they are to click on it when it comes up in a Google search. This improves your click-through rate (CTR), which, in turn, boosts your reputation with Google. Use your keywords to create titles that grab your target customers' attention. Post titles should be thirty to sixty-five characters and include your target keyword or phrase. WordPress will likely default to a URL for the post that matches the post's title. This may be fine if you've chosen a short, keyword-rich title, but I often see URLs that are far too long. Google recommends using a maximum of three to five words in your URLs. I also recommend keeping them between thirty and fifty characters.

Include Design and Visual Elements

Although Google can't crawl images, it can identify posts that include visuals and it ranks posts with images higher than those without. Depending on post length, try to include at least one to three relevant images per post. Images that you've created or photos you've taken are always going to be more attractive to your visitor than stock images, but you can get high-quality royalty-free stock images from websites like Pixabay or Pexels, as well as through design tools like Canva. During the first two years of Millennial Money, I used only photos I took myself, but this became too difficult as the website scaled.

Large images tend to slow down page-load speed, which negatively impacts SEO, so resize the file to under 1.5 MB to ensure a good user experience. To improve search potential, you can also include alt tags and descriptions of any images through your content management system (CMS) platform.

Google also rewards posts that include videos. If you're not creating your videos at this stage, you can search YouTube for a relevant video and embed it directly into your post if it makes it more helpful. You should select videos that you think are awesome and that you think would add the most value to your reader. Don't add your competitor's videos to your site; you can find other experts to feature.

Provide a Call to Action

Even though you're giving this content away for free, if you plan to make money primarily by selling a product or service, you need a certain percentage of your visitors to buy that product or service from you. While the main focus of your posts should be to engage and inform your reader, each is an opportunity to market your product.

Link to your conversion pages to make it easy for your customers to buy from you. You can do this through links in the post or by issuing direct calls to action, such as "For more information on how to do *x*, sign up for my six-week online course."

CONVERSION PAGES ARE YOUR MONEYMAKERS

The ultimate goal of your website is to convert visitors into customers. You increase your chances of this in two ways. The first is by building compelling and clear product pages where people purchase your product. The second is to make it easy for visitors to subscribe to your email list through an opt-in page. We'll talk more about opt-in pages later in this chapter, so for now, let's focus on product pages. There are two types of product pages—product description pages and sales pages.

Product Description Pages

Product description pages share clear information about your product and make it easy for readers to buy. They are short, concise, and visually rich with images and video. A great product page has a clear and engaging description that makes it easy for your website visitor to understand what you're selling, who it's for, its unique benefits, and the problems it solves. It also includes high-quality images of the product, the product in use, or your services that illicit emotion. I see many new entrepreneurs skimp on image quality—don't.

Are you selling boutique teas? Show an image of someone cozied on the sofa on a cold day, drinking tea. Take your visitors to where they'll use your product, or try to make them feel what engaging with it is like. People connect with good images. An effective informational product page also includes transparent pricing, an easy way to buy, a list of frequently asked questions (FAQ), and an easy way for verified buyers to leave reviews. To see a simple but well-converting product page design, check out any product listing on Amazon.com. Most product page templates that integrate with your Shopify store or cart should have a solid framework you'll want to customize.

Sales Pages

Sales pages are typically longer than informational pages and go into deeper detail about the product and why you should buy it. Sales pages are designed to form a more intimate connection with your visitor, and great sales page writers leverage core principles of psychology to make you feel you can't resist buying the product. Sales copy can be so powerful and profitable that top copywriters can command up to $100,000 to write a single sales page that converts well and generates millions of dollars.

That is how powerful a single website page can be. But you don't need to spend money to learn how to be a great copywriter. It just takes some study and practice. While we won't go deep into this, many high-converting sales pages are built on a simple structure. For an example of a good sales page, check out the one I use for my community at https://grantsabatier.com/community.

HOW TO STRUCTURE A SALES PAGE FOR MAXIMUM CONVERSION

1. **Identify a Pain Point:** To get people interested in your product or service, talk about a problem or challenge they might face. This is called a pain point. For example, if you're selling a personal finance course for couples, you can talk about how many people struggle with money and how it's the number one cause of divorce and marriage stress. This helps your readers relate to the issue and makes them more open to hearing about your solution.

2. **Make a Promise:** Once you've highlighted the problem, it's time to offer your solution, aka your promise. Tell your visitors how your product or service can help them overcome the pain point. Sticking

with the above example, you can promise that your personal finance program will help couples be less stressed about money and build a stronger marriage. You can also promise it will help them build a life they want to live together.

3. **Introduce the Product or Service:** Provide specific details about your product or service, including its features and benefits. Features are what the product includes (e.g., 25+ videos, in-depth conversation guides, a community of other couples, a personal coach, etc.). Benefits include accountability, support, and the desired result. Explain how everything works and why it's the best solution to the problem you've mentioned.

4. **Provide Testimonials:** Share success stories, testimonials, and case studies to show that your solution is effective. People want to see how you have solved the problems of other people like them and how their lives have improved as a result. Share written or video testimonials from a diverse set of your customers. Keep a backlog of these testimonials and record new ones whenever one of your customers has a great experience, then add the best ones to your sales page. You can also take screenshots of Amazon reviews, social media mentions, and other reviews to include on your sales page.

5. **Show Social Proof:** People often feel more comfortable buying something when they know others have had a good experience. Share reviews, ratings, or endorsements from satisfied customers. Take screenshots of social media comments, emails, and messages

your customers write about your product. Include these screenshots on your sales page. This social proof builds trust and credibility.

6. **Answer Common Objections:** Potential customers will have many doubts and questions about your product. Answer the most popular questions and objections directly in your landing page's frequently asked questions (FAQ) section. Address these objections by providing clear and honest answers. By answering as many of the popular questions that potential customers have up front in your FAQ, you're building confidence with the visitors and removing their objections to purchasing.

7. **Include Bonuses:** Everyone wants to get as much value for their money as possible, and they might be more inclined to buy something if you can sweeten the deal. On your sales page, include bonuses people get for purchasing from you, like e-books, swag, or free products. You can easily include other things you've created or small bonuses that add a lot of perceived value to the purchase. Outline all these bonuses and try to quantify the monetary value of the bonuses for visitors to make the price of your product seem like a great value.

8. **Add Calls to Action:** Tell your visitors what you want them to do next and make it easy for them to do it. Encourage them to take action, such as clicking a "Buy Now" button or signing up for your newsletter. Make these call-to-action buttons noticeable and compelling. You want to make it as easy for them to buy from you as possible.

9. **Add Upsells:** An upsell is an additional product or service offer presented to a potential customer after they show interest in or decide to purchase the main product or service featured on the page. The goal of an upsell is to increase the average transaction value and boost revenue while offering customers products or services that align with their interests and needs. For example, if you're selling boutique teas, you could feature upsells like tea strainers, teapots, or another blend of tea similar to the one they want. To add extra offers to your sales page, start by finding products or services that complement what you're selling. Make them seem like a great deal by providing discounts or special packages. Place these offers where customers can easily see them on your sales page after they decide to buy your main product, but before they complete the purchase. Provide clear choices with buttons like "Add to Cart" or "No thanks."

10. **Create Urgency:** One way to make people more interested in your product is to create a sense of urgency by introducing scarcity into your sales page. This means letting visitors know they must act quickly to get a special offer or access. For example, you can say that your offer is available only for the next two hours and add a countdown timer on the page. People who feel they might miss out are more likely to take action. I open my FIpreneur community only two or three times a year to ensure everyone has a great experience, so those interested in joining have to act quickly when I open the community to new people. I put the countdown timer on the landing page so visitors know how long they have to

sign up before the offer expires. When I'm not accepting new members, I provide a link to a form potential future members can use to sign up for the waiting list.

11. **Money-Back Guarantee:** You should have a transparent refund or money-back policy on your FAQ and cart pages. I'm a big fan of offering a no-questions-asked thirty-day money-back guarantee to ensure my customers have the best experience possible. This guarantee takes all the risk away for the buyer since they know they can get their money back. You can make it harder for your customers to get their money back or make them jump through hoops by creating requirements for them to get their money back (like requiring them to complete all course modules and assignments), but this never felt right to me. You should get your money back if you don't think I've delivered on my promise. Ultimately, this leads to happier customers and builds a stronger brand.

While it might take some time for you to learn how to write strong converting sales pages, the time will be well worth it and it is an essential skill to at least know the basics of if you want to make money online. Even if you decide to hire an expert copywriter, good ones aren't cheap, and you can save a lot of money and become a much better all-around marketer if you invest the time to learn how to write sales pages.

Monitor Your Progress

As you set up your website, you should also set up the tools that will allow you to monitor your website traffic, engagement, and sales. If you sell products on your website, you must set up an online shopping cart and a payment processor. As of this writing, Shopify is the most popular online product sales platform, and Stripe is the most popular payment processor.

While there are several free and paid analytics tools, the most popular is Google Analytics, which you can set up for free. Within Google Analytics, you can easily integrate your sales data with your website data. This is valuable because you'll be able to see what website pages generated your sales and where the website traffic that generated the sale originated. In addition to using Google Analytics, you can also set up Google's Looker Studio, which allows for even more customizations across many different tools and platforms.

A few important key metrics to pay attention to at this stage are: unique website visitors, visitors by traffic source, page engagement, bounce rate (percentage of users who leave after viewing one page of the website), time on the website, and conversion events that show the number of visitors converting into sales and subscribing to your email list. You should also start analyzing your revenue per website visitor and work to increase it over time. In the affiliate marketing industry, we maximize our earnings per click (EPC) on our website and track it closely across our portfolio.

CULTIVATE YOUR CUSTOMERS WITH COMPELLING EMAILS

Once you've attracted potential customers to your website, you want to keep them engaged with your brand. No matter what type of business you have, email allows you to reach, cultivate, and monetize your audience. It is your direct line to both your current and future customers. You can use it to target specific content and offers directly to the people who care about and are interested in what you're selling. You don't need an extensive email list to start making some serious money. Once you hit 1,000 high-quality subscribers, you should be able to make consistent revenue from your list.

Email keeps your brand at the top of mind for anyone subscribing to your email list. It also allows subscribers to forward your content to others they think might be interested. Because you own and operate your email list directly, you have complete control over the messaging and delivery. You can easily use your collected data to gauge which messages lead to the most engagement and sales.

Emails can be pure gold, but they must be delivered and managed well. This all starts with the email copy. You must share content that engages, informs, and inspires subscribers to act. Email copywriting is an art form, but you don't need to be a great copywriter to harvest incredible value from your email list. You need to know what your audience cares about. These are your people! Your subscribers have either intentionally signed up to receive your emails or submitted their email addresses when purchasing. They care about what you're selling. Be yourself and don't get too stressed. The important thing is to get started.

As of this writing, email deliverability is starting to drop a bit because Gmail (the popular email provider owned by Google) is showing more ads in email, and its sorting algorithms are making it more difficult to end up in an inbox instead of the promotions folder. Unfortunately, the deliverability of your owned email list will still be impacted by the company managing your subscribers inbox. But the more relevant and engaging your content is for your newsletter subscribers, the higher your open rates will be, and your emails will have a higher percentage chance of ending up in your subscribers' inbox. Here are other ways to increase the effectiveness of your email marketing:

Step 1: Choose a Good Email Service

Email management platforms can be expensive and challenging to switch from one to another once you have everything set up across your website. That's why it's worth taking some time to research all the options available. Also, because every email subscriber costs you money, you should ensure that the service you choose makes it easy to unsubscribe. I also recommend investing in a service that offers high-quality automation services. You can set up email sequences to go out at certain times or when subscribers take a specific action without monitoring everything on your own. For current recommendations on good email providers, visit grantsabatier.com/tools.

Step 2: Set Up a Capture Mechanism on Your Website and Social Profiles

Make it easy or even mandatory to get someone to sign up for your email list. Include a call to sign up for your newsletter from all your social profiles and in the following locations of your site:

1. **Sidebars:** Include a box on the side of every page where people can sign up. Include a call-to-action that is relevant to your target customer, complements the type of emails you plan to send out, and includes a one-time offer (more on these below). Here are some examples from some of the businesses profiled in this book. You can also check your competitors' sites for inspiration:

    Millennial Money: Get free access to Grant's best tips, exclusive videos, podcasts, courses, and more.

    Student Loan Planner: Get the best student-loan calculator anywhere.

    Gold City Ventures: Learn How to Start a Business Selling Printables on Etsy!

2. **At the end of every blog post:** Since most first-time visitors will likely come to your site through a page they find in a Google search, include an opt-in box at the end of every blog post.

3. **Pop-up page for desktop site:** Pop-ups can be annoying, but they're also effective and make it evident immediately that you have something valuable to offer, like an immediate discount for signing up. However, use a pop-up form only on your desktop site, not mobile, as mobile pop-ups can impair the user experience and negatively impact your SEO.

4. **Locked content:** This can be viewed only if a user gives you their email address. Typically, you'll show a few

hundred words as a preview but then require an email address for the visitor to read the rest.

Set up these placements as soon as you build the website. Otherwise, you miss a huge opportunity to capture any traffic you receive, especially in the early days, when it's crucial for growth.

Step 3: Provide an Incentive

Offer visitors something in return for their email address. One of the most effective ways to get subscribers is to use a quiz that requires visitors to provide their email addresses to receive personalized results. People love quizzes because they provide valuable information in a personalized way, but they're certainly not the only option and they might not make sense for your business. Consider a discount code, a free download, premium content, or a trial service. The more value you can offer, and the more unique that value, the more subscribers you will get.

Step 4: Design Automated Email Sequences

A drip campaign is a series of emails you set up to be sent automatically and in a particular sequence when a subscriber takes a specific action. Use your email service to set up a drip campaign whenever someone registers their email address for the first time. You will also want to set up campaigns when they take specific actions, such as purchasing or downloading a resource from your site.

For now, focus on setting up these four emails in a welcome sequence that new subscribers receive over four days:

1. **Welcome Email:** The purposes of this email are to confirm they're on your list, share what a subscriber can expect, and include the incentives you promised in your registration form (e.g., a coupon code or link to a download) and links back to your website. Also, discuss what you plan to deliver in your email newsletter. Example: In our regular

weekly newsletter, you can expect (a) Valuable content related to [insert your niche], (b) Insights and tips from industry experts, and (c) Exclusive offers and promotions.

2. **Introduction to Your Brand and You:** This email introduces you and starts forming an emotional connection using your story. You can model this email from the About and home pages you wrote for your website.

3. **Your Favorite and Most Popular Content:** This email should deliver high value by directing subscribers to some of your most popular content. For years, my Millennial Money sequence included a list of the ten best posts I'd written, presenting a broad perspective of my thoughts on money. If subscribers read through all of them, they will learn a lot about me, the brand, my philosophy, and more. This further established trust and a connection with my readers.

4. **Favorite Resources and Exclusive Offer:** This email aims to highlight other resources you like and include an exclusive offer for your product or service. For this stage of my Millennial Money sequence, I included my favorite tools for tracking my personal finance journey. When a subscriber signed up for them, I received an affiliate commission. Once I'd created a course, I included an exclusive offer for the course. You can say, "As a special thank you for being a new subscriber, I wanted to share this exclusive offer with you . . ." then offer a discount for one of your products or services. This email will likely generate sales for you after all the value you provided in the previous email.

Step 5: Establish a Cadence for Correspondence

How often should you email subscribers? The answer depends on how much you can handle, when you can add value, and what your audience wants.

If you're a real estate agent, your subscribers likely care about new listings, trends in the neighborhoods they're interested in, and your thoughts on the market. I subscribe to the email newsletter of a Realtor in my neighborhood who marshals more than twenty-five years of experience to analyze local sales and listings. Once a month, he sends his thoughts on the market to all his subscribers. This is a good frequency for this market update and doesn't require too much time commitment. I've never corresponded with this guy, but I read every one of his emails and feel like I have formed a relationship with him. If I want to buy another investment property in Columbus or sell my house, who do you think I will call first?

We all get many emails, so don't just send as many emails as possible. I've never understood why I get so many emails from retailers like West Elm, Crate & Barrel, or L.L.Bean. They all email me at least once a day and sometimes more. I'm sure they have data that indicate that approach works—and they certainly have the budgets to do so. But as with any marketing strategy, you need to align your email cadence with your goals for your business. How many do you need to send out to add value to your audience without taking time or energy away from other areas of your business (not to mention life)?

Sending out a daily or even a weekly email would stress me out and would probably result in lower-quality content, so I focus on staying consistent with thoughtful, provocative biweekly emails. Stay with whatever form and cadence you can send consistently.

Step 6: Keep Delivering Value

While there are many forms your regular newsletter can take, try to add as much value to your subscribers as possible. Highlight extraordinary stories and products from your industry, share interviews, link to the best new content on your website, link to podcasts and videos you think your audience will like, share tips and tricks related to your products or services, and curate great content from others. The good news is that because you're already creating great content on your site, you can often repurpose it in your newsletter.

Whatever format you choose, stick with it. People will come to expect certain things and you want to make sure you deliver. In the current version of my newsletter, I share a 1,500-to-2,000-word piece (which only subscribers get) on a topic that is on my mind that week. I also include "What I'm Reading, Watching, & Listening To," which is a list of four pieces of media I've recently enjoyed, accompanied by a summary and links to each. Because my audience is interested in my thoughts on money, entrepreneurship, and life, that's exactly what I share with them. If I have a special offer, I include it in the email with everything else, but I share those only a few times a year when I'm opening up my membership community to new members.

Unless you're a product company, it's important that you not try to sell too much. Even then, you should still try to deliver roughly 90 percent valuable content and 10 percent sales pitches. You want to gradually form a relationship with your subscribers over time so that when you do want to sell something, they are open to buying.

To learn more about building effective email funnels, email copywriting, and next-level marketing strategies, I recommend checking out *Scarcity* by Eldar Shafir, *Launch* by Jeff Walker, and *The Ultimate Sales Letter* by Dan Kennedy. This is an exceptionally rich field for entrepreneurs who want to become better marketers.

CHAPTER 6

A SIMPLE BUSINESS FOUNDATION

"For every minute spent in organizing, an hour is earned."
—Benjamin Franklin

"Where the !?&$ is my money???"

I was starting to sweat. This was the third email I'd gotten from Melissa, a developer helping me with a website for a Chicago real estate brokerage. I owed Melissa $7,500 for the work she'd done, but my clients hadn't paid the $30,000 invoice I had sent them over two months ago for the website I'd already delivered. I had three clients who owed me over $80,000 in total, my business credit card was maxed out, and I now had a negative balance in my business account, so my bank was threatening to close my account.

I also had no money in my personal account, so I had to take money out of my stock index funds to cover the gap, paying taxes on the withdrawal. It was my first year owning my agency, and the situation forced me to start planning for worst-case scenarios. I needed a stronger foundation.

Running a business, no matter what stage of growth you're in, will add complexity to your life. The key to keeping your business sustainable is to set up systems early on that help you manage the complexity so you can focus on more important things. The more you grow, the more advanced and plentiful these systems will become. But always do your best to keep them manageable.

As an Experimental Entrepreneur, you want to optimize your revenue and expenses to have as much cash as possible to invest back in the business. Unlike the previous chapters, this chapter covers the technical and practical—less about the power of story and more about the power of good accounting.

Taking the time to understand how cash flows in and out of your business, how to optimize your tax and savings rates, and how to improve your balance sheet will make your business stronger now and well into the future. It will also allow you to make better decisions and set yourself up for maximum profitability no matter how big you choose to get.

SET UP AN LLC

As soon as you start generating consistent revenue from your business and/or if you plan to grow it, you should register it as a separate business entity. While you can manage your business under your personal name, doing so limits the tax benefits you can receive for running a business. You also need to establish a legal business to open a business bank account and business credit card, which make it easier to separate your business and personal assets and gain access to capital you can use to grow your business.

There are many ways to classify a business, but you're best off registering as a limited liability company (LLC) at this stage. Among other advantages, an LLC protects your personal assets, like your house and car, from being seized by creditors or anyone who sues your business. If you have a separate bank account and credit cards for the business, the LLC designation also protects your business assets from any personal lawsuits. LLCs can also take out loans and own assets outside your personal assets. This makes it easier for you to access capital for your business without having to use your personal assets as a guarantee.

LLCs also offer several tax benefits. An LLC can save you money because profits aren't taxed at the business level. Instead, the profits are passed through to you and your partners based on your ownership percentage. This reduces your tax burden compared with corporations, which are typically subject to double taxation, at the corporate level and again when they distribute dividends or profits to share-holders.

An LLC can also help you save money on self-employment taxes if you register as an S corporation with the IRS and pay yourself, your business partners, and any employees a regular paycheck. I'll dig into how to do this later in the book, but thinking about and setting up your LLC and tax classification early in your business can help you keep more money in your business and put more money in your pocket over time.

It is easy to set up an LLC, but there are some expenses as well as administrative and legal things to consider before you do so. First, you need to pick a name for your company. I typically recommend that you name your company whatever you've named your business (for example, MillennialMoney.com was managed by Millennial Money LLC). You don't need to turn your LLC into its own brand, but if you want to, make the name memorable and descriptive of what you do.

The setup costs of an LLC range between $500 and $1,000 because of the state filing and legal fees. The least expensive way to do this is directly through the states's website where you want to register the LLC. But using a service like LegalZoom, ZenBusiness, and Rocket Lawyer can help you set up the paperwork and will then file it on your behalf in the state of your choosing. These services can also help you determine what business licenses you may need. You can use an attorney, but costs can vary widely, as can the attorney's expertise.

While most LLC operating agreements are simple and templated, especially if you're a sole proprietor, one of the many benefits of an LLC is how flexible you can make the operating agreement if you have business partners or a complex situation. An operating agreement details how profits will be shared among partners and how the company will be managed. You should have one in place if you are working with business partners. A good operating agreement will help ensure that everyone knows their responsibilities during this process, including what happens when someone wants to leave or sell their shares of ownership in your company in the future.

In addition to the setup fees, you will be responsible for specific recurring fees, like an annual business registration fee you pay to the state where you registered the LLC. Finally, once you receive your formation paperwork from the state where you set up the business, you'll want to register your business with the Internal Revenue Service (IRS) to get what's known as your employer identification number (EIN). This is like a Social Security number for your business, and you'll need it for everything from setting up your business bank accounts and credit card to filling out your W-9s when you get paid. Setting up your EIN online is easily done by filling out a simple questionnaire at https://irs.gov.

You don't need an LLC to start your business. I wait until my idea is making at least $1,000 a month before creating one. It's a worthwhile investment. While LLCs are U.S.-specific, there are similar structures in many other countries where you can get similar liability and legal protections.

SEPARATE YOUR FINANCES

Whether you're making $100 or $100,000 a month, it's essential to separate your personal finances from those of your business. Set up a separate business checking account, either at your current bank or another one, and deposit directly into that account any money you receive from selling your product.

If you accept payments online or have an online store, set up your payment processor to automatically transfer available funds into your bank account daily or weekly. You should never leave money in Stripe, PayPal, Square, or any payment processor because your account could get locked and you might not be able to access your money for any number of reasons.

Transferring the money to a bank account will also make it easy for you to track precisely how much the business is making, especially come tax time, when you will need to report your personal and business income to the IRS. Any payments you need to make for your business will come from your business account. You can also set up a business savings account to store your business's cash buffer so it stays separate from your checking account.

You should also open a business credit card. You can use a regular credit card, but those designed for businesses usually come with specific perks and bonuses. Set up a payment due date for thirty days after you get paid so you can make sure you have money in your account to pay off the balance each month. For example, if you invoice on the last day of the month, set your credit card due date for the thirtieth of the following month.

Use your credit card for any expenses associated with the business. Need supplies or to ship something? Taking a client to lunch? Attending an industry conference in another city? Have any recurring advertising expenses? Charge all these expenses to the card and pay the balance in full monthly. Doing things this way allows you to delay paying vendors by a few days or weeks, since you won't need to produce actual cash until your credit card bill is due.

You can usually find business cards that charge 0 percent APR for the first year. This allows you to pay off any large up-front costs to help set up your business over time without accruing any interest or taking out a loan. A separate credit card also allows you to easily compare your monthly expenses and revenue by looking at your checking and savings accounts and credit card statements to ensure you're taking in more than you're paying out.

Plus, you can accrue points that you can redeem for travel and other rewards, further lowering your overall overhead costs. At MMG Media Group, we get almost 1 million points a year, putting our advertising spending on our business credit card, which we redeem for plane tickets when we travel to conferences. You can also use your business points for personal trips.

A nice perk about credit card points is that they are tax-free. Whether you plan to use these points for travel or cash back, you can earn considerable rewards by putting everything on a business credit card. If you're opening a new business bank account or credit card, you might qualify for a cash or points sign-up bonus. This can range anywhere from $200 to $1,000. Check out all the up-to-date account bonuses at my website: https://grantsabatier.com/bonuses.

SET UP ACCOUNTING AND BOOKKEEPING TOOLS

Bookkeeping is the practice of creating a reliable and organized record of financial transactions to establish a detailed record of your revenue, expenses, and liabilities. Accounting is the practice of using the data collected through bookkeeping to provide insights into a company's financial health, profitability, and overall performance.

Both are essential for a well-run business, and while I recommend you outsource them to professional experts as soon as you can afford to do so, in the beginning, you should—and will likely need to—handle these responsibilities on your own. Not only will this save you money, but it will provide you valuable insight into how your business runs. This will allow you to make better decisions now and after you grow.

I've tried many online accounting platforms, and QuickBooks is the best. You can set up an account, connect your bank account, and connect your credit card in about ten minutes. After that, QuickBooks automatically pulls your transactions into the software, where you can easily track how much money you're making, when that money is hitting your bank account, how much money you're owed, how much money you're spending, and how much profit you're making. You can also categorize transactions by type (Is this revenue or an expense? Who is it from/to? What is it for? and so on). It's pretty intuitive, though I recommend spending a few hundred dollars to have a QuickBooks-trained accountant set it up for you.

IMPROVE CASH FLOW AND REDUCE EXPENSES

Cash is the lifeblood of your business. It doesn't matter how much money you expect to make in the future, how much you're owed, or even how much you're making right now. If you don't have enough money in the bank to cover your operating expenses, you won't be able to stay in business. The more positive cash flow you have (the more cash you have coming in versus going out), the more opportunities you have to reinvest in your business or spend in other areas of your life. Cash-flow management is an acquired skill, but it's easy to learn. Here are some simple strategies to help you get started.

Create a Buffer

If you've ever studied personal finance, you know that, in order to grow, you should have money in an emergency fund before you invest. The same is true in business. Uncertainty in business is inevitable, and planning for it is essential. The best way to do this is always to ensure you have enough cash in your bank account to cover expenses if cash flow slows down or something else threatens your bottom line. Far too many businesses, like many people, live paycheck to paycheck. If something goes wrong, they're forced to take out a high-interest loan just to keep the lights on. Or worse, they're forced to shut down the operation entirely.

It's up to you to decide how much money you need to save to sleep at night, but I always have four to six months of anticipated expenses in cash in a business account. This allows me to cover payroll for myself and my partners and essential expenses to keep the business running. I also like having enough on hand to spend on certain discretionary expenses to help grow my business. I don't want to invest so much time and energy in my business and risk it vanishing so easily. I want to buy time to adjust or pivot if something unexpected happens.

Saving this much will take some time, especially as you try to increase and maintain a steady cash flow. The simplest way to do this is to set aside a certain percentage of your monthly revenue until you've built the buffer you want. Aim for at least 20 to 25 percent as soon as possible to reach your target buffer quickly. If your cash flow increases, increase your savings rate temporarily to take advantage of it. Once you have your target amount saved, you can slow down or stop saving altogether and reinvest any extra revenue back into your business. While you can have more than twelve months of expenses saved, your money will be worth more if you put it to work growing your business.

Create a Time Gap between When You Get Paid and When You Pay Others

You can't pay for your expenses if you don't have money in the bank. Ensure your revenue is hitting your bank account before your bills come due. The easiest way to do this is to get paid up front for your product or service, then pay your vendor and contractor invoices as late as possible (while still paying on time).

Getting paid up front can be challenging, depending on the type of industry you work in, but it's becoming more common and accepted. Even if you can't get paid in full until later, see if you can ask for some of the money up front, especially if you must procure materials or spend time preparing before you fulfill the service. Think of contractors who have to buy materials before renovating a house or tattoo artists who have to spend time sketching designs before their client sits in their chair.

Unfortunately, in affiliate businesses like the ones I run, it's impossible to get paid up front, as you only get paid after a visitor to your site takes a specific action with the affiliate. Even then, you usually have to wait thirty to ninety days after that conversion happens to receive the money. If you can't get paid earlier, you'll want to start keeping cash on hand to serve as a buffer. I always keep at least six months of expenses in cash to cover our costs until our affiliates pay us.

In addition to increasing the speed at which you get paid, try to delay the time you have to pay others. As discussed earlier in the chapter, one strategy is to set up a late credit card due date. You should also ask any vendors from whom you require invoices to invoice at the same time and as late as possible. I always try to get the writers we hire to invoice us once a month at the end of the month for all services they've delivered in that time frame. But even though we ask them to invoice after they've rendered a service, we are also sure to pay them quickly—usually within one to three business days of receiving their invoice—because their work is essential to our business and we want to keep them happy.

Reduce Expenses

How you manage expenses will determine how quickly your business grows and how much profit it can make. You will eventually need to increase your business expenses if you want to scale, but the earlier you start creating systems that allow you to keep those expenses as low as possible, the better. These savings compound over time, and you'll get better at identifying an essential expense that will help you grow versus a discretionary expense that you might not need right now.

As businesses grow over time, one-off and recurring expenses can start adding up and are one of the biggest reasons businesses fail. Expenses get too high for the revenue the company generates. I recommend you analyze all your regular expenses at least once a year to reduce any you no longer need. Naturally, as a company grows, you acquire some expense bloat along the way.

Some simple questions to ask yourself: Do I need this? Is this helping me grow my business? What has the return on investment (ROI) been on this expense over the past six to twelve months? Does this help me save valuable time or money?

It also helps to classify your expenses as either essential or discretionary. Essential expenses are the ones you need to run your business. Discretionary items are those that are useful but optional. Keeping your essential expenses low will give you more options with your discretionary expenses so you can cut back if cash flow gets tight or double down if you have a surplus of cash you want to reinvest in the business.

Below is a breakdown of some of our essential and discretionary expenses, to see the difference. I encourage you to analyze your expenses by breaking them into each bucket once a quarter.

ESSENTIAL EXPENSES	DISCRETIONARY EXPENSES
Website Hosting	New Blog Posts from Writers
Email List Platform	Travel

Company Email Platform	Slack for Team Communication
Asana Project Management Software	Digital PR
Keyword Research Tools	Executive Assistant
General Business Liability Insurance	Podcast Editing
P.O. Box	New Computer
Registered Agent Fee for Delaware LLC	Link Building

Your essential expenses will depend on what type of business you have, but I typically recommend spending money on decent website hosting, a good email management platform (which is usually inexpensive for your first 1,000 subscribers), and whatever else you need to sell your products or services. Most businesses, especially asset-light businesses, don't need much. I also typically recommend getting a good general business liability insurance policy, but that can wait until the next level of entrepreneurship.

An often overlooked but valuable way to reduce expenses is to negotiate lower rates with your vendors, especially for recurring expenses you usually pay. Since I run many content-driven websites, our most significant discretionary expense is hiring writers. Our average cost per word is $0.11, about 50 to 75 percent less than the industry average for a personal finance-focused writer. I've been able to negotiate this lower fee because I can promise them at least $2,000 worth of assignments per month, and as noted above, we pay exceptionally quickly. The result is that we save a lot of money and our writers are still happy.

You can negotiate with software and website-hosting companies, who would rather have your business at a lower fee than not have it at all. For large essential expenses, I'll always ask if we can get a better deal when I first sign up or when I need to upgrade to a larger plan.

Salespeople and account managers might have room to negotiate because margins are so high for most technology services. It's always worth asking if there's room to negotiate.

You can also reduce your expenses through simple bartering. While this is easier to do when you're part of a community of entrepreneurs, if you have a valuable skill set, you might be able to trade it for something you need in your business. When I started Millennial Money, I bartered SEO audits for several services, like helping with JavaScript and building some calculators that still live on the website. This is also where networking and collaborating with your competitors can help.

Many of my early competitors wanted to learn how I could get so much media coverage for my story. In exchange, they taught me how to project-manage my content strategy and build a link-tracking system. One even shared how much money affiliates were paying him for sign-ups. All of these accelerated my learning and helped me immediately negotiate higher affiliate payouts for some of my partners, leading to more revenue for my business.

How to Pay Yourself

Determining how much to pay yourself as an Experimental Entrepreneur can be complex and depends on various factors, including your business's financial health, personal financial needs, and long-term-growth objectives. Many Experimental Entrepreneurs take out too much money from the business too quickly and don't reinvest enough in the business to help it reach a point of sustainability. Or they don't take enough out of the business to support their living expenses and the business ends up making them miserable. The key is to balance the two extremes and pay yourself enough, but not too much.

When I was experimenting as an entrepreneur, all the money I made with my side hustles I either kept in the business or invested in the stock market. I never used it to pay my living expenses because I was focused on wanting to grow the money and accelerate my journey to financial independence. But this was my singular focus. Later in the book, I'll dive deeper into the topic of how much to pay yourself as your business grows.

Here is a simple framework to help you determine how much to pay yourself now and over time:

1. **Assess Your Financial Needs:** Start by evaluating your personal financial situation, including your monthly expenses, savings goals, net worth, and outstanding debts. Calculate how much you need to cover your basic living expenses and financial obligations.

2. **Consider Your Business Finances:** Review your company's financial position, including cash flow, revenue, and profitability. Determine how much the business can afford to pay you while having enough money for expenses and growth.

3. **Set a Fixed Percentage:** Some entrepreneurs pay themselves a fixed percentage of the company's profits. This approach ensures that your income increases proportionally as the business grows and becomes more profitable.

4. **Compare Market Rates:** Research the salaries and compensation levels for similar roles in your industry and location. Understanding what others in your field earn can provide a benchmark for your salary.

5. **Fortify Your Personal Emergency Fund:** Maintain a personal emergency fund that can cover your living expenses for six months in case of unexpected financial setbacks in your business. You never want your personal financial situation to jeopardize the business.

6. **Monitor and Adjust:** Regularly review your personal financial needs and the financial health of your business. Be prepared to adjust your salary as circumstances change. As the business becomes more established and profitable, you can increase your compensation accordingly.

Optimize Your Taxes

The U.S. tax code favors small businesses, but you need to know how to use it to your advantage. First, be sure to pay all your expenses through your business accounts. This helps to keep your finances separate and makes it easy to spot possible deductions come tax time. You can deduct most of the expenses you incur while growing a business, allowing you to effectively "grow" your business tax-free as long as you track everything properly.

Whether you have an LLC or not, when you're first starting and making less than $100,000 in revenue per year, it makes sense to get taxed as a sole proprietor or partnership (if you have a business partner or partners) and pass the tax burden through your business onto your personal taxes. If you do this, you should expect to pay your regular income tax level on the profit your business makes (at the federal, state, and city level), plus a 15.3 percent self-employment tax to cover your Social Security and Medicare contributions. Note that while you only have to pay Social Security tax (which accounts for most of the self-employment tax) on the first $160,200 of profit (as of 2023), the amount you pay to Medicare increases as your income grows.

One of the best ways to reduce your taxable income is to reinvest more of your profit in the business by paying as many expenses as you can before the end of the year. You can also contribute to a tax-advantaged investment account, like a solo 401(k) or a SEP-IRA, specifically designed for business owners and independent contractors. As with a regular IRA or 401(k), you won't pay tax on any contributions you make until you withdraw from the account.

Another way to potentially reduce your taxes is to elect to be taxed as an S corp, or S corporation. An S corp requires you to pay yourself a reasonable salary based on your role and current market rates for a similar position. It's worth researching S corp calculators and talking with an accountant to evaluate how much money you can save by structuring your LLC to be taxed a specific way.

While you can hire an accountant or registered agent to file your business taxes, I encourage you to file them yourself using a platform like TurboTax or H&R Block, at least for the first year or two. Doing so will help you learn what expenses can and can't be deducted and see their impact on your taxable income. You can also pay an accountant or registered agent for an hour or two of their time to answer your questions or get advice on setting up your business for maximum tax advantages. I did this until I could afford to hire my accountant to do my taxes for me. As you make more money, there are many tax-optimization strategies you can use, but there's a lot of gray area in the tax code. This can get you in trouble. Find an an accountant you trust and keep it simple.

Monitor Your Progress

As with any experiment, it's worth keeping a close eye on your progress to decide whether or not it's worth continuing to build or scale your business. Here's how to assess your business's overall health and viability at this phase and beyond.

1. THE PROFIT AND LOSS STATEMENT (AKA INCOME STATEMENT)

Your profit and loss statement (P&L) shows how your business has performed over a certain period by showing how much money you made (revenue), how much money you spent (expenses), and how much money you have left (profit). I recommend looking at your P&L each month and quarter, and at the end of each year. In addition to helping you assess and optimize your business, your P&L is also essential if and when you decide to sell your business because potential buyers will want to see it before they make an offer.

A P&L shows your net income (aka your bottom line or profit) by deducting all the money going out of your business (expenses, salaries, loan payments, etc.) from all the money generated through sales of your product or service (revenues). In other words, your net income is the amount of money you keep after all your expenses have been paid.

The better you understand your P&L, the more informed business decisions you can make. Which business lines or products generate the most profit and are therefore worth doubling down on? Where are you losing money and how can you reduce or eliminate those losses? I always see new things when I look at my P&L and often look across expense categories to evaluate which expenses are worth the money I'm spending.

A P&L also tells you what your business is worth at the end of each period. This information helps with financial planning, such as budgeting future profits and losses, setting goals for increasing profitability, and deciding whether it's worth investing further in an area of your business or cutting back.

Let's look at how to read a P&L, using the sample below.

INCOME STATEMENT	JAN 2023	FEB 2023	MAR 2023	APR 2023	MAY 2023	JUN 2023	JUL 2023	AUG 2023	SEP 2023	TOTAL
Income										
4100 Advertising income	7,923	10,678	4,359	6,170	12,560	11,987	8,641	5,679	9,081	77,078
4500 Sponsorship Income	2,500		12,988		5,000					20,488
4650 Digital Product Income	1,179	385	385		397		280	280		2907
Total Income	11,602	11,063	17,732	6,170	12,957	16,987	8,921	5,959	9,081	100,473
Cost of Goods Sold										
5105 Subcontractors	1,605	1,901	1,250	1,980	1,579	4,204	3,817	1,809	3,703	21,848
5130 Affiliates and Commissions					1,320		900			2,220
Total Cost of Goods Sold	1,605	1,901	1,250	1,980	2,899	4,204	4,717	1,809	3,703	24,068
Gross Profit	9,997	9,162	16,482	4,190	10,058	12,783	4,204	4,150	5,378	76,405
Gross Margin	86%	83%	93%	68%	78%	75%	47%	70%	59%	76%
Expenses										
Total 6200 Payroll Expenses	1,500	1,500	1,500	1,500	1,500	1,500	1,500	1,500	1,500	13,500
Total 6300 Merchant Processing Fees	125	125	125	125	125	125	125	125	125	1,125
Total 6400 Office + Admin Expenses	200	200	200	200	200	200	200	200	200	1,800
Total Expenses	1,825	1,825	1,825	1,825	1,825	1,825	1,825	1,825	1,825	16,425
Net Income	8,172	7,337	14,657	2,365	8,233	10,958	2,379	2,325	3,553	59,980
Profit Margin	70%	66%	83%	38%	64%	65%	27%	39%	39%	60%

QuickBooks has default expense categories, as does the IRS. There is some overlap, but I default to the IRS categories and adjust my QuickBooks accordingly, so it's easier to break them out when doing my taxes.

At the beginning of each month, I'll analyze my business P&L from the previous month. I'm looking at three things in particular: how much cash we've made, how much money we've spent (our expenses), and how much profit we've made.

First, I'll dig into our expenses to see if anything is out of the ordinary and how much we've spent on key categories like legal, marketing, and contractor expenses. Early on in a business, keeping a close eye on all your expenses makes sense because cash flow and revenue are usually light. But once you have a good handle on where your business spends money, and you're hitting your target profit margin, it is more effective to do this at a high level each month and then do a deep dive every quarter.

Next, I dig into the profit. Our business's target profit margin is 70 percent or above, so I evaluate whether or not we're at our target level. We might be higher or lower for a given month if we have a jump in revenue or have ramped up some investments, so I will factor that into my assessment of the numbers. I also look at trends over the past three, six, and twelve months since businesses naturally ebb and flow due to many factors. If I notice that we're below our target profit margin for several consecutive months, then it's likely because we've acquired or invested in another website or that revenue is down because of seasonality (in personal finance, site traffic is usually greatest from January to May, when more people are thinking about their finances).

Suppose I notice that we're at 80+ percent profit for a month. In that case, I look seriously at ways to invest the additional profit back into the business to grow it in the best way possible—whether that's ordering new content, building out new functionality, or testing new ad campaign ideas. This is a great problem to have.

2. BALANCE SHEET (BUSINESS NET WORTH)

A balance sheet shows what an entity owns and owes, along with the amount invested by investors. It's a snapshot of the company's financial position at a given point in time. Unlike a P&L, the balance sheet accounts for all the company's assets and any liabilities it owes, not just the money flowing in and out regularly.

Balance Sheet	9/30/2023
Assets	
Total Bank Accounts	41,092
Total Other Current Assets	0
Total Fixed Assets	25,000
Total Assets	66,092
Liabilities	
Total Other Current Liabilities	331
Total Credit Cards	7,187
Total Long-Term Liabilities	2,509
Total Liabilities	10,027
Total Equity	56,065
Total Liabilities and Equity	66,092

Balance sheets help you see where all your money comes from, how much your company is worth, whether your company has enough money to pay its debts on time, and whether it is profitable. Learning how to read a balance sheet will help you run your business and make you a better stock investor because public companies release their balance sheets. And if you ever decide to acquire or invest directly in another company, balance sheets can help you quickly assess the risk involved.

The balance sheet has three main sections: assets (what you own), liabilities (what you owe), and equity (the difference between what you own and what you owe). Assets are anything your company owns and can be either tangible (cash, inventory, business equipment, real estate, etc.) or intangible (patents/rights and trademarks). Liabilities are the money your company owes and can be divided into current or long-term liabilities. Current liabilities are due within a year and include accounts payable (money owed to vendors) and short-term loans. Long-term liabilities are due more than one year after the balance sheet date and include things like mortgages, leases, and longer-term loans. Your equity is your business's net worth and is calculated by deducting your liabilities from your assets.

3. STATEMENT OF CASH FLOWS

While P&Ls show your business's profitability, cash-flow statements reveal the financial reality of your operations. Your statement of cash flows shows how much cash is coming into your business from sales, investments, loans, and other sources, and how much is going out for expenses, debts, and investments. I look at my statement of cash flows every month.

Statement of Cash Flows	9/30/2023
Cash at Beginning of Year	15,981
Operations	
Cash Receipts from Advertisers	78,109
Cash Paid for Written Content	8,179
Salaries	5,500
General Operation Expenses	1,200
NET CASH FLOW FROM OPERATIONS	63,231
Financing Activities	
Cash Paid for Loan Payment	(4,105)
NET CASH FLOW FROM FINANCING ACTIVITIES	(4,105)
NET INCREASE IN CASH	59,126
Cash at End of Year	49,807

A cash-flow statement helps you predict your short-term cash flow and ensures that you have enough cash to cover essential expenses like payroll, rent, and utilities. Cash-flow statements also help with business growth planning because they help you assess whether you have the necessary cash reserves to expand, hire more staff, purchase equipment, or invest in marketing.

Also, by regularly analyzing your cash-flow statements, you can identify trends and patterns in your business's cash management. You can also spot problems early and work to take action, such as reducing your expenses or seeking additional funding if your cash flow is restricted. Paying attention over time can also help you anticipate seasonal cash fluctuations, trends, or periods of increased or decreased cash flow throughout the year that you can plan for.

Check In with Yourself

Life is too short to do something you don't love. Being an Experimental Entrepreneur is not just about setting up your business for maximum sustainability; it's also about experimenting with how it feels to be an entrepreneur. It's about testing the waters to see how entrepreneurship can help you live the life you want and become the person you want. Throughout this phase, I encourage you to check in with yourself and remember Truth #2: Trust what you feel before what you think.

Are you excited enough about your idea that you're thinking about it throughout the day? Are you working through the next steps as you stand in line at the grocery store? Are you excited to sit down and keep building? Or are you more exhausted than excited? Are you just going through the motions because it's what you think you should be doing? Are you curious to figure it out or dreading your next work session? I've already said it a few times in the book—this isn't easy, but you should still be excited to figure it all out. If you're not, you don't yet have the right idea, support, momentum, or all three.

If you're not excited or intrinsically motivated to work on your business, you will not be able to build and sustain momentum when things get tough. Truth #7: Momentum is the most powerful force in business.

One of the biggest challenges in being an Experimental Entrepreneur is not giving yourself enough time to find the right idea, test, learn, and prove your business. I experimented for over a year before I found my first profitable ideas, but I kept at it because I craved the freedom I believed becoming an entrepreneur could give me. I didn't believe in who I was, but I did believe in who I could become.

It helped that I've always hated working for someone else and being stuck in the nine-to-five, so the default status quo didn't appeal to me. I knew if I kept learning, I'd figure things out eventually—and I was right. The more you learn, the more that learning accelerates and compounds. It's like any other compounding curve: slow at first and then rapidly accelerating. When you invest more time and energy up front, the more it will compound.

Far too many people quit or pivot too quickly after just a few months because they're not making as much money as they want or get bored too quickly. Without fail, almost weekly within my community, an entrepreneur who is thinking about quitting on their idea or business reaches out to me. It's always the same story: they're not gaining momentum quickly enough, they're not making enough money, or the worst one is—I don't have the time. Ahh, that one always gets me. Wait . . . You don't have time for yourself? You don't have time to build a life you love? You don't have time to create more options and freedom in your life?

They quit before they've even begun.

That's fine if you want that to be your life. But I know you don't, because you wouldn't have read or listened this far into the book if you did. Obviously, you should feel free to pivot or abandon your business idea if it's not making enough money, you're not enjoying it, or both. But if you're serious about being an entrepreneur, try to spend at least six months actively focused on your business before you throw in the towel or decide it's not for you.

Now, if you've already found an idea you love, you're making some money, and you're excited and have some momentum, you're ready for the next level.

LEVEL 2
THE SOLOPRENEUR

The Solopreneur level is when your business grows from a side gig into a real, sustainable business—one built for long-term growth. This level is all about building sustainability: a sustainable and growing community that buys your products, sustainable cash flow that covers and then exceeds your living expenses, and sustainable systems powered by technology and people so you can free up your time.

Solopreneurs can have the freedom of being an entrepreneur, but one of the challenges with solopreneurship is that your business and your life are often intertwined. Many Solopreneurs make the mistake of viewing their life as a business, often letting it take over most of their time. They lose control or get in so deep that it becomes tough for them to disentangle their personal lives from their business. This is one reason it's so valuable to be conscious and intentional from the beginning. If you start to feel stuck, this is the stage where it's relatively easy to make adjustments. And the more you stay true to what you *really* want to build, the more likely you will be able to create a business that supports your life.

As you start generating more consistent revenue, you will still likely need to trade a fair amount of your time for money. But you can start to use your increased cash flow to build simple systems and outsource work to contractors so that you can have the freedom to choose how to spend your time—growing the business or just living your life.

At this stage, you want to gather enough data to understand exactly how your business works, what efforts are working and which are not, and where you should invest your time and energy for maximum impact. You want to learn how to use numbers alongside your intuition, to make sure you're making decisions that push your business forward, help increase your profit, and inject your life with energy.

You're going to make some mistakes and wrong choices, but what's important is that you keep making choices and moving forward. Once you establish and sustain your momentum, good is usually good enough. Though, when anything in life loses momentum or energy, the business will suffer, and the joy it brings to your life will also start to wither. Many companies just run out of oxygen because the business owner lost their momentum. As an entrepreneur, especially a Solopreneur, it's essential to cultivate this energy early and often.

The people with whom you surround yourself will either feed your energy or try to suck it up. This is why finding the right people to work with is vital. Just because you're a Solopreneur doesn't mean you need to be a business of one; in fact, surrounding yourself with great people will only enrich your business and your life.

In many ways, the Solopreneur stage is the make-or-break moment for your business. Do you lay the foundation to automate, systemize, and outsource, or do you burn out from trying to do it all yourself? Do you build a sustainable community who are excited to support you as customers and will evangelize on your behalf? Or do you chase short-term marketing tactics that everyone else is using? Do you build a business that makes you feel alive? Or do you get stuck in just another job?

The answers to these questions will determine the future of both your business and your ability to build a life you love. In the next chapter, I discuss the exact strategy I used and encourage you to take it and make it your own. The heart of this strategy is you and your story. It's what will make people pay attention despite all the noise online and our increasingly deteriorating attention spans. It's your business; build it how you like.

CHAPTER 7

CREATE YOUR COMMUNITY AND A SUSTAINABLE CUSTOMER BASE

"To lead people, walk beside them."

—Lao Tzu

I pulled out my phone and opened my email while waiting in line at Chipotle. There it was: "Hi Grant, I just wanted to write and say thank you. You saved our marriage. We've never been able to talk about money but now we talk openly because of you. I hope we have the chance to thank you in person one day. Keep doing what you're doing."

Time stood still. I was speechless. I can still hear the chicken hitting the grill and remember the face of the woman who served me on this otherwise unmemorable day. It was the first email like this that I had ever received from a reader. All of a sudden, all of the late nights of writing were worth it. I was doing exactly what I was supposed to be doing.

Some people thought I was crazy or dumb for being so open about my life and struggles when I started Millennial Money, but others loved it. The people who loved it got invested in my story, in me, and in what I was building. They shared my content online and with their friends. And I started getting emails like the one I received while in line at Chipotle.

When you engage with an audience in an open, transparent, and vulnerable way—by sharing about your life, asking for their advice, and asking them to contribute to your mission—your audience will be more invested in you and your story. They are more likely to follow along, root for you, join your community, and buy your products. But for it to work, you actually need to be open; you can't fake it. You can try to fake it, and you might make some connections, but it won't feel good—to you or your audience—and it won't last.

In the early days of Millennial Money, I obsessively tracked my website traffic in Google Analytics. But even as traffic started to build, I didn't *truly* understand the impact I was making until readers started reaching out to me personally. It brought the human element into my work. It dawned on me that every single website visitor was a real person with a story, a family, hopes and dreams, and a relationship with money.

Now when readers meet me in person, some of them give me hugs, bring me blueberry pies (because I mentioned them once on a podcast), and tell me that the "me" they read and listen to online is the same as the "me" in real life. Sometimes they cry. Sometimes I cry. I love meeting readers in person. When I started, I wanted to help my friends and maybe a few other people. There was no way I could have envisioned the scale of what it would become.

Money is an emotional topic. It wasn't until I was on my book tour in 2019, meeting so many readers, that I realized it wasn't the money tactics or investing strategies I had shared that people connected with. It was my vulnerability and authenticity. It was my tone. I actually cared about them, even though I'd never met them. My story inspired them, and my content made them believe they could do what I did. I helped them see the world a bit differently and recognize that you don't have to accept the status quo, work until you're sixty-five, and toil in a job you hate. But I didn't just tell them—I showed them how to do it. This changed their lives, and it also changed mine.

No matter what kind of industry you're in or the product you sell, you're in the people business. If you're not consistently adding value to your community, they'll lose interest. If you can't keep your community happy, satisfied, and coming back, you won't stay in business very long. Many business owners, especially Solopreneurs, obsess over customer, website, and sales data instead of remembering why they built the business in the first place. They let data drive their decisions instead of staying closely connected with their community.

Customers may buy from you once because an ad followed them online for a week or you offered a good incentive, but they come back because they love and trust your brand and want to support it. Any decent marketer can find customers, but the best brands build community. This community keeps coming back (which helps you grow), they refer others to your business (which expands your growth), and they save you resources, since you don't have to put as much effort into engaging them as you would a first-time visitor.

Building a community takes time, and it can feel intimidating to start if you're an introvert like me. That's okay. If you remember your purpose, honor your limits, and stay true to your values, your authenticity and unique approach will help you stand out against your competition, and your audience will come to you.

While it will take some work, if you focus on consistency of connection, quality over quantity, sharing openly, and optimism instead of fear, you'll have a significant advantage over others who give up or pump out generic content.

Here are five steps to help you cultivate a community and turn it into a sustainable customer base:

STEP 1: BUILD IN PUBLIC TO CROWDSOURCE SUPPORT

"Building in public" describes the process of sharing your creative or entrepreneurial journey with others, typically through social media, blogs, or other online platforms. More than just a phrase, it's a group of individuals who believe that this is the best way to attract an audience (who may convert into customers and help them grow) in an authentic, human way.

The idea is to document and share your progress, challenges, and insights as you work on a project, business, or personal development. It can be a powerful strategy for building an audience, gaining feedback, and establishing credibility.

My friend Caitlin Pyle left her retail job and leaned on her strengths for detail orientation to start a proofreading side business freelancing for court reporters. She then documented her experience of building her business on Facebook and her blog *Proofread Anywhere*. Over time, there was so much interest in her story that she launched a proofreading community and course in 2014 to help proofreaders build their own businesses. She also built this business in public, which drove even more customers her way, creating the momentum for her business to scale. Over 15,000 students ended up buying her courses, and Caitlin sold her business in 2022 for $4.5 million.

I recently invested in Carry, a personal finance platform for business owners. Once a month, cofounder Ankur Nagpal openly shares the company's revenue, user numbers, big projects, pain points, and plans for the upcoming month to an email list that anyone can sign up for. Ankur is very open, transparent, and even a little vulnerable in the letter. He shares when things aren't going well or if something didn't work, while celebrating new features and growth milestones.

As an investor, I get a slightly different version of this email, which includes a list of the company's assets under management (AUM), but other than that, it's the same email that any other subscriber gets. He ends with a section titled "How You Can Help," where he lays out how readers can support the company's goals. These are usually simple things, like testing a new feature and providing feedback, sharing a new product or feature with friends, or referring great contractors and professionals interested in working with the company. Ankur's openness with an engaged group of followers and investors who want to support Carry opens up a large audience with resources to help. Subscribers quickly respond to these requests for help because they feel connected to Ankur and the company and want to contribute.

This community-first approach is accelerating the growth of his business. The "build in public" movement has expanded rapidly beyond software developers (where the movement started) to all types of entrepreneurs. You can join them by sharing your own business and life journey at the level you feel comfortable. You don't have to share everything, of course, but the more open and transparent you can be, the more trust you can transfer, relationships you can build, and help you can get.

In addition to discussing the product or service you're trying to sell or commenting on your industry, you reveal the reality of being an entrepreneur and discuss all the challenges you're facing and the decisions you're trying to make. When I first launched Millennial Money, I didn't try to be perfect or pretend I had everything figured out. Instead, I leaned into my vulnerability and shared it with the world, often in real time.

Building in public helps people connect with you on a human level. When this happens, you become more than a brand or a product; you become someone your customers can root for and remember. It also lets you connect with other entrepreneurs, who can become allies and advocates on your journey. I often go to my network for advice or perspective on something I'm struggling with; most of those confidants started as people whose work I followed or who followed me.

Here are some things you can share and ways to take advantage of building in public. We'll dive deeper into a few of these throughout this chapter:

- **Build a Platform:** Create a central hub, such as a blog or a social media profile, where people can easily follow your journey. Use relevant hashtags to make it easier for others interested in your niche to discover your content.
- **Project Updates:** Share regular updates on the progress of your project. This could include new features, milestones achieved, or any setbacks you encounter. Transparency about your journey will create a sense of trust with your audience.
- **Challenges and Lessons:** Document your challenges and what you learn from them. Sharing your mistakes and how you overcome them can be both informative and relatable to your audience.
- **Behind-the-Scenes Content:** Give your audience a glimpse of your daily work, whether it's a home-office setup, a workspace, or a peek into your creative process. People are often curious about the work that goes on behind the scenes. I shared the entire process of writing my first book, which built up excitement and generated early sales.

- **Engage with Your Audience:** Respond to your followers' comments, questions, and feedback. This engagement can foster a sense of community and build a loyal audience.
- **Personal Growth:** Share your goals, progress, and tools or techniques you use to improve. This can inspire others on a similar journey.
- **Networking:** Building in public can also help you connect with like-minded individuals. Reach out to others who are building in public and collaborate when possible. Attend relevant events or conferences, either in person or virtually.
- **Feedback and Iteration:** Use your audience as a source of feedback for your project. You can sometimes poll your audience or seek their input when you encounter decisions or changes.
- **Establish Credibility:** Building in public can help establish your authority in your niche. Over time, as you share valuable insights and showcase your expertise, people are more likely to trust your opinions and advice.
- **Stay Authentic:** Be yourself and share your true experiences. People connect with real stories and people, not polished, overly curated images.

Remember that building in public is not just about self-promotion; it's about sharing your journey and creating a sense of community and mutual growth. It can be a powerful way to connect with others who share your interests and goals.

STEP 2: EXPAND YOUR CONTENT TO BUILD TRUST

Content creates leverage. Some posts I wrote in 2018 still generate over $500 a month in revenue to this day. Vicki Robin, whose book *Your Money or Your Life* changed my life, reached out to me after I recommended it in an interview and someone shared it with her. People reach out to me after reading blog posts that I wrote in 2017. I get questions and opportunities almost weekly from people who have read my book *Financial Freedom*, which came out in 2019. Other creators, investors, and brands reach out to me after coming across an interview with me. Rachael Ray saw me in a CNBC video interview in a taxicab, and I got invited to her show. While I sleep, the content that I created as a Solopreneur continues to build my brand and my businesses.

At this stage, you should expand your platform by creating more of the highest-quality content you can, across the platforms you enjoy using. Double down on your strengths and the platforms you enjoy. Publishing content allows people to engage with you on their terms— on their computer at work, when they're just killing time online, or when they're playing with their phone before bed.

A single piece of great content you repurpose across platforms, and that will remain relevant for a long time, is worth more than dozens of lesser-quality, time-sensitive or trend-based content. As a Solopreneur, you won't be able to spend as much on things like advertising as your more established competitors, and you won't yet have reached the scale where you can dominate SEO by posting ten times a day. This is your biggest advantage. Playing the numbers game is fine for short-term growth or quick wins, but building something people love is far more rewarding. It is also much better for growth because quality content takes on a life of its own and continues to gain traction long after you've sent it into the world.

Here are some tips to help you build trust through your content:

1. **Practical + Personal:** My most successful posts have been the ones that combine personal anecdotes and elements of my story with practical strategies and perspectives. This is true for every content creator I've met. Storytelling is one of the most powerful ways to convey information because people respond to narratives more than ideas. Good stories also prove that you know what you're talking about and give people a memorable example to follow.

2. **Quality > Quantity:** There are so many new content-creation tools available (including AI), and competition for

attention is fierce. Until you can outsource some content creation to others, you also have limited time to create worthwhile content. This is why I always lean toward quality over quantity. Deliver valuable, well-researched, and well-structured information in order to rise above the crowd.

Focus on creating content that solves problems, answers questions, or meets the needs and interests of your target audience. Share diverse types of content, including stories, tips, and educational content that helps customers make the most of your product or service. The more your content benefits and engages your audience, the more trust you'll build. Helpful, informative, and entertaining content will earn trust more effectively than a high volume of mediocre content.

3. **Share Your Expertise:** You must distinguish yourself as an expert in your field to get people to trust you. It doesn't matter what field you're in—whether it's high finance or horticulture—use the content you produce (a product description, a newsletter, or a social media post) to demonstrate you know what you're talking about. Share in-depth insights, case studies, and real-world examples. When your audience sees that you know what you're talking about, they're more likely to trust your guidance. Writing what you know will also simplify the process, making you more likely to stick with it and build momentum.

4. **Focus on Optimism, Not Fear:** The media has always preyed on people's fears and insecurities to attract attention. With the rise of algorithm-driven platforms, this has only gotten worse. Most marketers encourage you to identify people's anxieties and then communicate in a way that capitalizes on those anxieties by creating a sense of urgency and FOMO.

But what kind of energy does this put out into the world? Clickbait headlines might get you some quick engagement, but you can build more customer trust by leading with hope and optimism than with fear. When you have to manipulate people to get them to buy from you, you must ask yourself what value you're providing. When positioning stories or planning your marketing strategies, consider how you can improve people's lives, not remind them of what they're lacking.

5. **Transparency and Authenticity:** Be open and transparent about your intentions, process, and potential conflicts of interest. If you make a mistake, admit it and show how you plan to correct it. Transparency builds credibility. Be yourself and share your personal experiences when relevant. Authenticity allows your audience to connect with you on a human level and builds trust. Feel free to share both your successes and your challenges.

6. **Care, and Honor Your Promises:** Show empathy and understanding for your audience's concerns and challenges. Let them know that you genuinely care about helping them. Never talk down to them, shame them, or make them feel bad. Deliver your content with care, love, and support, and people will feel it. If you make promises or commitments in your content, make sure you fulfill them, including delivering on deadlines and honoring any guarantees you provide. Both have been very important to me and helped me stand out. Just do what you say you'll do and keep showing up.

7. **Maintain a Consistent Schedule and Style:** While I've already covered this, it's important enough to repeat. Consistency in your content creation and sharing schedule builds trust and helps your audience depend on you.

Whether you're posting daily, weekly, or on another schedule, stick to it. Maintain a consistent style and tone in your content, including using the same colors, fonts, and imagery. Consistent branding can make your content more recognizable and trustworthy.

8. **Share Testimonials, Cite Sources, and Provide Clear Calls to Action:** Social proof, such as testimonials or case studies from satisfied customers or clients, demonstrates that your expertise and advice have been valuable to others. When you use data, statistics, or information from other sources, cite them properly. If your content includes calls to action, make them clear and relevant. If your audience finds value in your content and you offer a next step, they'll be more likely to take it.

9. **Stay Informed:** Continuously update your knowledge and expertise. The more you stay up-to-date in your field, the more trustworthy you become. But just because something is trending doesn't mean you have to care about it.

    It's tempting to want to ride the waves of people's attention, but if you follow the path everyone else is taking, it will become more and more challenging to stand out from the crowd. It's okay to write about trending topics, but don't feel pressured, and only do so if you want to and have something valuable to add to the conversation.

10. **Repurpose:** Repurpose the strongest existing content you have into formats that work on other platforms. If you like podcasting, you can record your podcast on video and then post it to YouTube; then, you can have small snippets of your interview cut up and turned into YouTube shorts, Instagram Reels, and TikTok videos. You can post the video or audio on Facebook, LinkedIn, or within your Telegram or Discord community.

You can then transcribe your podcast and use it as a video transcription for the YouTube video and use parts of the transcription as the outline for a new blog post that you can write or assign to another writer. That transcription can also be repurposed for newsletter copy, where you could link to the blog post, YouTube video, and audio file.

While this may sound like a lot to consider, many technologies and people can help you repurpose content for free or cheap. Newer AI tools are particularly helpful. But once again, choosing to do the right things well instead of trying to do everything at this stage is very important. Go where your audience is and prioritize the work you enjoy doing, which creates, instead of takes, more energy in your life. It can take time to establish a solid reputation in your field; however, consistently delivering valuable and trustworthy content will help you build a loyal and engaged audience.

STEP 3: ASK AND ENGAGE

The closer you live to your customers and market, the better product and market-fit feedback you will get. The more and better feedback you can get from your customers, the better you can serve them. Happy customers buy again, recommend your business to their friends, and leave positive reviews. Without satisfied customers, you can't build a sustainable or growing business.

The best way to learn about your customers is to talk to them directly and make it easy for them to connect with you. Consistently provide outstanding customer service. Address their questions and concerns promptly, resolve issues quickly, and go the extra mile to exceed their expectations. Being available when things go wrong is one of the best ways to build trust, and customers are more likely to return and recommend you to others if they have a positive experience interacting with your brand.

But quality customer service is just as proactive as it is reactive. By inviting feedback from your customers, you demonstrate that you care about who they are and what they need. Make it easy to give feedback when customers are ready and only ask occasionally. Provide your contact information prominently in the footer and on the Contact page of your website. Have a call number where customers can reach your support team. Don't be one of those companies that makes it so difficult to contact you that customers get frustrated, leave bad reviews, and never buy from you again. Yes, customer service can be time-consuming and expensive, but it's one area where you shouldn't cut any corners. Think about how you would like to be treated as a customer. Then, go above and beyond that. Nothing will pay bigger dividends over time.

Most companies do the bare minimum or they cut corners. Customers can tell. If you simply keep your promises, deliver what you sold, and try to go above and beyond when you can, you'll easily set yourself apart.

Create surveys that solicit specific and open-ended feedback and share them with your email subscribers, blog readers, and on social media if you use it. Don't overdo it; no one likes to be asked to provide feedback every time they do something similar, like buy a plane ticket or contact customer service. Invite and share customer reviews on your website and respond to them publicly—especially the negative ones. Don't delete legitimate negative reviews. Respond to comments on your blog and answer questions as quickly and thoroughly as possible. As you grow, you'll need to share or outsource this task to manage everything, but at this stage, being hands-on will provide high-quality insights into your earliest—and most likely to be loyal—followers.

You can also learn from "bad" customers. By "bad" here, I mean customers who aren't a good fit for your service. Even if someone subscribes to your email list or buys from you once, it doesn't mean they're a good customer. If someone unsubscribes from your email list, ask them why they unsubscribed. If you find that multiple people who unsubscribe came to you from the same place, you might redirect efforts to a different place to attract better customers. Ideally, you *want* these customers to unsubscribe from your email list because it will save you money on your email subscription fees and give you better metrics (like open and conversion rates). Bad customers are also more likely to leave bad reviews.

Turn Your Customers into Evangelists

This involves creating such a positive and memorable experience that customers are willing to share and promote your brand to others. The best way to turn your customers into evangelists is to make sure your product or service delivers on its promise. If it does, you create trust. Then your customers will not only buy more, they'll also share it with their friends. Here are some other strategies to help you create customer evangelists:

- **Tell Customer Stories:** Share compelling stories about your customers' successes or how your product/service has positively impacted their lives. Authentic stories resonate with other potential customers.
- **Improve Your Product:** Continuously strive to improve your offering based on customer feedback and new information. Demonstrating a commitment to their satisfaction can turn customers into loyal fans.
- **Surprise and Delight:** Occasionally surprise your customers with unexpected perks. Small acts of kindness, like handwritten thank-you notes, surprise discounts, or free offers, can go a long way in building your community.
- **Connect Your Community:** Create or facilitate a community forum around your brand. This can be in a Reddit forum, social media group, or any platform where customers can connect, share experiences, and support each other. You can use many excellent community technology platforms, such as Circle, Skool, Thinkific, and others, to bring your community together.
- **Establish a Loyalty Program:** This rewards customers for their repeat business. Offer discounts, exclusive access, or other perks to incentivize loyalty. Make the program

actually valuable so people will want to use it—not something unrealistic like needing to make dozens of purchases to get 20 percent off. The higher the program's value, the higher the participation and the more recurring revenue it will generate.

- **Solicit User-Generated Content:** Encourage customers to share their reviews, testimonials, photos, and videos with you and on social media. Reshape the best posts and tag them. Create social contests to encourage sharing. Sharing user-generated content can enhance your credibility and provide social proof for potential customers by showing them your products are being used.
- **Set up a Referral Program:** Referral programs incentivize customers to refer friends and family to your business. Offer discounts, gifts, or other rewards to the advocate and the referred individual.

According to Nielsen, "92% percent of consumers worldwide say they trust word-of-mouth or recommendations from friends and family, above all other forms of advertising. Beyond friends and family, 70% of people trust online reviews written by other consumers as much as they trust recommendations from personal contacts." Once this cycle is activated, it will work and compound on its own, but you can accelerate the compounding by continuing to share stories, create content, and connect with your customers.

STEP 4: SELL AND REENGAGE

After you've spent so much time adding value to someone's life and building trust, your community will pay attention when you're ready to sell. Whether you're releasing a new course or a skin care cream, you'll have cultivated a community of eager buyers. While most of your community will be silent, rest assured that they are there and getting value from what you're doing. Even if only a tiny percentage buy from you, you can see who's engaging by checking visits to your site and the open rates of your emails.

The "marketing rule of 7" was initially developed in the 1930s by movie studios, which determined that consumers needed to see an advertisement for a movie seven times before buying a ticket to see it, and the concept is just as relevant today. Most people will need to engage with your content at least seven times, if not more, before they buy anything from you. They'll read your blog, subscribe, listen to a few podcast episodes, and watch some of your videos, and if they find it interesting, educational, or inspiring or connect with it in some way, they'll keep engaging. I'm always surprised when a reader emails me that they've been reading my blog for five years, but have just bought my book. They might have engaged with my content hundreds of times before purchasing.

While it varies considerably based on industry and the quality of your email subscriber list, the average rate of people who buy something from a brand is 3 to 5 percent of total subscribers. So, if you have 1,000 subscribers, you should anticipate thirty to fifty sales from that size audience on the first email send, although it could be considerably more if you're offering something they really want. It's not unheard of to get a 30 percent sales rate off an email list that small for a highly anticipated product release.

One thing you should make sure you're doing is reengaging email subscribers who didn't buy on the first email. Resend the email to anyone who didn't open it, and also send a follow-up email to everyone with a reminder about the sale. A sale won't typically happen on the first email, so keep up your sales promotion over three or four days— ideally with a deadline or built-in scarcity. "Get 30% Off Everything Site Wide through Sunday Night" will generate more sales than a subject line without the discount or the deadline.

You should also be reengaging website visitors who left without making a purchase, visitors who added items to their shopping carts but didn't check out, and previous customers who are potential candidates to become repeat buyers. We'll dig deeper into paid marketing strategies in the Level 3 section "The Growth Entrepreneur," but it can be worth spending some money on ads to reengage website visitors, those who abandoned their shopping carts, and customers who've previously bought if you have something specific to offer them.

Since these ads are so low in the sales funnel and all about reengaging and making sales, you should be able to manage them profitably.

Some additional tips for increasing your sales and making them more sustainable:

- **Experiment with Your Pricing Strategy:** Experiment with different prices and pricing models, such as tiered pricing, subscription models, or bundles, to find the most profitable price for your audience.
- **Upsell and Cross-Sell:** Encourage customers to purchase more by offering upsells (higher-tier versions of your product) or cross-selling related products or services. This can increase the average transaction value.
- **Diversify Your Products or Services:** Look for opportunities to add complementary products or services that appeal to your existing customer base.
- **Increase Customer Retention:** Focus on retaining existing customers by providing exceptional support and incentives for repeat buyers. Loyal customers are more likely to make sustainable, long-term customers.

To build sustainability, keep growing your reach, platform, repeat customers, and email list so that whenever you're ready to sell a product, you'll have a larger community to release it to. The more customers you get, the more evangelists you can get, the more repeat customers you'll get, and the growth continues.

STEP 5: OPTIMIZE VISIBILITY, ENGAGEMENT, AND SALES

It's important to use both the qualitative data you're getting from talking with and surveying your customers and the quantitative data you're getting from your website analytics, email management platform, and sales data to improve your marketing and sales funnel. Steps 1–4 above will generate a lot of data, which, if you monitor and analyze it correctly, you can use to generate a bunch of actionable information.

For example, by analyzing your most popular posts or product pages, you can see what content and products resonate most with your customers. You can also take it a step further and see which posts are driving the most sales and work to improve the calls to action on those posts to see if you can increase sales even further. Or you can identify posts that used to lead to sales but have now dropped off and then try to improve those posts and test different calls to action.

This might feel like a lot to monitor at first, but correctly using the correct tracking tools does a lot of the heavy lifting for you. Then, over time, it also gets much easier to spot patterns and understand what's happening so you can quickly make improvements that generate more traffic and money. While you can outsource this to someone else, I'd recommend learning as much of this as possible and managing it yourself first so you can always understand what's going on and uncover ways to keep improving such a vital part of your business.

Below are the quantitative data points that I find most valuable, how I read them, and how I use them across three categories: Visibility, Engagement, and Sales.

Visibility

The metrics below measure how many people see your content, website, social profiles, and brand. You want to track your visibility over time and work to keep growing it. Here's how you evaluate it:

1. **Total Website Impressions (Google Search Console):** This is the total number of times a page from your website has been displayed in search results to users. Impressions can occur when a web page appears in the search results, regardless of whether or not the user clicks on the page. You should see your impressions increase over time as you create more content and Google ranks it. If you're not seeing growth after three to six months of launching your website, then the quality of your content is likely too low, or there are technical issues with your website that are impacting

how Google is crawling it. Look at the Page Experience and Core Web Vitals tabs in Google Search Console to see if they've identified any technical issues with your website.

2. **Impressions and Reach (Various Social Media Platforms):** Impressions represent the total number of times your content has been displayed on users' screens. It includes all views, whether from the same user or multiple users. Reach represents the number of unique accounts that have seen your content. While this varies slightly across social media platforms, it's essentially the same type of metric. Track your impressions and reach over time at your account and individual-post level. Double down on the types of content that are getting the most impressions and reach to expand your account visibility.

Engagement

The metrics below measure what content visitors are engaging with, how many are returning, how many are signing up for the email newsletter, and what percentage of email subscribers are opening your emails and clicking on the links.

1. **Total Website Clicks (Google Search Console):** The number of clicks users have made on your website's links in Google search results. It tracks how often users click on your website's pages or content from search results. Just like impressions, you want to see this growing over time.

2. **Unique Website Visitors (Google Analytics):** The number of distinct, individual users who visited your website within a specified time frame.

3. **Returning Website Visitors (Google Analytics):** Users who have visited your website and then returned for another visit later. This is a crucial metric, since returning website

visitors have found enough value in your content to come back for more. Work to increase this over time by driving newsletter subscribers back to your website, creating a reason for users to come back regularly (weekly updates, for example), and offering premium experiences that offer exclusive content or offers in exchange for a fee. Adding a discussion forum to your websites can also be an effective way to increase returning visitors.

4. **Website Traffic by Source (Google Analytics):** This tool provides information about the channels or sources that drive traffic to your website. It can include organic search, direct traffic, referral traffic from other websites, social media, paid advertising, and more. It helps you understand where your visitors are coming from.

5. **Popular Posts (Google Analytics):** This shows you which pieces of content, such as articles or blog posts, have garnered significant attention, engagement, or views. Write more posts like the ones that are performing.

6. **Events—Email Sign-Ups (Google Analytics and Your Email Management Platform):** Events, tracked in both Google Analytics and email management platforms, represent actions that users take on your website or in emails. "Events—Email Sign-Ups" refers to the number of users who have signed up for your email list. One of your primary calls to action should be getting visitors to sign up for your email list.

7. **Email Open Rate (Email Management Platform):** This is a key email-marketing metric that calculates the percentage of recipients who have opened and viewed your email. It measures the effectiveness of your email subject lines and the overall engagement of your list. Email titles significantly impact open rates, so you should be testing different

headline formats and A/B testing two headlines against each other in your email platform (almost all platforms have this feature). Industry averages are typically 25 to 45 percent. One way to increase your open rate is to remove email subscribers who haven't opened your emails in the past six months since you don't want to pay for subscribers who never engage with your content. Be sure to check for any email deliverability issues because it's becoming increasingly difficult to get an email to land in a Gmail inbox without going to spam.

8. **Email Click-Through Rate (Email Management Platform):** The email click-through rate (CTR) measures the percentage of email recipients who have clicked on one or more links in your email. It gauges the level of engagement and interest generated by the email content. The average CTR is 1 to 3 percent in most industries.

Sales

The metrics below are essential to track in order to optimize your business. Pay close attention to these metrics in your sales platform, on your P&L, through Google Analytics, and in your email management platform.

1. **Total Sales (Sales Platform):** Total sales is the total revenue generated from selling products, services, or goods within a specific time frame. You should track this across all products and traffic channels to see which products are selling the most and which channels are driving the most sales.

2. **Average Order Value (Sales Platform):** The average order value (AOV) is the average amount of money customers spend per order or transaction, which is calculated by dividing the total revenue by the number of orders during a given period. You want to track and work to increase your

AOV over time by offering add-on products, upsells, and bundled deals.

3. **Gross Profit (P&L):** Gross profit is the profit a company makes after deducting the cost of goods sold (COGS) from its total revenue. It does not account for other operating expenses like marketing, rent, or salaries.

4. **Lifetime Value of a Customer (Sales Platform or Self-Calculated):** A customer's lifetime value (CLV) is the estimated total revenue a customer is expected to generate for a business over their entire relationship. It helps companies to understand the long-term value of acquiring and retaining customers. I'll dive into how to calculate and optimize for CLV later, in chapter 9.

5. **Email Click to Conversion Rate (Self-Calculated):** This metric in email marketing measures the percentage of email recipients who clicked on a link in the email and subsequently completed the desired action, or conversion, such as making a purchase or signing up for a newsletter.

These are the metrics that I paid the closest attention to as a Solopreneur, and they represent a good foundation for analyzing and improving the performance of your business. But depending on the type of business you have or the insights you're looking for, you may need to edit this list or add to these metrics. The important takeaway here is that to build predictability and sustainability into your business, you need to create a set of core metrics that you track, which help you identify what's working well and the areas for improvement. This gets much easier to do over time.

CHAPTER 8

UNLOCK SUSTAINABLE CASH FLOW AND MAXIMIZE YOUR INVESTMENTS

"Entrepreneurs believe that profit is what matters most in a new enterprise. But profit is secondary. Cash flow matters most."

—Peter Drucker

Hey, can you chat quickly?" The text message came out of the blue one night while I was out to dinner. I hadn't heard from Luke in over a year, but I called him back later that night, figuring it must be important. Luke owns a company that sells school supplies to parents at wholesale prices through parent-teacher associations. He makes it easy for schools to help parents get the exact school supplies their kids need at a significantly lower cost than they could get from a store. The school reaps the added benefit of getting free school supplies to help some of its students in need. It's a nice niche business, but unfortunately, the profit margins aren't that great. It's also asset-heavy, since you need a warehouse full of school supplies to assemble the shipments.

"I don't know what to do." I could immediately tell that Luke was stressed-out. "I've run out of money. I'll be out of business in a few weeks if I can't find a solution. What should I do?" Like many entrepreneurs, the pandemic hit Luke's business hard; you don't need school supplies when kids are learning remotely. He didn't have enough cash coming into the business to keep paying his employees. I advised him to downsize his team immediately, negotiate his warehouse lease, and try to get a loan based on the value of his existing inventory.

Thankfully, he significantly reduced his expenses and got a loan to keep him afloat for the next two years until the kids started returning to school in person. The silver lining of this story is that, when kids went back to school, Luke could capitalize on surging demand because he was one of the few companies like his to stay in business through the pandemic. Coupled with his much-reduced expenses, this increase in demand significantly increased his cash flow and profit in 2022, setting his company up so well that he could sell it in early 2023.

The biggest reason businesses fail is that they run out of money. They don't have enough cash in the bank to keep the lights on. This can happen to the local BBQ restaurant down the street, just like it can happen to Silicon Valley Bank, a bank with billions in assets that lost its cash flow and went bankrupt in only a few days.

Cash-flow management is often the biggest challenge for Solopreneurs, especially when you're going from having a steady, dependable paycheck to having to pay yourself, either on a regular schedule or more irregularly, when you have cash from the business to spare. Many Solopreneurs go through feast or famine periods where their cash flow can fluctuate significantly. This can be stressful and derail any entrepreneur. The key is building more predictable cash flow and cash-flow planning into your business.

If you want to be a world-class athlete, you can't simply train hard and expect to stay at the top of your game forever. You also have to monitor your physical health and metrics to ensure your body functions optimally. Your heart rate, diet, blood pressure, spinal alignment, muscular health, and many other factors can affect your performance just as significantly as how fast you run or how much you can deadlift. An undetected injury or health condition could ruin your career before you notice it.

The same is true for business. You can throw all your profit into growing your business, but if you're not paying attention to where your money is going and how it's impacting your business, you could run out of cash and the ability to operate before you even realize why.

Beyond having enough cash to cover your monthly expenses, you want to set up a system that makes your cash flow more sustainable.

Being able to predict and depend on consistent cash flow makes your business more resilient so you can weather uncertainty, allows you to plan for the future from a position of strength, and makes you more agile so you can capitalize on new opportunities as they arise.

The more cash you have available, the more freedom you have.

And once the cash is flowing, you can use the profit to increase the freedom you have in your personal life and business. At the Solo-preneur stage, your goal should be to grow revenues while establishing the best cash-flow system to help you build a sustainable, dependable company. If you're working another job, the work you do at this stage should allow you to quit your day job and work on your business part-time or full-time, but with more time to spend with your family, on your hobbies, or on any other activity that brings your life energy.

After you've built a sustainable cash-flow system, you can also focus on scaling it and unlocking even more freedom in your life while simultaneously increasing the value of your business.

MEASURE AND MANAGE CASH FLOW

As discussed in chapter 5, at its most basic definition, cash flow measures how easily you can pay your bills in full and on time. Good cash flow means you have enough money coming in before your bills come due. Poor cash flow means you often have to scramble to cover your expenses while you wait to get paid (or because you're not generating enough revenue). Your cash flow is the lifeblood of your business. It makes everything run smoothly and ensures you can profit from your business or grow it if you'd like.

Generally speaking, there are three levers you can pull to optimize your cash flow:

Expenses: Keep costs as low as possible and spend additional money only when you know you can afford it. Many first-time and early-stage entrepreneurs spend too much too quickly and then have trouble generating enough revenue to keep pace down the line.

Revenue: There's a limit to how much you can cut back on expenses, since you will need to shell out some money to run the business. However, there's no limit to how much revenue you can earn if you make good decisions and run the business efficiently. You can increase your customer base, prices, average order value, customer lifetime value, and more. Beyond a certain point, focusing your energy on maximizing revenue rather than minimizing costs is always better.

Net Profit: This is the amount of revenue you have left over after you deduct all your costs of goods sold and expenses. You can reinvest this profit in the business, take it out of the business to invest in other asset classes, or use it to pay for your personal life. The lower your net profit margin, the tighter your cash flow will likely be, and the more challenging it will be for you to make enough to invest in other areas of your business unless you have a massive scale.

First-time entrepreneurs often assume that if their business is profitable, that's enough to keep it healthy. This is a mistake. A business can be profitable and still fail, and you can grow a business on thin margins if you manage your money well.

One of the reasons I recommend selling digital or physical products online is that there is relatively low overhead or cost of goods, so your profit margin is typically higher. Brick-and-mortar restaurants and retailers, by contrast, have low profit margins; even the most successful businesses often operate on a razor-thin line where a couple of bad months or a disruption in service could put them out of business forever.

That's why it's essential to not only pay attention to the bottom line of your P&L but also monitor and measure your cash flow so you know exactly how much money you have and how it's being used.

You can generate several reports in your accounting software to help you do this. You should handle your financial and accounting responsibilities independently when you're starting—at least for a while. Even if you turn this responsibility over to someone else, you should schedule regular check-ins with that person to ensure you have a complete picture of your company's financial health. Doing this will give you a deeper understanding of how your business functions and enable you to make better decisions.

Create a Cash-Flow Forecast

I recommend you create a cash-flow forecast that outlines your expected weekly, monthly, and quarterly income and expenses. This makes it much easier to forecast how much cash you will have on hand in the near future and will help you anticipate cash shortfalls and surpluses.

While you can build a manual system, it's a lot less complicated and time-consuming to use software that connects to your bank accounts and can do this for you. QuickBooks currently has a cash-flow forecast feature, and other cash-flow management software, like Xero, Wave, FreshBooks, and Quicken, all include similar features. At MMG Media Group, I use the forecast from QuickBooks, and I've custom-built one with my accountant in a Google Doc. It's simple but essential for me to see how much money we're owed and when I should expect the cash to hit our bank account. Since our partners pay us on Net-30- to Net-90-day payment terms, we're always owed a lot of money.

Knowing exactly how much cash we're owed and when we should receive it makes it easier for me to determine how much money I can invest in the business in the next several months and what our expense liability will be. While you should develop a detailed cash-flow forecast, you should customize it to your business and what you'd like to know.

HOW TO IMPROVE CASH FLOW

You can improve your cash flow by increasing your revenue, which involves getting more customers, increasing your prices, and increasing your average order value. You can also increase your cash flow by reducing your costs by cutting discretionary expenses, unnecessary overhead, and labor costs. But to improve your business's cash flow, you should create the biggest time gap between when a customer pays you and when you have to pay your suppliers. To do this, you should track and monitor your accounts receivable, accounts payable, and expenses by vendor reports closely. Here's how:

Get Paid Quickly

Accounts receivable (A/R) reports are generated in QuickBooks and other accounting software to show how much money you're owed, who owes it to you, and when it is due. It's a valuable report for cash-flow management because you can easily see when money is due and past due. Because you can see when you will get paid in the future, you can make decisions about making investments in your business and manage your bills based on the expected cash flow.

When you see money that's past due, you can follow up with the person who owes it to you and request payment. I use this report to see how much cash our business is owed and who is late in paying it.

Here's a breakdown of the data that accounts receivable reports show, what numbers to look at, the type of data they contain, and how you can customize them to your needs:

1. **Recording Transactions:** In your accounting system, you record all customer sales or services. Each transaction includes details such as the customer's name, invoice amount, date, and payment terms. Recording a sale is recognized as revenue in the P&L, even if you haven't been paid yet. As you receive payments, they offset the accounts receivable, affecting the P&L positively. Unpaid receivables can also be considered bad debts and impact your expenses.

2. **Aging Schedule:** The aging schedule shows which payments are current (typically due within a 30-day payment period) or overdue by 30, 60, 90, or more days. This report reflects the timeline of unpaid invoices and helps you

monitor the promptness of payments, by understanding which invoices are due and when businesses can better predict their cash inflows and outflows. This information also helps you recognize which invoices are overdue and by how many days, allowing for prompt follow-up and collections. You can also use the aging schedule to analyze whether customers consistently pay within terms or frequently pay late. In QuickBooks and most accounting software, you can automate email reminders to customers when their payments are overdue.

3. **Total Accounts Receivable:** This report provides the total amount of money you're owed. It may be broken down by customer or invoice.

4. **Source Breakdown:** You can generate reports that show which customers or sources owe you money or have the most overdue balances. Reach out to customers who haven't paid, to ask why and push them to pay you what they owe you promptly.

You should track accounts receivable regularly, at least once a week, or daily for larger businesses. It's essential to monitor overdue invoices and follow up with customers who are late on payments. The aging schedule is especially important in assessing the health of your receivables.

Effective accounts receivable management ensures your business has a healthy cash flow and minimizes the risk of bad debts. If you notice an increase in aging receivables or overdue payments, you should try to address the issues immediately with your customers who owe you money.

Here are other ways to improve your accounts receivable:

- Send invoices promptly and ensure that your invoices are accurate and easy for customers to understand. Include all necessary information, such as invoice number, due date, payment instructions, and a breakdown of charges.

- Provide customers with various payment methods, such as credit cards, electronic funds transfers, and online payment portals.
- Communicate your payment terms to customers from the beginning of the business relationship. Include any penalties for late payments in your contracts and on invoices.
- Use invoicing and accounting software to automate the invoicing process and send customer payment reminders. Automation reduces the chances of human error and ensures timely follow-ups.
- Offer discounts for early payments to encourage customers to pay faster.
- Establish a consistent and effective collections process for overdue payments.
- If you offer subscription-based services, set up automated recurring billing for customers.
- For large projects or significant purchases, request prepayments or deposits from customers. This up-front cash can help cover costs and improve cash flow.
- Maintain strong and open communication with customers. Building positive relationships can encourage timely payments and reduce disputes.

Pay on Your Terms

Accounts payable (A/P) reports how much money you owe, to whom you owe it, and when it's due. This tracks all your outstanding bills and debts. Recording a bill you owe is not recognized as an expense in your P&L until you pay the bill. Once you make the payment, it decreases your expenses in the P&L. Proper management of payables helps control costs and impacts your profitability.

Regularly tracking accounts payable helps you manage your cash flow, budget for upcoming expenses, and maintain strong relationships with your suppliers. If you notice an increase in overdue bills or other concerning trends, it may indicate a need to pivot or add additional working capital to the business.

Here's how accounts payable reports are generated, what data they contain, key numbers to look at, and how to customize them to your needs:

1. **Recording Bills:** In your accounting or financial management software, record all bills you receive from suppliers and vendors. These entries typically include the supplier or vendor name, invoice amount, due date, and other relevant details.

2. **Aging Schedule:** The accounts payable aging schedule categorizes your outstanding bills into aging periods, such as 30, 60, 90, and over 90 days overdue. This report reflects the timeline of unpaid bills.

3. **Total Accounts Payable:** This report provides the total amount of money you owe to all your suppliers and vendors. It also breaks down the amount owed by individual suppliers. This is an essential number to track to know how much money you owe and to whom.

4. **Source Breakdown:** You can generate reports that show which suppliers or vendors you owe money to. This helps in managing your payables efficiently.

When paired with the accounts receivable report, your accounts payable report is useful for cash-flow management because you can see how much money you're owed versus how much money you owe. When you subtract these two numbers, you can get a more accurate representation of your free cash flow, or how much cash you'll have at any point in time if you receive all the money you're owed and pay all the money you owe within the time it's due.

Free cash flow is the extra money you have left over after paying for everything you need to run your business. It's the money you can use however you want. You can save it, buy more supplies, or use it to pay yourself a salary. With free cash flow, a company can pay down debt, invest in new opportunities, cover unexpected expenses, or return money to investors or owners. Potential investors or acquirers of your company will look at your free cash flow to see how efficiently you convert revenue into cash flow. Companies that have high free-cash-flow margins, above 20 to 25 percent, typically get higher valuations.

You should track accounts payable regularly, usually weekly or biweekly, to stay on top of how much money you're owed. The aging schedule is vital for assessing how timely you are with payments to avoid late fees or supplier disputes. Maintaining healthy relationships with your suppliers is crucial, since replacing them can be expensive and difficult. Remember that businesses are built on relationships, so you should keep your customers, employees, vendors, and suppliers happy.

Here are other ways to improve your accounts payable:

- Negotiate favorable payment terms with your suppliers. Request extended payment periods to align with your cash-flow cycle.
- Take advantage of early-payment discounts offered by suppliers if the discount is significant.
- Take advantage of vendor credit programs, where suppliers may offer financing options or lines of credit to help you manage cash flow. Carefully review the terms and interest rates associated with such programs.
- Ensure that you pay critical suppliers promptly to maintain essential business operations.
- Extend payment terms with suppliers whenever feasible, as long as it aligns with your agreements and doesn't harm your relationships.
- Invest in accounts payable automation tools and software to streamline invoice processing and payment approvals. Automation reduces manual errors, speeds up processes, and improves efficiency.

- Monitor and manage your payment schedule to avoid late fees.
- Set up an invoice approval process to ensure that invoices are reviewed and approved before payment. This reduces the risk of paying incorrect or fraudulent invoices.

Cut Unnecessary Expenses

The expenses by vendor report details how much money you're paying vendors over a defined period. Our largest expense at my company is content, and we spend a lot on contract writers every month. I use the expenses by vendor report to see exactly how much we spend on writers and how much we pay each writer.

I look at the past months, and often year-to-date, to see how much we're spending. I also know how much each of the writers charge on a per-word basis, so I can calculate the number of words we've written that month based on this report, as well as look for ways to reduce our expenses by negotiating long-term deals with writers to whom we are outsourcing a lot of content. Here are a few ways to optimize your vendor expenses:

- Review and cut unnecessary or discretionary vendor expenses.
- Consider outsourcing or automating tasks to reduce labor costs.
- Negotiate better terms with service providers and vendors.

THE CASH CONVERSION CYCLE: THE LITTLE-KNOWN METRIC YOU SHOULD USE

One of the best ways to measure your cash flow is to use a metric most new entrepreneurs often overlook: the cash conversion cycle (CCC).

The CCC measures how many days it takes for the cash you're owed to reach your bank. This is important because the faster you have money in the bank, the more quickly you can use it to manage and grow your business. When your customers pay you before you have to pay your vendors, you will never have to worry about running out of money or being forced to take on debt. In addition, as long as you know you will recoup the money in time to pay your vendors, you can use the cash you have on hand to grow your business. This is the entire concept behind preorders: by taking cash up front from your customers before you have to deliver your product or service, you can use the money they give you to fund the creation of the product.

By contrast, if you wait to get paid by your customers but owe vendors and suppliers money right now, you'll be forced to "float" money. This means you need to use whatever money you currently have to cover your expenses while you wait to get paid. If this float gets too big, it can cause significant cash-flow issues, forcing you to take out a loan (thus further increasing your expenses) or to close your business. Unfortunately, it's common for a company with a great product, great marketing, strong demand, and a robust profit-and-loss statement to go out of business because their float gets too large and they can't get paid quickly enough.

CCC is measured in days; the lower the number, the better. A lower CCC generally indicates a business is more efficient at creating and managing its cash flow. There are many ways to calculate your CCC, depending on your business, so I encourage you to study this topic further and figure out the CCC of your business. The CCC is commonly calculated using the following components:

Days Inventory Outstanding (DIO): The average number of days for a company to sell its inventory. It's calculated as:
DIO = (Average Inventory / Cost of Goods Sold) x 365

- Average Inventory is the average value of inventory held during a specific period. You can set up QuickBooks to track your inventory and calculate the average value of your inventory by using QuickBooks inventory-management features.

- Cost of Goods Sold (COGS) is the total cost of producing the goods sold during the same period. You can calculate this in QuickBooks and show it on your P&L.

Days Sales Outstanding (DSO): The average number of days for a company to collect customer payments. It's calculated as: **DSO = (Accounts Receivable / Total Credit Sales) x 365**

- Accounts Receivable is the amount of money owed by customers. You can generate this from the A/R report in QuickBooks.
- Total Credit Sales are the total sales made on credit during the period.

Days Payable Outstanding (DPO): DPO represents the average number of days a company takes to pay its suppliers or vendors. It's calculated as: **DPO = (Accounts Payable / Cost of Goods Sold) x 365**

- Accounts Payable is the amount of money a company owes to its suppliers. You can generate this from the A/P report in QuickBooks.
- Cost of Goods Sold (COGS) is the same as in the DIO calculation above, which you can pull from your P&L in QuickBooks.

With these three components, you can calculate the Cash Conversion Cycle (CCC):

$$CCC = DIO + DSO - DPO$$

A CCC below zero means you're collecting cash that number of days before you pay your vendors. For example, if your CCC is −8, your customers pay you, on average, eight days before you have to pay your vendors. Fun fact: Apple's CCC is −48 days, and Amazon's is −21 days. It's widely believed that Amazon's low CCC is why it survived the dot-com bust in the early 2000s. For comparison, Walmart's CCC is +2, which means they don't collect their cash from customers until, on average, two days *after* they have to pay their vendors. This is okay for Walmart, since they compete on such a massive scale that they can negotiate favorable terms with their vendors and float any cash if necessary.

One of the countless benefits of selling products online (digital and physical) is getting paid before the customer receives the product. This is also another benefit of productizing your service and setting up either a monthly recurring or annually recurring subscription model (more on this below).

But when you own a service business like a painting company, you do the job, send an invoice to your customer, and then wait to get paid. So you don't get paid until after the job, and since some customers will be slow to pay or might not pay at all, this will negatively impact your cash flow. Even with a regular service business, although not typical, you can ask to be paid in full or in part up front for the service. Always try to get all or as much money as you can up front, set a deadline for payment, and charge a fee for late payments to encourage customers to pay promptly.

THE FIVE PHASES OF CASH-FLOW MANAGEMENT

One way to monitor your cash-flow management is to think of it in phases, each representing a new stage of freedom for both yourself and your business. The best way to figure out which phase you're in or want to pursue is to ask yourself, "What's the best use of this $1 for my business and life?"

The answer to this question will change depending on your goals, but it often depends on how much freedom you already have. Should you reinvest this dollar in the business to keep it growing? Should you pay it to yourself as a salary or an owner/partner distribution to cover your living expenses? Should you invest the money in a retirement account or some other asset to diversify your investments?

I like to think of cash-flow management in terms of five distinct but related phases:

Phase 1: Consistent Positive Cash Flow: This is the most fundamental phase, which you reach when you're consistently generating enough revenue to pay your expenses in full and on time each month. This is when you are breaking even.

Phase 2: Save a Cash Buffer: In the event your cash flow is disrupted, you'll want to make sure you have enough cash on hand to cover your expenses while you improve the business. As I've mentioned, I'm conservative and always like to have four to six months of expenses on hand. Save this money in a high-yield business checking or savings account.

Since we've already covered Phases 1 and 2 earlier in the book, let's examine the last three phases in more detail:

Phase 3: Cash-Flow Financial Independence

Live off your profit and maximize your freedom.

At this stage your business is generating enough revenue to cover your personal living expenses. I reached financial independence by saving $1.25 million in an investment portfolio so I could live off the income my investments generated. But a faster way to reach financial independence is to live off the income you generate from your business. If you're generating enough revenue to consistently cover all your personal living expenses—rent/mortgage, car/insurance payments, food, clothing, etc.—then you've reached cash-flow financial independence, aka Cash-Flow FI.

When you reach this stage, you can take advantage of the freedom it gives you and do whatever you want with your extra time. Logan Leckie, whom I mentioned in chapter 3, makes $5,000 in profit from selling on Amazon every month. This covers his living expenses, so he can spend the rest of his time working on other, more meaningful entrepreneurial ventures without needing a salary. Logan got to Cash-Flow FI within six months of starting his Amazon FBA business and now has more options and time to invest in other ventures.

If you've already separated your business and personal finances, as suggested in chapter 5, then it will be relatively easy to manage a Cash-Flow FI business. You need to figure out how much money you need to cover your living expenses and tax liability each month and set up automatic payments from your business checking account to deposit in your personal checking account on a set schedule. I walk through a detailed method for calculating your living expenses in the third and fourth chapters of my book *Financial Freedom*.

There are two obvious perceived risks to the cash-flow financial independence model:

1. Your expenses increase over time and your cash flow from your business no longer covers the cost of your living expenses, or

2. Your product or service becomes less competitive and your cash flow declines.

This is why the Lifestyle Business Cash-Flow Method described below protects you in case your business fails or you don't want to run it anymore. You can either move to this phase after you reach Cash-Flow FI or work toward it simultaneously.

Phase 4: Lifestyle Business Cash-Flow Method

Acquire more freedom today and tomorrow by accelerating your journey to financial independence.

This phase allows you to not only live off the revenue your business generates but reach financial independence by diversifying your assets and amassing enough personal wealth so that you don't need to work if you don't want to. We've already talked about the power of building your business around your life instead of your life around your business. This cash-flow method helps you make that possible, as it allows you to pay yourself from the income of the business (as you do in the Cash-Flow FI method), grow your business, and invest in diversified asset classes outside your business (like stocks, bonds, and real estate) for retirement or other income generation.

The ultimate goal is to accelerate your journey to financial independence inside and outside your business. The most efficient and effective ways to do this are to reduce your taxable income so you have more money to invest, increase your savings rate to increase the amount of money you invest, and diversify your investments to maximize returns while minimizing risk.

There is a direct correlation between your savings rate and the time it will take you to reach financial independence. The higher the percentage of your personal and business income you invest, the faster you'll get there.

SAVINGS RATE TO YEARS TO FI

The higher your savings rate, the faster you can reach financial independence.

Your savings rate is the total percentage of your income that you're saving in all your accounts. It's easy to track:

1 year of freedom = 1 year of expenses covered by savings

No matter how much money you're making, here's how long you have to work to save one year of living expenses:

ANNUAL SAVINGS	
Bank Accounts	
Savings 1	$5,000
Savings 2	$2,000
INVESTMENTS	
Pretax	
401(k)	$18,500
Roth IRA	$5,500
After Tax	
Brokerage	$9,000
Total Saved	$40,000
Income	$100,000
Savings Rate	40%

10 percent savings rate: 9 years of work $(1 - 0.1) / 0.1$

25 percent savings rate: 3 years of work $(1 - 0.25) / 0.25$

50 percent savings rate: 1 year of work $(1 - 0.5) / 0.5$

75 percent savings rate: ½ year of work $(1 - 0.75) / 0.75$

To calculate your savings rate, add up all the dollars you save, both in pretax accounts (for example, 401(k)s and IRAs) and after-tax accounts (brokerage), and divide that total by your income. Here is an example of how it looks if you have a $100,000 income and a savings rate of 40 percent.

An easy way to monitor your savings rate is to use a spreadsheet that you update monthly, or use the savings rate calculator that I've built. Both are available at https://grant sabatier.com/tools.

Below are seven steps to help you optimize Phase 4, the Lifestyle Business Cash-Flow Method. While we are veering a little deeper into personal finance here, the point of these recommendations is to reduce your taxable income from your business.

STEP 1: MAXIMIZE YOUR TAX-DEDUCTIBLE BUSINESS EXPENSES

As you know, the U.S. tax code is designed to incentivize small-business owners because small-business growth creates jobs and grows the economy. But to make the most of these incentives, you must take all the expense and tax deductions you're entitled to. Tax-deductible business expenses are costs associated with running your business that can reduce the amount of business income subject to taxation.

When you realize you're going to have a profitable year in your business, you can reduce your business profit and thus your tax burden by prepaying as many of your expenses this year for next year from your profit. At my company, come November, we will try to offset our profit for the year by prepaying our website hosting expenses, conference registrations, and more anticipated expenses for the following year.

Many of your vendors will be happy to allow you to prepay because it immediately puts cash into their business. Of course, you should do this only if you have more than enough cash in the bank and a strong enough cash flow to ensure that reducing your tax burden doesn't compromise your business.

It's essential to keep detailed records and receipts for these expenses to support your deductions using expense tracking and accounting software like QuickBooks. While the specific deductible expenses can vary based on your business structure, industry, and location, common tax-deductible business expenses include:

- Advertising and Marketing
- Office Rent or Lease
- Utilities
- Phone and Internet
- Office Supplies
- Business Insurance
- Salaries and Wages

- Contract Labor
- Professional Services: Fees paid to professionals such as lawyers, accountants, and consultants for services related to your business
- Interest Expenses: Interest paid on business loans, credit card interest related to business expenses, and mortgage interest for business property
- Depreciation: Since certain business assets, such as equipment and vehicles, may provide critical service to the business but depreciate in value over time, you can deduct a portion of their cost each year as a business expense to account for their decreasing value.
- Travel and Meals
- Vehicle Expenses
- Licenses and Permits
- Home Office Deductions
- Employee Benefits
- Software and Technology
- Employee Education and Training
- Charitable Contributions
- Rent or Lease of Equipment

STEP 2: REDUCE YOUR TAXABLE INCOME

Not all income is created equal. One of the goals of efficient tax optimization is to minimize your W-2 taxable income because it's what is taxed at the highest rate. You want to ensure that your "effective tax rate" is as low as possible each year since these W-2 taxes cost you the most money. To calculate your effective tax rate, you can use your recent personal tax return and plug the numbers into the following equation:

Effective Tax Rate = (Total Income Tax Paid / Total Income) x 100%

In addition to ensuring that you get the most from your tax-deductible business expenses, you want to minimize the tax on the profit your business generates—since that tax burden passes through to your personal taxes as an LLC pass-through entity.

One of the easiest ways to reduce your taxable income is to take advantage of tax-advantaged retirement accounts and defer as much of your tax liability as possible into the future. This allows you to delay paying taxes on your investment gains until you finally sell those assets, at which point you'll pay capital gains taxes, which are significantly lower than regular income tax rates.

STEP 3: MAXIMIZE YOUR RETIREMENT CONTRIBUTIONS TO REDUCE YOUR TAXABLE INCOME

One of the most important things you can do at this stage is to set up a retirement account. These tax-advantaged investment accounts, which include employer-based 401(k) and Individual Retirement Accounts (IRAs), are one of the most efficient ways to increase your wealth while reducing your tax burden—and they are easy to set up.

As an entrepreneur, you can set up a Simplified Employee Pension Individual Retirement Account (SEP-IRA) or a solo 401(k) plan.

Simplified Employee Pension Individual Retirement Account

SEP-IRAs are the least complicated of these two account types and can be set up in a few minutes through a brokerage like Vanguard, Fidelity, or Charles Schwab. When you contribute to a SEP-IRA, the maximum contribution is based on a percentage of your net profit, not your gross profit.

It's also worth noting that the SEP-IRA contribution is typically made by the employer (you, if you're self-employed), not the employee, and is a tax-deductible business expense. Remember that specific rules and limits can change, so it's advisable to look up the current limits and regulations when you make your contributions for the year.

Solo 401(k)

A solo 401(k) requires a little more paperwork and annual maintenance, but it allows you to make contributions as an employee *and* employer. This means you could potentially save more money than you could with a SEP-IRA, especially if your net earnings are on the low side. Even if you have access to a 401(k) from your full-time job, you can still set up a solo 401(k) for your side business, but you'll have to make sure you don't exceed the employer contribution levels that are set cumulatively across all accounts by the U.S. government.

In 2024, for instance, you could contribute up to $23,000, or $30,000 if you were fifty or older. As the employer, you could contribute up to 25 percent of your net earnings from self-employment, or up to 20 percent of your net adjusted business profits if you're a sole proprietor or single-member LLC. This contribution is subject to certain IRS limits, and the total contribution limit for 2024, including both employee and employer contributions, is $68,000, or $75,500 for those aged fifty and older. These rates tend to change every few years, so it's worth looking up each year to make sure you're within the limits.

To establish and contribute to a solo 401(k), you need to have some self-employment income and not have any employees. You can set up a solo 401(k) through many financial institutions or companies like Carry, which I'm an investor in. Once your solo 401(k) is set up, you can contribute funds to the plan and invest them in various financial instruments, such as stocks, bonds, mutual funds, real estate, etc.

STEP 4: MAX OUT YOUR HEALTH SAVINGS ACCOUNT CONTRIBUTIONS

In addition to the solo 401(k) and SEP-IRA, you should look into opening a health savings account (HSA). HSAs allow you to make pretax contributions to the account to cover future medical expenses when or if they arrive. HSAs offer a unique triple tax advantage. Contributions are tax-deductible, earnings grow tax-free, and withdrawals for qualified medical expenses are tax-free. Any interest or investment earnings on the money in your HSA are tax-free. Your HSA funds can grow over time without incurring capital gains or income taxes. This combination of tax benefits is not found in other types of accounts.

Unlike flexible savings accounts (FSAs), which require you to spend all the money you invest every year, you can let HSA contributions and investment gains continue to grow and roll over year after year. This allows you to use HSAs as additional retirement accounts. Like SEP-IRAs and solo 401(k)s, HSAs are portable, meaning you can keep your HSA account even if you change jobs or health insurance plans. Your HSA is not tied to your employer.

As of 2024 you can invest pretax income up to $4,150 if you are single, $8,300 if you have a family, and an additional $1,000 catch-up contribution if you're over the age of fifty-five. HSAs are also accessible exclusively to individuals and families enrolled in high-deductible health insurance plans, which can be more costly than lower-deductible plans, but the overall tax advantages over time of an HSA should significantly offset the cost increase and are often well worth it when you run the numbers.

The typical advice when optimizing HSAs is to always pay your medical expenses out of pocket and save the receipts. Then you can reimburse yourself at any time in the future, using those receipts after your HSA balance has grown from increased contributions and investment gains. Given these incredible tax advantages, HSAs can be an effective tool for managing health care costs, saving for retirement, and reducing your overall taxes.

STEP 5: MAX OUT YOUR IRA ACCOUNTS

The next account you should open and max out, if you haven't already, is an Individual Retirement Account (IRA). Both Traditional and Roth IRAs are personal investment accounts, not attached to your business. The biggest difference between the two is how they are taxed. Contributions to a Roth IRA are made with after-tax dollars, meaning you pay income tax on the money before you contribute. The advantage is that qualified withdrawals, including contributions and earnings, are tax-free if the account has been open for at least five years and you meet specific distribution requirements, such as being age fifty-nine and a half. Contributions to a Traditional IRA are often tax-deductible, which means they can reduce your taxable income for the year you contribute. However, you will pay income tax when you withdraw funds from a Traditional IRA during retirement.

One valuable feature of a Roth IRA is that you withdraw your contributions (but not earnings) without penalties or taxes at any time for any reason, making a Roth IRA a de facto emergency fund if you need it. However, I'm not recommending you do this unless it's an emergency and you've depleted your regular emergency fund. Roth IRAs have income limits that can affect your ability to contribute. If your income exceeds these limits ($161,000 if you're single and $240,000 if you're married and filing jointly), you may be restricted or ineligible to contribute directly to a Roth IRA. There are no income limits for contributing to a Traditional IRA. However, your eligibility for tax-deductible contributions may depend on your income and whether a retirement plan at work or as an entrepreneur already covers you or your spouse.

Choosing between a Roth IRA and a Traditional IRA depends on your current financial situation, your expected future tax situation, and your retirement goals. Many people also combine both types of IRAs to diversify their tax planning. If you qualify for a Roth IRA, it's almost always the better choice for most people because investment gains can grow tax-free.

If you are above the income limits to contribute to a Roth IRA, I encourage you to look into and consider doing a Roth IRA conversion, which is when you have contributed money to a Traditional IRA and then convert the money into a Roth IRA and pay taxes on the conversion. Setting these up is beyond the scope of this book, but I write about them in more detail in my book *Financial Freedom*.

STEP 6: OPEN AND KEEP INVESTING THROUGH A BROKERAGE ACCOUNT

If you've maximized your contributions to your 401(k) or SEP-IRA, your HSA, and your IRAs, then the next account you should open is a brokerage account. Although brokerage accounts don't give you any up-front tax advantages, and you can invest money only after you've paid tax on it, the accounts give you unlimited flexibility in what you can invest in, and you can withdraw money at any time.

One recommendation: if you invest in stocks in your brokerage account and hold those investments for at least a year, you have to pay capital gains tax only when you sell the assets. You do, however, have to pay regular income tax on any stock dividends for stocks you hold in your brokerage account. Every year, when I was pursuing financial independence, I was able to max out all my tax-advantaged accounts and had money left over to invest in my brokerage account, which I continue to add to regularly. Over time, I've let my retirement accounts continue to grow to maximize their tax advantages, and I withdraw funds from my brokerage account whenever I want to make a big purchase or need to top up my cash buffer.

STEP 7: INVEST IN REAL ESTATE

In addition to benefiting business owners, the U.S. tax code offers incentives for real estate investors. Investing in real estate is a great way to add diversification and tax savings and reduce your reliance on your business income. Diversifying into real estate can provide a hedge against the volatility of traditional investments like stocks and bonds.

Rental properties can also generate regular rental income, providing a steady cash flow that can be used to cover expenses, repay loans, or reinvest in your business. In addition to increasing rental income, real estate properties have the potential to appreciate in value over time and increase your personal net worth.

You can buy property as an individual or through your business. Either way, you can deduct business expenses related to the property, such as maintenance, repairs, insurance, and property management. Real estate also offers various tax benefits, including deductions for mortgage interest, property taxes, and depreciation. As long as you are buying a building or property to use for your business, you can benefit from depreciation deductions by utilizing them to claim depreciation losses against business income, which can help offset your business taxes.

It's important to note that while real estate can offer many advantages, like any investment, it also comes with challenges and risks, such as property management and market fluctuations. Take the time to learn about real estate and set up your investment criteria before diving in. A few good books to read are *How to Invest in Real Estate* by Joshua Dorkin and Brandon Turner; *The Millionaire Real Estate Investor* by Gary Keller, Dave Jenks, and Jay Papasan; *The House Hacking Strategy* by Craig Curelop; and *The Small and Mighty Real Estate Investor* by Chad Carson.

While there are many other ways to diversify your investments outside your business, stocks and real estate are historically the most dependable performers. To learn more about my recommended investment strategy, read chapter 10, "The Seven-Step Fast-Track Investment Strategy," in my book *Financial Freedom*.

Phase 5: Growth Maximization Cash-Flow Method

Reach financial independence as quickly as possible by betting on yourself and your business.

In this phase, you strive to maximize your business's value and minimize your taxable income by reinvesting as much profit as you can in the business. This is a great method for people who don't need to draw an income from their business to cover their living expenses. Since I achieved financial independence several years ago, any income I might draw from my businesses wouldn't improve my life much (if at all) and would just increase my tax burden.

I view my businesses as investments, and since I have more control over them than over other asset classes, such as the stock market, I want to reinvest my business earnings in the business because I believe that can generate higher returns over time than investing in another asset class. This is a core part of my investment diversification strategy.

The idea here is to take advantage of the tax benefits of growing the business by writing off the investments as expenses, and instead of taking profit out of the business, defer your tax gains into the future, when you will be able to sell your business and be subject to capital gains tax on the profits, which is much lower than income tax. This can be highly profitable but also extremely risky because if the business goes under, you've lost all the value you created.

That's why I recommend holding off on pursuing this strategy until you've, at the very least, created a cash buffer to shield your business in the case of reduced revenue or increased expenses. You can decrease your risk even more if you reach financial independence before you reinvest so that any blows to the business don't impact your personal finances. I'll explore exactly how to identify the best ways to reinvest in your business in chapter 9 and in the Level 3 section "The Growth Entrepreneur."

Cash-flow management becomes easier over time. You can significantly reduce your business's risk by keeping a large enough cash buffer, monitoring the cash coming in and out of the company, and planning using your cash-flow forecast.

BUILD SUSTAINABLE SYSTEMS SO YOUR BUSINESS CAN RUN ITSELF

"Every system is perfectly designed to get the result that it does."
—W. Edwards Deming

As I write this, I'm in year three of building a new company, the seventh business I've launched. So far this morning, we've made about $5,000 in profit and it's only 1:00 p.m. I haven't yet logged into my email, sat in meetings, or taken phone calls. I've been writing this book. I just checked our revenue-tracking sheet, most recent P&L, Google Analytics, and link-tracking performance report. Within ten minutes, I can get a detailed picture of the business's performance and identify areas that appear to be working well or might need improvement. This allows me to make quick, efficient decisions in an industry that demands I move quickly.

There are many advantages to being a Solopreneur, not least of all the freedom and flexibility that comes from working alone. But one of the challenges of this style of entrepreneurship is that your business and your life can become so intertwined that it can be hard to separate the two. Many Solopreneurs need to spend more time working on and in their business; but at the same time, they need to remember to create a business around their life instead of vice versa.

It's easy to see and feel the warning signs: your business is keeping you up at night because you're stressed about covering your living expenses; you constantly worry about losing your biggest customer or client; you're unhappier than you were when you were working for someone else; or you're not present in other areas of your life because you're always thinking about your business. If you don't set up good habits and systems early on to keep this from happening, it can be challenging to course correct later on, especially as your business starts to grow and there's more work to do.

Some people are naturally better at setting boundaries than others, and it gets easier to do, the more intentional you are. Once again, this comes back to testing your limits and being honest about your strengths. It's also easier and often more profitable to build as many systems as you need to support your business without trading your time for money. How you use people and systems is key to freeing up more time for your life.

To scale, you need to automate and outsource as much work as possible so you can focus on long-term planning and strategy and put your energy toward the activities you love most. Chances are there is some system, technology, or other people who can do most of the tasks you need to run your business. The more you grow and the more money you make, the more you will be able to buy back your time, but you can do so only if you have the systems in place to allow your business to run without you—or at least with less of you. Your time is inherently limited. Systems ensure that more work can get done without your having to trade a proportional amount of time to do it.

As you're transitioning into the Solopreneur stage, you probably won't be generating enough revenue to afford to hire a bunch of contractors or to subscribe to a bunch of fancy automation systems. But if you start by building small and strategic systems, you can build on these systems as you grow. This chapter will cover the most essential systems to set up during this phase of your business.

MONITOR YOUR BUSINESS WITH A PERFORMANCE DASHBOARD AND REPORTS

One of the myriad benefits of running an online business is that you can access a ton of up-to-the-minute data with little effort. With a few clicks, I can see website traffic, link clicks, affiliate conversions, course sales, earnings per click, our top partners, and current revenue today or over any period.

In my last business, we used business intelligence software (Looker Studio and then Tableau) to integrate all this data in one place, so I was able to see all of it on one central dashboard that I checked a few times a week. Most business intelligence software platforms give you the ability to connect all your data sources, such as Google Analytics, Shopify, Stripe, QuickBooks, your bank accounts, email management platforms, and more, and then isolate the key data points you'd like to pull into the dashboard, and organize the data however you'd like.

Some platforms also give you the ability to use the dashboard as an entry point to deeper data analysis if you build out additional reports. You can also sort data by date range and more. This is all to say that it's highly customizable.

I encourage you to set up a simple business performance dashboard (using Looker Studio, Domo, Tableau, or similar software), or if you don't create a dashboard, you should at minimum have a performance report that integrates your key metrics in Google Sheets or something similar. You can pull data from most systems into a simple Google Sheet or Looker Studio to keep your costs down. Check out the Google Chrome extension Coefficient, which allows you to connect almost any data source to Google Sheets, with no coding required!

This dashboard or performance report should be customized to show exactly what you need to know to manage your business effectively. You should keep it as simple as possible to show the data you'll use. These dashboards or reports will save you a lot of time from having to review all your data sources, and they can also help you more easily see how well your business is performing and where you might want to dig deeper. They will also help you have more effective conversations with your business partners and teams, because you're all looking at and accountable to the same data.

BUILD STANDARDIZED SYSTEMS TO
MANAGE YOUR BUSINESS

In addition to the reports that help us *monitor* the business, we have an intentionally designed set of systems that help us *manage* the business. By leveraging the increasingly advanced capabilities of technology and software and the efficiency of remote and contracted work, these systems are fine-tuned so our small team of nine gets the maximum leverage for our time.

Our systems help us manage millions of unique visitors a month across our websites, more than 400 partnerships, a content-creation strategy that produces 100 to 200 new blog posts per month, and endless requests from our advertising partners. As artificial intelligence advances and becomes more accessible, this technology will become even more powerful, giving business owners more opportunities to leverage their time.

Here is a selection of some of the systems we've developed that help us manage our business:

- System for Creating New Blog Posts
- System for Managing Advertising Partners
- System for Revenue Optimization
- System for Managing Employees and Contractors
- System for Managing Finances

The systems you create will depend on the type of business you run. For example, you might require a customer service or inventory management system. Regardless, the sooner you identify and develop these systems, the more efficient you will become and the easier it will be for you to grow.

Now let's dive deeper into the exact steps to build these systems:

Step 1: Identify the Key Processes within Your Business

Create a six-column table in Notion, a Google spreadsheet, in an Excel doc, or on a piece of paper. Name the first two columns "Process" and "Tasks." Name the remaining four columns as follows: "Like/ Love/Hate," "Technology/Person," "SOP," and "Next Steps." Under the first column head, list all the essential functions your business requires in order to run. These should be broad but discrete. For example, you might include things like accounting/taxes, customer service, affiliate/partner relations, inventory management, blog post creation, etc. Below is an example of the table layout:

PROCESS	TASKS	LIKE/ LOVE/ HATE	TECHNOLOGY/ PERSON	SOP	NEXT STEPS

In addition to listing the processes you already do, you can use this spreadsheet as a strategy document and list any processes you would eventually like to add to the business, such as digital advertising, public relations/media strategy, or video creation. This is a living document. It should be comprehensive, but it doesn't have to be perfect.

Step 2: Break Down Each Process into a Series of Step-by-Step Tasks

In the "Tasks" column, list each step required to fulfill the process. For example, this is what such a list might look like when creating new content in a content-driven affiliate marketing business:

PROCESS	TASKS
New Content Writing	Pick a keyword from the keyword tracking sheet
	Create a content brief for writers in Asana that includes the target keyword, an outline, competitors ranking for the keyword, and any FAQs

	Assign the content to a writer
	Writer writes in a Google Doc and when they're done, they add the Google Doc link to the Asana task

Step 3: Identify the Tasks You Like, Love, and Hate

Under column three, indicate whether you like, love, or hate each task or process. The more you can focus on the tasks you love and less on the ones you hate, the more energy and excitement you will have about your business and the more momentum you will naturally generate. Be honest with yourself here. Me? I love writing blog posts and handling the basic accounting functions for my business, but I hate managing social media posting.

Even if a task you hate doesn't take a ton of time, the stress or procrastination that can come with knowing you have to do it can kill your momentum and bleed into other parts of your business. It might not be possible to outsource or automate everything you hate doing right away, but it's useful to recognize this limit for yourself now so you can strategize how to move it off your plate later on.

Step 4: Identify Technologies or People to Automate or Outsource Each Task

Under column four, "Technology/Person," indicate what kind of technology and/or professional you could (or currently) use to automate or outsource each task. For example, you could use bookkeeping software like QuickBooks to track and manage your books, and you can also hire a professional bookkeeper to oversee this process so you don't have to.

Below is an example:

PROCESS	TASKS	TECHNOLOGY/PERSON
New Content Writing	Pick a keyword from the keyword tracking sheet	
	Create a content brief for writers in Asana that includes the target keyword, an outline, competitors ranking for the keyword and any FAQs	Project management software (Asana)
	Assign the content to a writer	Asana
	Writer writes in a Google Doc and when they're done, they add the Google Doc link to the Asana task	Freelance writer/ Google Docs/Asana

In addition to the above, we use an email marketing platform to automate and manage our email system, and we use a payroll and HR benefits technology to manage all our employee needs, compliance, and insurance. We use a link management system to manage and optimize our partnerships with affiliates. We've also built many of our own back-end systems and custom databases to power all our websites, push and pull data across our portfolio, and many of the features of our websites. Our websites are built on a central theme so the system behind it allows us to manage our entire portfolio more efficiently because we can roll out new updates across all the websites simultaneously.

Most technologies have entry-level plans that are free or relatively inexpensive for you to use when you're just starting. While it can be easy to get overwhelmed by all the available software, don't worry. Research and test the most popular tools; they are often popular because they're the best and can be a good place to start.

It's easy to go overboard with the technology and take on unnecessary expenses, so testing out a technology or a few before signing on for a longer subscription is always useful. Prioritize outsourcing or automating the tasks you hate doing and/or those that someone else could do more efficiently. By removing this low-hanging fruit from your plate, you immediately buy back some of your time and can return to the other tasks later when you have the resources to do so.

Step 5: Create Standard Operating Procedures

A standard operating procedure (SOP) is a detailed step-by-step outline of exactly what you do to accomplish a specific business task, the tools you should use, and the links to any relevant documents. SOPs are what you give to someone you hire to show them how to do exactly what you want them to do. They are like recipes with precise instructions. SOPs also make your business more attractive to a potential acquirer because they make it easier for them to integrate your company and systems into theirs.

When I sold Millennial Money, the SOP for creating new blog posts, optimizing them for SEO, and getting them posted was over forty pages long. While this might be extreme for your business, the more thorough you can be, the more detail you can add, and the easier the SOP is to understand, the better. It's also valuable for you, the business owner, because it forces you to dig into your business's details, which will help you make better decisions and uncover inefficiencies.

You can write out an SOP or film a short video (walking through the steps of what and how you do something), using a screen-capture video service like Loom or using a hybrid approach, with links to the videos embedded in the written version. I like the hybrid approach because it's much easier to edit a Google document or rerecord a short video when revising a process than it is to rerecord a long video. When you've created the SOP for a specific task, add the SOP document link to your spreadsheet's SOP column. This will create a master document of your business's tasks and SOPs.

The more standard operating procedures you have, the more you can outsource and automate your business. This is an ongoing process, and as soon as you can off-load one task, you should refer back to your list to see what you can tackle next. Use the last column, "Next Steps," to jot down your plans for this task, even if you're not yet able to realize them. The more you do this, the more time you will be able to buy back until you can focus solely on the aspects of your business where you create the most value.

TURN YOUR SERVICE INTO A PRODUCT

If you're the only person responsible for delivering the product or service or creating content to attract advertisers and affiliates, the value you can provide is automatically limited to how much time you have. This is less a problem for product-oriented businesses, since you can sell a product forever once you've invested the up-front time, costs, and energy in creating it—especially if you're selling digital products that don't require keeping up with inventory or shipping.

Service and affiliate businesses are more complex. With a service business, you're trading your own time for money. With an affiliate business, you must constantly produce content to keep your audience coming back so that partners and advertisers will be interested. This requires a steady investment of time, and the more readers you get, the more diverse offerings you should have to keep them interested.

If your service is straightforward and you design a SOP for it, you can hire contractors to do it for you. For example, in *Financial Freedom*, I told the story of Matt, who started a dog-walking business as a side hustle. He could walk only so many dogs in a given day, thus limiting the number of clients he could take on. But it's pretty easy to hire and train people to walk dogs, as the process is neither unique nor requires any particular skill.

Thus, it was easy for Matt to scale his business by paying

contractors a portion of the fee he charged to clients. He no longer had to trade his time for money, and if he wanted to continue growing his revenue and there was enough demand for his services, he could hire additional dog walkers to provide those services.

Scaling becomes more complicated when your work is more specialized, skilled, or unique. This is especially true when you're selling expertise or creativity. For example, if you're hiring a graphic designer, you tend to choose based on their style and skill. Whose work do you vibe with more? If that person then subcontracted your project to someone else, how would you know you're going to get the same design quality?

Or, if you're writing a blog and need to produce more content than you can personally handle, how can you outsource some of the writing while ensuring the finished posts retain your voice and authority? This was precisely the problem I faced when trying to scale Millennial Money, and it's similar to the problem many entrepreneurs face when their business is centered on content or a customized service. If you've chosen this path for your business and want to scale and/or stop trading your time for money, you must first figure out how to create a SOP for your core offering. This is also known as "productizing" your service.

Productization is the act of turning any skilled or creative task into a standardized, replicable offering that allows for consistent quality no matter who is performing it. The best-productized businesses offer something unique or a feature that distinguishes their offering from their competitors'. For example, Matt's dog-walking business could offer services and prices similar to those of other nearby dog-walking companies. But to help Matt's stand out, they could offer special recreational activities for their dogs or cater to skittish dogs that don't like going out in public. Matt could build this offering into his SOP to ensure that any of his contracted dog walkers know how to provide the service, and he could market that process to his customers as a competitive advantage.

The trap many Solopreneurs fall into is that, instead of focusing on selling their service, they focus on selling themselves. The most in-demand designers, photographers, lawyers, dance instructors, marketing advisers, etc., create a reputation as "the best," so people want to work only with them specifically. But what happens when you're not there if your business is centered on you, or you have to perform a specific task personally to command the highest price from customers? What happens if you want to vacation, handle a personal emergency, or do something new without spending as much time offering your service? Short answer: the business suffers.

When you focus instead on selling *what you offer*—with or without you attached—you can hire and train others to provide it, while making it clear to potential customers that they will receive the same quality service no matter who is providing it. This is exactly what Travis Hornsby did with Student Loan Planner. When he first launched the business, he did all the consultations because he had done all the research and could give tailored advice to clients. But when it came time for him to scale, he figured out a way to teach others how to offer the same thing by creating a replicable product from his service.

Regardless of how much you plan to scale, it's worth figuring out how to productize your offering so you can scale or sell whenever you want to. Here's a guide to help you figure out how to do so:

1. **Understand Your Service:** Clearly define the nature of your service, outlining its core features, benefits, and unique selling points. A comprehensive understanding of your service and who benefits from it is essential.

2. **Understand Your Competitors:** Analyze your competitors, pricing models, and different product types to identify opportunities and potential challenges.

3. **Create a Prototype:** Develop a prototype or minimum viable product (MVP) that showcases your product's key features and benefits. This prototype is a tangible representation of what your productized service will offer.

4. **Standardize Processes:** Establish clear workflows and procedures to ensure consistency and efficiency through your SOPs. Standardizing processes is crucial for scalability and maintaining high quality and replicability.

5. **Automate:** Integrate automation into your processes to enhance efficiency and scalability. Automation can reduce manual effort, minimize errors, and facilitate a smoother workflow.

6. **Establish Pricing Strategy:** Establish a pricing model aligned with the value your productized service provides. Consider market prices, customer willingness to pay, and operational costs when determining a fair and competitive pricing strategy.

7. **Create Marketing Materials:** Develop a suite of marketing materials, including adding the product to your website. The messaging should effectively communicate to your potential customers the benefits and features of your productized service.

8. **Customer Support:** Implement an effective customer support process to address inquiries, issues, feedback, and refunds. Providing excellent customer support is crucial for building trust; ensuring customer satisfaction; and getting repeat customers, referrals, and testimonials.

9. **Launch:** Plan a strategic launch to your email list and the broader market. Before a broader release, consider starting with a soft launch to select audience members to gather initial feedback and make necessary adjustments.

10. **Gather Feedback:** Collect feedback from early adopters and customers. Use this input to improve and refine your product based on real-world user experiences.

11. **Iterate and Improve:** Continuously improve your product based on customer feedback and market trends. Stay agile and be willing to make necessary adjustments to enhance the value proposition of your productized service.

12. **Scale:** As demand grows, scale your operations accordingly. This may involve expanding your team, improving infrastructure, and exploring opportunities to reach new markets.

For more information on how to productize your service, check out *Built to Sell* by John Warrillow and *The E-Myth Revisited* by Michael E. Gerber. Both explore the traps many entrepreneurs fall into when creating a business around themselves, and they offer specific strategies for reengineering your business so it can run with or without you.

HOW TO HIRE AND MANAGE YOUR DREAM TEAM OF CONTRACTORS

The next step in building sustainability into your business is to hire the right people for the right roles, first as contractors and then as full-time employees if they add tremendous value to the company and you can afford to have them on the payroll. One of the many reasons it's easier to build a business now than before is that you can find talent anywhere. The internet makes it easier to identify and recruit job candidates, and many jobs can be performed remotely, further deepening the hiring pool. You can also now use platforms to find highly skilled professionals for almost any role internationally, so you can hire experts for specific roles more cost-effectively.

The best way to find contractors is through your personal and professional networks. All the best contractors I've worked with have been referred to me by someone I know, and the same will likely be true for any Solopreneur. All you have to do is let people know you're hiring. Start by creating a simple job description that outlines the role, the responsibilities, the time commitment, the experience you're looking for, and whether the role is full-time, part-time, or freelance.

That last part is important to share since some people want to work only freelance, while others want to work for only one employer. This is an easy way to save yourself the hassle of sifting through unwanted résumés. Then you can share it on LinkedIn or any other social media platforms you use, email, your website, and with friends or colleagues who might know someone interested.

You can also approach people directly if you think they'd be a good fit or you're eager to work with them in some capacity. I occasionally do this, especially with people recently laid off by one of our competitors. If they say they aren't interested in working with us, I ask if they'd be open to doing a consulting project for us instead. I've learned an immense amount by paying my competitors' former employees a small fee for some consulting and their perspective. I've also found a few good contractors with a ton of relevant experience by paying attention to layoff discussions on LinkedIn.

If you can't find someone through your network and can afford it, you can post your job listing on various recruitment websites or pay to run a job ad on LinkedIn. Since it's so easy to apply for jobs on LinkedIn, this latter tactic has always led to many applicants, but it takes a ton of time to sort through them (even for my assistant!) and find good fits.

Of course, when you're still in the early stages of growth, you likely won't be able to afford a lot of contractors, so you'll want to prioritize the ones who will give you the most bang for your buck and allow you to grow most efficiently. Here are my top recommendations about whom a Solopreneur should hire.

#1. Executive Assistant

An assistant is the most important person you can bring on, and you should do so as soon as possible. When you think of an assistant, you might think of someone who answers the phone, manages your schedule, and gets you coffee. But that's not what I mean. You can and should train your assistant to take as many of your responsibilities off your plate as possible. While it will take some time to train your assistant when they first start, the SOPs you created should help them get up to speed quickly, allowing you to focus on managing the business.

My executive assistant, Emily, manages all my emails, aggregated from my four email accounts. Her job includes writing back to as many people as she can so I don't have to, forwarding outside requests to the correct team member, and only putting emails in my "Grant" folder that I need to see or respond to. The "Grant" folder is the only folder I check. If it's not in there, then it's not essential. Combined with the more than 50 filters I use to limit the emails that reach my inbox, I can triage over 500 emails daily, resulting in fewer than 20 that typically need my direct attention or response. In addition to managing my email, Emily manages countless other tasks for me as well, freeing up much of my time. When new projects come up, I create a new SOP and email it to her, answering most of her questions over email.

In the beginning, Emily and I worked together to clarify which emails I cared about and to answer any questions she had about my SOPs; these days, we rarely talk more than once a month. Having Emily around not only saves me loads of time but also gives me peace of mind to know that the business will keep running if I'm traveling, busy with some other priority, or unable to work for some reason. Oh, and did I mention that she does all this part-time as a contractor for about ten hours a week? She lives in the United States and is semi-retired from a marketing career.

I run a multimillion-dollar business with the help of a part-time contractor who manages almost all my core day-to-day responsibilities. But you don't need to make much money to hire someone to take specific tasks off your plate. While many people hire virtual assistants who live in countries where they are more affordable, I've always hired U.S.-based assistants with a lot of experience so I can turn more work over to them sooner and trust them to handle more complicated or delicate tasks. Your strategy will depend on your needs and budget level. Once you have detailed SOPs for all the tasks your assistant manages (and that your assistant can update as systems change or as they take on more responsibilities), it should be relatively easy to change assistants in the future if you need to.

#2. Bookkeeper

You can't manage and grow a business if you have inaccurate numbers or don't know your numbers. Thankfully, you can hire bookkeepers pretty inexpensively. Current market rates are $200 to $1,500 a month, depending on the complexity of your business. If you have a few services or products you're selling, you should get excellent bookkeeping support for less than $500 per month.

If you have the revenue to hire a bookkeeper, it's well worth doing so. Look for a bookkeeper specializing in your industry with at least five to ten years of experience. Typically, the more experience they have, the more expensive they are. The best way to find a good bookkeeper is through industry communities or groups—join a Facebook community for entrepreneurs in your industry and ask for bookkeeper recommendations who are QuickBooks-certified. Another way to find one is to visit the Find an Accountant page on QuickBooks and search through their database of QuickBooks Certified ProAdvisors, where you can filter by location, business type, and industry.

I usually always hire a bookkeeper when I start a new business, though with my recent company, I hired an accounting firm that does our bookkeeping for us. While more expensive, combining the two services saves us money in the long run because the professionals we hire can uncover savings and tax optimization strategies more immediately than someone without full access to our books and tax records.

#3. Accountant

While I'm a big fan of doing my taxes, I still work with an accountant to do our business taxes and help us make decisions throughout the year to minimize our tax bills. While I think it's beneficial for all business owners to learn how to optimize their taxes independently, the reality is that more than 150,000 words are added to the tax code every year, which means it can get complicated quickly.

Working with an accountant who specializes in your industry can be particularly beneficial as many tax-savings opportunities are industry-specific. Our accountant primarily works with online businesses, so she is proactive about bringing us ideas that can save us money. While we pay a monthly retainer fee for our accountants, you can easily find a good accountant to pay per hour.

#4. Lawyer

Find a lawyer who specializes in your industry and understands its specific risks. We work with a lawyer who specializes in business law and mergers and acquisitions in the online space. His expertise has helped us generate millions more dollars in revenue. This has easily amounted to a 40 to 50 times return on the money we've paid him. Given his industry experience, he also acts as our business adviser. Whenever I think about acquiring a new website, he's always the first person I call. Talking through the opportunity with him helps inform my decisions because he knows the market, our team, and our business well.

A good lawyer is valuable, but they can get expensive quickly if you don't define a scope of work and a budget and pay close attention to how they bill. Most lawyers bill per hour, and small time blocks can add up quickly. Unfortunately, it's common for them to bill for more time than they spent on your work. Our lawyer routinely bills us for ten-minute blocks of time and has never overcharged us. As your business grows, I encourage you to consider working with a law firm instead of a solo practitioner. While we have one primary lawyer as our main point of contact, he works at a larger firm and has, therefore, been able to consult his colleagues with deeper expertise on specific issues when needed. For example, his tax and trademark attorney colleagues have helped us multiple times.

While there are many other contractors that you might want to hire for specific tasks (like writing, design, editing, social media management, etc.), I can't stress enough how important it is to keep your expenses low until you have enough revenue to cover their fees easily. Far too many entrepreneurs invest too heavily in outside help too early, hurting their businesses. From the beginning of my entrepreneurial journey—and even today—I have tried to rely on technology as much as possible. This saves us money and the headache of having to manage more people. We use technology to manage our payroll, health insurance, 401(k), human resource support, podcast editing, email funnels, and more. AI is making this even more accessible and affordable. As I write this, several new and promising bookkeeping and accounting AI tools are coming to market.

A SYSTEM FOR SANITY: PLANNING IN 1-MONTH, 2-MONTH, AND 4-MONTH WINDOWS

A significant difference between successful and unsuccessful entrepreneurs is that successful ones engage in strategic planning and continually work to improve their businesses. This doesn't have to take much time, nor does it have to be perfect to be effective. The key is to fall into a consistent rhythm that works for you and helps you make more immediate progress in your business. As with almost everything in business, this gets easier over time.

Research in behavioral economics, psychology, and decision-making suggests that humans are less accurate in predicting distant or long-term events than short-term or near-future events. This phenomenon is often called the prediction paradox or the forecasting fallacy. We give more weight to immediate outcomes and are less accurate at predicting events that are further in the future.

I encourage you to manage your business in one-month, two-month, and four-month windows instead of planning years ahead. While it's worthwhile to plan for the upcoming year, I find focusing on smaller time frames and sprints is much more effective. Remember, the goal is to make at least two to three good decisions for your business every day. If you do that consistently five days a week, that is 40 to 60 decisions every month, 80 to 120 decisions every two months, and 160 to 240 decisions every four months. You can accomplish a lot quickly, especially with limited time.

Below are some guidelines for strategic planning in the short term, though you should customize these to work for you. I keep track of my plans in a simple Google Sheet and then review it every thirty days, but you can also use a project management platform like Asana to keep track. The goal is to consistently evaluate what you want to accomplish in the next one month, two months, or four months and then review these plans each month to determine how your efforts paid off.

1-Month Plan

1. **Review and Analyze:** Review the previous month's performance. Analyze key sales and engagement metrics, financial statements, and customer feedback. Review your P&L, balance sheet, cash-flow statement, and cash-flow projections for the previous month.

2. **Short-Term Goals:** Set specific, achievable goals for the next thirty days. How much content will you create? Which new promotion do you want to run and how many sales do you want it to generate? These goals should align with your overall business strategy and address immediate challenges.

3. **Prioritize Tasks:** Identify critical tasks and projects that need attention in the short term. Prioritize based on urgency and impact on your goals. Break out your goals into sprints whenever possible for larger projects.

4. **Improve Daily Operations:** This could involve refining processes or SOPs, improving efficiency, adjusting workflows, or addressing immediate issues. The goal here is to keep making your business more efficient and sustainable.

5. **Align Your Team:** Communicate the short-term goals to your partners, assistants, contractors, and other team members to ensure everyone is aligned on the priorities for

the next thirty days. A simple email outlining these goals should suffice.

6. **Build in Public:** Share your monthly update with your community. Indicate how they can help you and ask how you can help them.

2-Month Plan

1. **Evaluate Thirty-Day Goals:** Assess the success of the goals set for the previous month. Identify what worked well and areas that need improvement.

2. **Identify Medium-Term Goals:** Set new goals for the next thirty to sixty days. These goals should build on the achievements of the previous month and address more intermediate challenges like increasing sales, improving customer service, improving your website, or anything that needs to get done over the next sixty days.

3. **Engage Your Community:** Double down on community engagement by doing something that delights them. Offer a giveaway, host a live Q&A, organize an in-person meetup, collaborate with another brand, or share something inspiring. The point of this exercise is to ensure you're consistently adding value to your community.

4. **Engage Your Customers:** Gather feedback, address concerns, and implement product improvements based on customer input.

5. **Strategize Business Development:** Identify five to ten potential new partners, advertisers, or others in your industry and reach out to them. This helps expand your network and opens up unforeseen opportunities.

6. **Review Your Finances:** Conduct a thorough financial analysis, including a review of cash flow, profit margins, and overall financial health. Adjust your cash-flow projections.

4-Month Plan

1. **Conduct a Quarterly Review:** Conduct a comprehensive review of the past ninety days at the end of every month. Evaluate achievements, challenges, and overall progress.

2. **Set Next-Quarter Goals:** Set long-term goals for the next quarter. These goals should align with your annual business plan and contribute to the overall success of your business.

3. **Engage in Strategic Planning:** Evaluate market trends, the competitive landscape, and industry changes. Adjust your business strategy accordingly.

4. **Evaluate Your Systems and Technology:** Once a quarter, I do a deep dive into how well our systems are working and look for ways to improve them. I also try to identify what repeatable tasks we're doing that could benefit from a new process.

5. **Brainstorm Marketing and Sales Strategies:** Consider which marketing and sales initiatives you could perform to boost revenue quickly. Doing this monthly could lead to customer fatigue. Consider promotions, discounts, or targeted campaigns.

6. **Explore Opportunities for Market Expansion:** Consider new products, services, or target markets to increase and diversify your revenue.

7. **Explore Strategic Partnerships:** Reach out to whom you can collaborate with and who can contribute to your business's growth and sustainability in the long term.

8. **Develop Risk-Management Strategies:** Identify challenges that could arise in the next quarter and create contingency plans.

9. **Forecast your Financials:** Review your P&L, balance sheet, and cash-flow statement, and create cash-flow projections for the next quarter.

I was naturally prone to burnout when I was younger, but I don't suffer from it anymore because I have reliable systems and work with great people. I also have enough money saved and invested so that I don't have to rely on my business for income.

I don't feel any pressure or stress in my business anymore. Yes, I want my businesses to be successful, profitable, and to grow, and I want my business partners to be happy, but it doesn't keep me up at night. Even when facing a big problem, I find I can let go of it without impacting my day-to-day life. I trust myself and my intuition to solve the problem or find the answer. I don't get hung up on big decisions. I use data and intuition to make a decision quickly. Then I make decisions, plan, and execute to keep the momentum going. Running a business is a constant process of refinement and adaptation. Keep moving and evolving. Then decide how you want to grow—a topic we'll dive into next.

LEVEL 3
THE GROWTH ENTREPRENEUR

Growth becomes inevitable at a certain point in a business's life cycle. If you've built something that brings people value, people will talk about it. And if you've set up efficient systems, people will find you even if you stop doing any active promotion. If you want to stay small, you will have to actively fight against this growth. You'll have to turn clients away or pass up new opportunities, so you'll have to develop additional systems and frameworks to help you decide where to focus your energy and time.

Limiting growth also increases your risk because opportunities that exist today will inevitably not be available in the future. It may be that you will one day need to grow just to sustain your business, but you might not have that opportunity when you need it. Salary expectations also increase over time, so without growth you might not be able to keep with the incentives your team wants. Most businesses have to grow to survive.

Growth minimizes risk. When you have income from many sources, it's easier to recover if you lose clients or the market shifts in a way that no longer favors a particular product. You also have more resources—time, money, and people—at your disposal to help you spot opportunities and potential roadblocks and stay up-to-date with market trends. This becomes especially necessary as you get older and adapting to new technologies and staying relevant to your market becomes more difficult.

At some point, you will need to exit your company, either by choice or by force. You could just shut it down when this time comes, but then you lose all the value you've created and leave clients without a product or service on which they've come to rely. Selling your company on your terms and timeline is much better, but doing so requires some forethought. Staying small will make that more difficult. Potential buyers want proof that the asset they're buying will appreciate over time. If you don't already have a growth strategy and mechanism for managing it, your business will be less attractive, even if it's otherwise well run and sustainable. Your risk exposure also affects how potential buyers will assess the value of your business.

By staying small, you limit the number of customers you can serve and the community you can build. You limit the opportunities and experiences you can have and the number of people you can work with. You limit the number of people you can help financially—through employment, affiliations, or joint ventures. If you are running a mission-driven business, you limit the reach and impact you can have.

Or consider Anita Roddick, who founded the Body Shop with a mission to create a beauty brand that promoted ethical consumerism, social impact, human rights, and environmental sustainability. She did not set out to become a billionaire or create a globally recognized brand. But as she grew, she began to understand the impact she could have by choosing to grow. If she had opted to stay small, the business world would not have her example to follow and the consumer would have been forced—at least for a while—to continue to buy less-ethical or lower-quality products.

You don't have to know how you're going to grow to choose the path of the Growth Entrepreneur. This stage is about building an engine to accelerate growth while gathering the necessary information to decide where to direct that energy. Moving to this stage is like climbing a ladder: the higher you go, the farther you can see. It wasn't until I reached this stage that I realized I had been thinking too small when I started. The more I grew, the more I learned and the more opportunities opened up. Today I am having a much greater impact than I could have imagined at the time.

As passionate as I am about the power that growth can have, I don't advocate growth for its own sake. Conventional wisdom holds that anything that helps you grow is worth doing. Growth is natural, but it is not neutral. Some strategies will lead you closer toward building the life you want, and others will take you further away. Unmitigated, careless growth has led to some of the worst economic and social disasters in recent history: Enron, the dot-com bust, the 2008 housing crash and recession. Responsible, sustainable growth requires limits. The next few chapters will explore how to test and set them.

CHAPTER 10

DOUBLE DOWN ON WHAT WORKS TO ACCELERATE GROWTH

"You will either step forward into growth or you will step back into safety."
—Abraham Maslow

I've been working in marketing for over fifteen years, and I've managed hundreds of millions of dollars in marketing spending. I've tried every growth hack out there and I'm not a fan of most of them because they don't build sustainability into your business. While I'm all for growing as quickly as you want to, most growth hacks are short-term tricks that may generate a quick boost in sales or email subscribers but rarely work long-term and can easily distract you from more strategic planning.

While he didn't invent it, Jim Collins popularized the "flywheel effect" idea in his book *Good to Great*. Using this principle, he explored how consistent, well-aligned actions, when repeated, can lead to significant business growth and success. Once the flywheel starts turning, you need to apply consistent effort to keep it moving. Over time, the cumulative impact of these consistent efforts starts to compound.

As the flywheel continues to turn, it gains momentum and becomes increasingly efficient. At a certain point, the flywheel becomes self-sustaining and generates its own momentum. It requires less effort to maintain the same growth rate as it did during the initial push. As the flywheel spins faster and faster, the business can achieve accelerated growth and success. The energy generated from earlier efforts contributes to this increased momentum.

Growth can be expensive, so to get the most leverage and highest ROI (return on investment) for your money and time, you should create a flywheel effect where every dollar you're investing in your business increases sales, which then increases repeat customers, which then increases referrals, which leads to more links back to your website, more organic website traffic, more newsletter subscribers—and the flywheel continues to grow your business. The whole is greater than its parts. For instance, a single positive customer experience often leads to improved retention and referrals.

The flywheel accelerates through consistent improvement of these four growth levers:

Lever 1—Acquisition
You can improve how a customer finds and starts engaging with you by expanding your organic content and paid advertising, building a simple acquisition funnel that explains who you are with a compelling call to action, and having a well-designed website and brand. Be up front, authentic, and transparent. Lead with your story, as well as the stories of others who are in your community.

Lever 2—Experience
Every touch point your customers have with your brand should be consistent and enjoyable—from the welcome email they receive after subscribing to your site, to the customer service they receive when they have a problem with their order. It's so difficult to build trust and so easy to lose it. Especially with an online business, there are so many touch points you might not be able to see or control. You can improve this lever by adding more personalization to the process, improving your customer service, and genuinely trying to make your customers happy and their lives easier.

Lever 3—Retention
Happy customers stick around if they like your products and the content you share. Engage with your customers regularly,

but don't force it. Be human. You can improve this lever by sharing great stories, content, exclusive offers, and products you know your audience will like. Invest in new content you think is awesome. Keep adding value to their lives, and your customers will stick around and tell their friends.

Lever 4—Referrals

How many customers refer you to their friends, family, co-workers, and the broader world? You can improve this lever by making it easy to recommend your products and incentivize recommendations. You can do this without being pushy—just be open about how referrals really help and lean back into your story. Many customers would love to share your products with others, but they might not know they should. You can also create an affiliate program and build partnerships where you pay a flat fee or commission on every sale that comes through a referral. Affiliate programs can be extremely powerful growth drivers because it's a win-win for you and your partners: you get a new customer and they make money from sending them to you.

You want to increase revenue with as much precision as possible. It's easy to waste money. At this stage, you will have consistent cash flow. Use some of that extra revenue to accelerate your growth by hiring writers to create more organic content, explore strategic partnerships, and expand your product or service offerings.

You can also start exploring paid marketing by running digital ad campaigns, but don't ever rely on ads alone. Many entrepreneurs fail because they focus exclusively on paid channels to generate short-term sales, and then when they get more expensive (which they always do) and audience preferences shift (which they always do), they no longer have a business.

This is why you need to invest in multiple channels to create the flywheel effect. While this isn't easy, it's more than doable if you pay attention to the numbers, keep testing, and don't waste money.

THE PROS AND CONS OF DIGITAL ADVERTISING

Before the internet, almost all marketing was awareness marketing. This is when you spend money to make someone aware of your company, brand, products, or services. Billboards on the highway, television ads, banner ads on websites, brand sponsorships of events or projects—those are all examples of awareness (aka "brand") marketing. The ROI on awareness marketing is typically difficult to track since it's hard to know how a particular ad or brand placement brought a customer to you.

Thankfully, now we can spend money much more efficiently through targeted marketing, also referred to as direct marketing. This type of marketing often has a desired customer conversion event attached to it, such as generating an email sign-up or selling a particular product. With targeted marketing, you can track which marketing campaigns generated sales, even in some cases down to the exact keyword the customer searched on Google, the ad they clicked on, and the headline of the ad that generated the sales. Depending on the marketing platform you use, you can target people based on a number of different factors, like geography, age, interests, and where someone is in the sales cycle for a particular product. For example, on Facebook and Google, you can target your ads to people who have indicated they are in the market to buy a specific product based on their recent search history and activity on the platform.

Of course, the more targeted your ads get, the more expensive they tend to be. Paid marketing costs have skyrocketed as Google, Facebook, Amazon, TikTok, Pinterest, X, Instagram, and other digital platform ads have become more competitive. Advertising is the primary way these companies make money and they have significantly increased the cost of running ads while simultaneously reducing the number of targeting options. This is partly due to privacy restrictions, but increased competition for ad space also makes these companies more money.

The more opaque the advertising companies make the targeting options, the harder it is for you to control the parameters and the more expensive it's getting. When Facebook ads first launched, you could buy highly targeted clicks for as little as ten cents. But the trend on all marketing platforms is always the same. Over time they get more competitive and expensive, making it increasingly difficult for a single brand to generate a positive ROI. Staying at the forefront of paid digital marketing is exceptionally difficult and requires a lot of testing.

All of this might suggest that running paid digital-advertising campaigns is a waste of time and money. I'm only sharing this information so you are aware of some of the challenges before you start experimenting with paid ads. Don't let the challenge dissuade you from running paid ads when you have the budget to do so, because when done well, they can be profitable and help accelerate your flywheel. I still know many online content creators running Facebook ads to build their email lists, which they then monetize by selling their courses and recommending products. Digital marketing is evolving rapidly, so it's difficult to predict what will be possible when you read this.

HOW TO GET STARTED WITH DIGITAL ADS

When you first start experimenting with digital ads, you likely won't have the budget to try all the platforms you want to, and that's okay. It makes sense to start small so you can learn what works—and what doesn't—before laying out a bunch of cash that might not yield a great return.

One quick recommendation: always set up and test your first campaigns yourself. It is easy to learn how to run a basic digital ad campaign. While there are many contractors and agencies who are more than willing to help you set up and run your ad campaigns for a fee, I'd be extremely skeptical about whether the cost will be worth it. I owned an agency that ran digital ad campaigns for many businesses, and while we were great at what we did, a vast majority of the other agencies I encountered did a very poor job and weren't worth the money. No one will care as much about your business as you, and hiring someone else to run your ads is an easy way to waste a lot of money.

I recommend you start with one platform at a time and test your first campaigns for at least a week or two to get enough data to determine if they are worth continuing and how to optimize them. Regular monitoring and optimization are essential for campaign success. Digital advertising is dynamic; be prepared to adjust your strategy as needed. As you gain experience, you can fine-tune your approach to achieve better results.

While there are many ways to start running digital ad campaigns, I've outlined a practical, high-level system that should help you figure out the best approach and help you set up your first few campaigns.

1. **Define Your Goals:** Start by clearly defining the goals of your campaign. In most cases, I'd recommend running campaigns with a goal to sell products. You can also test campaigns that generate email subscribers once you know how valuable an email subscriber is to you (aka how much money you make on average per subscriber). I've never found brand-awareness campaigns or buying ads to increase website traffic or social followers worth the investment.

2. **Choose Your Platform:** Select the most suitable advertising platform based on where your core customers are and how much the ads cost per click. Common options include Google, Amazon, and social media. I always start with Google Ads because the traffic is so high-intent, and you pay only when someone clicks your ad. But if most of your customers find you through another platform, you might be better off running ads there. Also consider where your most successful competitors run their ads; if it's working for them, it could work for you, too.

3. **Determine Your Budget:** I recommend spending $750 to $1,500 over the course of a week or two to give yourself enough time to ensure everything is set up and sales are tracking correctly. Start with a manageable budget until

you gain more experience and have enough performance data to ensure it's worth increasing the amount you spend.

4. **Research Your Target Audience:** Update the personas you designed in chapter 5 to include relevant demographics, interests, and behaviors based on data you've gathered from your audience, community, and customers. This data will help you target your ads more effectively across all platforms.

5. **Structure Your Campaign:** Begin with a few campaigns targeting the same audience so that you can minimize the variables among different campaigns to see what works when you're testing different variables.

6. **Write and Design Your Ad:** Craft compelling ad copy that is concise, relevant, and tailored to your target audience. You can write this yourself or use the help of AI writing tools—writing compelling ad copy is something they are particularly good at. Design visually appealing ad images or videos that align with your brand and message. Use the platform's ad guidelines for reference.

7. **A/B Test:** Create five to seven ad variations for each campaign. Test different headlines, copy, images, and calls to action. A/B testing helps you identify what resonates best with your audience and leads to the most conversions. Most platforms allow you to add different headline and copy options and upload several additional images. After running several variations, the ad platforms will identify which combinations performed best and will default to those going forward.

8. **Monitor and Optimize:** Let your campaigns run for a week or two while monitoring their performance. Assess critical data points such as the following:

- **Impressions:** The number of times your ad is displayed
- **Click-Through Rate (CTR):** The percentage of users who click on your ad after seeing it
- **Conversion Rate:** The percentage of ad clicks that result in a desired action (e.g., purchase, sign-up, download)
- **Cost per Click (CPC):** The average cost you pay per click on your ad
- **Return on Ad Spend (ROAS):** The revenue earned from an advertising campaign compared to how much you spent to run the ads. A ROAS of anything over 100 percent means you are making money, but you should be targeting at least 130 to 140 percent, which means for every $100 you spend on ads, you're making $130 to $140 in sales. A ROAS of 200+ percent is exceptional, but generating even higher returns is not uncommon.

9. **Adjust:** Based on your data analysis, make adjustments to underperforming elements. This could involve pausing or modifying ads, changing targeting options, or adjusting your budget. Many of the platforms will make recommendations for how you can improve your performance. While these can be very helpful, remember that some might be designed simply to get you to spend more money.

10. **Scale and Expand:** Once you have successful campaigns generating your target ROAS and profit, consider scaling them up by increasing your budget. While it's up to you to decide how much to spend, it makes logical sense to spend as much money as possible on any campaign that hits your target ROAS and profit since you know that the more money you put in, the more money you'll make. Still, always keep a close eye on your ad spend because campaign profits can change quickly. Once you've found a profitable platform and created a profitable campaign, keep it running at the highest budget level you can afford for as long

as it remains profitable. Meanwhile, you can explore additional audience segments on the same platform in a new campaign (that doesn't touch your profitable one), because you can often unlock even more scale adding new campaigns in a profitable platform.

11. **Continue to Learn and Test:** Digital advertising changes quickly and can be difficult to stay on top of. But stay updated on industry trends, best practices, and platform updates. Continuously learn and refine your strategies. As you scale the campaigns yourself, you can teach your assistant or hire someone with experience to run campaigns that are already running well.

OPTIMIZE YOUR MARKETING SPEND TO MAXIMIZE PROFITABILITY

While your ROAS tells you if a specific campaign is profitable, it analyzes results for only one platform at a time. To ensure you're generating as much profit as possible from your marketing spend, you need to get a broader view across all your organic and paid marketing efforts by paying attention to your customer acquisition costs (CAC) and your customer lifetime value (CLV).

CLV represents the total revenue a customer is expected to generate for a company over their entire relationship with the business. The more money you can earn on a single customer over time, the more you can afford to spend to acquire them.

CAC measures how much it costs to acquire that customer. To determine the long-term profitability of a customer, you compare CLV to CAC. If CLV is significantly higher than CAC, it indicates a profitable customer relationship. Minimizing CAC and maximizing CLV is the key to unlocking more profit.

CLV — CAC = Long-Term Profit from Customer

CUSTOMER ACQUISITION COST

As you ramp up spending, advertising will quickly become one of your biggest expenses. CAC is a critical component when calculating the return on investment for marketing efforts.

Understanding CAC is crucial because it helps determine whether your customer acquisition efforts are financially sustainable. If your CAC is too high, it can negatively impact your profitability. CAC allows you to evaluate the effectiveness of different marketing channels, campaigns, and strategies. It helps you identify which channels yield the best return on investment (ROI) so you can decide how much of your budget to allocate to marketing and sales efforts.

Your CAC is easy to calculate:

Marketing Costs / Number of Customers = Customer Acquisition Cost

You can run this calculation for your aggregate marketing costs across both organic and paid channels, but it's even more helpful to break those costs out by channel to see if some campaigns or platforms are more effective than others at generating new customers.

For example, let's say you spend $5,000 on Instagram ads and receive 100 new customers as a result. At the same time, you spend the same amount on Google Ads and receive 150 customers through those ads. Your CAC for each channel would be:

Instagram: $5,000 / 100 = $50 CAC

Google: $5,000 / 150 = $33.33 CAC

At least as far as your current campaigns are concerned, Google is the more effective platform. If all other things are equal (e.g., you're running the same or similar ads on each platform; the customers from each platform spend, on average, the same amount, etc.), you might decide to invest more money in Google and less in Instagram. But if you're still making over $5,000 in revenue from the Instagram campaign, you might decide to keep it in play. It all depends on your goals and your budget.

To assess the return on marketing investment (ROMI), you compare the revenue generated from those campaigns to the total CAC associated with those campaigns. ROMI is used to measure the effectiveness and profitability of a marketing campaign. Here's how you calculate it:

(Revenue from Marketing Campaign — Total CAC) /Total CAC = ROMI

Let's continue the example from above and say that you earn $200 in revenue on each product you sell, and you sold 100 units on Instagram and 150 units on Google. This generated a combined $50,000 revenue.

Your total ad spend on Instagram was $5,000 and on Google was $5,000, for a total ad spend of $10,000. This is your total marketing spend because you spent it all to get new customers. Using the equation above, you can calculate your return on marketing investment:

($50,000 — $10,000) / $10,000 = 4x ROMI

You spent $10,000 on ads and generated $50,000 in revenue, so you have a four times return on your marketing investment. When you use the formula, you're calculating how much revenue you've earned from the marketing campaign compared to the total cost of acquiring customers through that campaign. If the result of the formula is greater than 1, it means that your marketing campaign is generating more revenue than it cost to acquire customers, indicating a positive return on investment. If it's less than 1, your campaign gives you a negative return and you lose money.

Most entrepreneurs starting with paid marketing fall into one of two groups: they spend too much or too little on marketing. When I started buying ads at my marketing agency, I was very conservative about how much money I spent because I didn't have a system to know what worked.

When you have the data and understand your total CAC, your CAC per channel, and the ROMI, you know exactly how much of your hard-earned money is worth spending and where. Soon, you start to think of marketing as less an expense and more an investment—an intelligent step toward growing your business and strengthening it for the long term.

Here's how to make decisions using CAC data:

1. **Analyze by Channel:** Segment your CAC data by marketing channels, such as organic, paid search, social media, email marketing, and so on. This allows you to assess the performance of each channel individually.

2. **Compare Organic and Paid Channels:** To measure CAC across organic and paid marketing channels, you can calculate CAC separately for each. For organic channels, consider content creation, SEO efforts, and social media management expenses. For paid channels, consider advertising costs.

3. **Optimize Campaigns:** Optimize your marketing campaigns and strategies based on CAC data, especially when implementing changes. Be prepared to make adjustments to your strategy as needed. Experiment with different ad copy, targeting, and messaging to improve efficiency.

4. **Analyze Historical Trends:** Look at historical CAC data to identify trends. Has your CAC been increasing or decreasing over time? Are there seasonal fluctuations or specific events that affected CAC?

5. **Set CAC Benchmarks:** Establish CAC benchmarks that align with your business goals and industry standards. These benchmarks will serve as a reference point for evaluating your CAC. While CAC benchmarks can vary widely, depending on the industry and type of business, I've in-

cluded some rough guidelines in a text box later in this chapter.

CUSTOMER LIFETIME VALUE

Many entrepreneurs focus only on trying to get the next customer in the door. However, experienced entrepreneurs know that the real money is in retaining customers for as long as possible and maximizing the revenue you earn per customer over time. Retaining customers and increasing the customer lifetime value (CLV) will help improve your overall profitability. When customers are happy with your product or service, they'll continue to subscribe or will be more likely to return and buy from you again.

Retaining existing customers is also significantly cheaper (five to twenty-five times more so) than acquiring a new customer, and increasing customer retention by as little as 5 percent can lead to 25 to 95 percent more profit. The more money you make from a customer over time, the more you can spend on marketing to acquire that customer, which can be valuable in helping you scale and maximize profit across increasingly competitive digital marketing channels.

CLV measures how much revenue or profit you make, on average, from one customer for the entire time they're a customer. CLV can be calculated as revenue-based or profit-based (subtracting cost of goods, customer acquisition cost [CAC], and any other expenses related to the production of your product or service).

There are different formulas to calculate revenue-based CLV, but one commonly used formula is:

CLV = Average Purchase Value x Average Purchase Frequency x Average Customer Lifespan

Here's what each of these components means:

Average Purchase Value (APV): This is the average amount of money a customer spends on each transaction with your business.

Average Purchase Frequency (APF): The average number of transactions a customer makes within a specific time frame (e.g., per year).

Average Customer Lifespan (ACL): This represents the average duration a customer remains engaged with your business. This is the amount of time between their first purchase and most recent purchase.

Here's an example of how to calculate CLV using that formula:

Let's say you run an e-commerce business. On average, a customer spends $50 per purchase, they make four purchases per year, and they remain engaged with your company for five years.

$$\text{CLV} = \$50 \text{ (APV)} \times 4 \text{ (APF)} \times 5 \text{ (ACL)} = \$1,000$$

In this example, the estimated customer lifetime value is $1,000. This means that, on average, each customer is expected to generate $1,000 in revenue for your business throughout their engagement with your company.

It's important to note that this is a simplified example. CLV calculations can become more complex when you consider factors like customer churn and discount rates. However, this basic formula provides a good starting point for understanding the value of your customer relationships. You can refine your CLV calculations further, based on your specific business model and data.

Once you have your CAC per channel and profit-based CLV, you can determine the return on investment (ROI) for each of your marketing campaigns and platforms by comparing the CAC to the CLV. A CAC that is significantly lower than your CLV is a positive indicator of profitability.

Growing a Recurring Revenue Business

If you're running a recurring revenue or subscription business, you should track your average revenue per user (ARPU), churn rate, and net dollar retention (NDR).

Average Revenue per User

Average revenue per user (ARPU) calculates the average revenue generated by each user or customer over a specific period, usually a month or a year. By dividing the total revenue by the total number of customers, businesses can determine the average revenue they receive from each client within a given time frame. ARPU for subscriptions is the same as APV for transaction-based businesses, like e-commerce stores. The simple formula for ARPU is:

Total Revenue / Total Number of Users or Customers = ARPU

Churn Rate

Your churn rate is the rate that your customers are canceling or not buying again over a defined period. While you can look at churn rate week over week or month over month, it's more helpful to look at it over a more extended period, like twelve months. To calculate your churn rate, use the following formula:

**Total Number of Customers at Beginning of Period —
Total Number of Customers at the end of Period**

For example, if you had 100 customers twelve months ago and you have 50 customers today, then your churn rate would be:

(100 – 50) / 100 = .5 = 50%

Many companies look at their churn rate year over year, or the previous twelve months compared to the twelve months before, to see how they retain customers. The higher your churn rate, the worse you are at retaining customers; the lower your churn rate, the better you are. A negative churn rate means you have gained customers within the period in question. Of course, this is relevant only to businesses whose customers would be repeat buyers. There are many businesses whose customer might buy once every fifteen years (a patio umbrella, for example) or hire you only once (a front-door restoration company), where churn rate and customer retention don't matter. But even if you don't have repeat customers, you still need a steady or growing number of customers to have a sustainable business.

If your churn rate is high or CLV is low, it's often an indication of a poor product/market fit, lousy service, or poor customer service. The data is just the starting point here, and if you don't already know why customers are leaving you, you need to look deeper into your business to find out.

A simple way to do this is to ask your customers directly why they are canceling, through an exit survey or phone call or by reaching out to customers who previously bought from you and offering them an incentive (like a $20 Amazon gift card) to offer their feedback on your product or service.

Whatever you do, don't become one of those companies that makes it extremely difficult for customers to cancel. A few years ago, I wanted to cancel my membership to Planet Fitness, and the company told me I had to send a certified letter to the location where I had initially signed up. Unfortunately, this location had closed, and when I called the corporate phone number, no one could help me. The only way I could cancel it was to have my lawyer send a letter to their corporate office and the closest location to where I had signed up. It still took four months. This was all to cancel a $19.99 a month membership.

Planet Fitness gets additional revenue by making it difficult to cancel, but this sure soured my relationship with the brand. You don't need to do this to make money and have a successful business. In an age when it's difficult to get help on the phone, and brands make it so challenging to cancel, you can stand out by offering excellent customer service and simply making every transaction—including cancellation—a good experience for anyone engaging with your brand.

Net Dollar Retention

Net dollar retention (NDR), also known as dollar-based net retention or net expansion rate, measures the health of your subscription business. NDR assesses the revenue growth from existing customers over a specific period, taking into account expansions, contractions, and churn. It reflects the percentage of subscription revenue retained from existing customers, including revenue from upsells and price increases, even if no new customers are acquired. NDR can also be boosted by raising prices for existing customers without needing to attract new ones.

The simple formula is:

NDR = (current period annual recurring revenue) / (previous period recurring revenue)

The current period is defined as the past twelve months of total recurring revenue, while the previous period is the twelve months preceding the current period.

If your NDR is 100 percent, you've retained all the revenue lost when customers canceled but have not gained any new revenue. If it's less than 100 percent, you're losing customers and revenue faster than you are picking up new customers and revenue.

Anything below 100 percent means your business is in trouble. If it's over 100 percent, you're acquiring more new net revenue than you are losing. The higher the percentage, the stronger the subscription business. Some of the most profitable examples are Software as a Service (SaaS) businesses, which, of course, are digital software. Slack, the project management software, had an NDR of 143 percent when it went public in 2019, and Asana, the project management tool, had an NDR of 120 percent when it went public in 2020. The average for a public SaaS company is about 115 percent.

Improving net dollar retention for subscription products involves strategies focused on retaining existing customers, increasing their spending, and reducing churn. Here are several strategies to enhance net dollar retention:

1. **Customer Success and Support:** Invest in exceptional customer support and success programs to ensure customers are satisfied and receive value from your subscription. Proactive engagement can prevent cancellations and encourage upselling.

2. **Communication and Education:** Continuously communicate the value proposition of your subscription product. Provide educational content, tutorials, and resources that showcase additional features to increase usage and customer satisfaction.

3. **Personalization:** Segment your customer base and personalize interactions based on their behaviors, preferences, and usage patterns. Tailor offerings and messages to specific segments to address their unique needs and encourage upsells.

4. **Tiered Pricing and Upselling:** Offer tiered pricing plans that encourage customers to upgrade as their needs grow. Implement upselling strategies to introduce higher-tier features or additional services to existing customers.

5. **Renewal Incentives and Discounts:** Provide incentives for customers to renew their subscriptions, such as loyalty discounts, extended trial periods, or bonuses for long-term commitments.

6. **Engagement and Retention Campaigns:** Run targeted email campaigns, in-app messages, or other retention-focused marketing efforts. These can include personalized offers, usage tips, and reminders.

7. **Customer Feedback and Iterative Improvement:** Gather feedback from customers who churn and those who stay. Use this data to iterate and improve your product, addressing pain points and enhancing features to align with customer needs. Regularly update and improve your product based on customer feedback and market trends.

8. **Net Promoter Score (NPS)** is a tool that many companies use to see how satisfied and loyal their customers are. It helps them determine if customers would tell their friends about the company. To get this score, they ask customers one simple question: "On a scale from 0 to 10, how likely are you to tell a friend about us?" A high NPS means customers really like the company and might tell their friends. A low score may indicate problems with customer satisfaction that need to be addressed.

9. **Reactivation Campaigns:** Implement reactivation campaigns targeting inactive or canceled customers. Offer incentives or showcase new features to encourage them to return.

10. **Community Building:** Foster a sense of community among your subscriber base. Encourage user-generated content, testimonials, and referrals. Loyal customers often become advocates, aiding in retention and acquisition efforts.

11. **Data and Metrics:** Continuously monitor key metrics like monthly recurring revenue (MRR), churn rate, net dollar retention (NDR), and average revenue per user (ARPU) to identify trends and areas needing improvement. Two other important metrics to consider monitoring are expansion rate (additional revenue generated from existing customers by upselling or cross-selling additional products or services) and net promoter score (NPS).

HOW TO BUDGET FOR MARKETING

While investing in marketing for growth is important, it's not advisable to allocate 100 percent of your profits to the effort. You need to maintain a sustainable cash flow and reserve funds for other operational needs. However, I recommend spending as much as possible if you're hitting your revenue or engagement targets. Start-ups and early-stage companies tend to allocate more of their budgets to marketing, but doing so is an easy way to waste a lot of money if you don't measure and manage your spending to maximize sales and profit.

The old-school way of thinking about marketing was to allocate 10 to 15 percent of your revenue to marketing activities, and many companies still use this calculation. But this is not how I like to budget. Because modern tools make it easy to measure exactly what's driving sales, I use acquisition, sales, and customer data to drive my marketing decisions. Allocate your marketing budget to channels and strategies demonstrating the best CAC-to-CLV ratio.

A healthy CAC-to-CLV ratio is typically considered to be around 1:3 or better. When the CAC-to-CLV ratio is around 1:3 or higher, the customer's lifetime value is significantly greater than the cost of acquiring them. This suggests a profitable customer acquisition strategy. A higher ratio indicates a more efficient use of resources in acquiring and retaining customers.

However, ratios can vary widely across industries. Some industries with longer customer retention and higher average purchase values might have higher acceptable ratios, while others, such as subscription-based services, might aim for even higher ratios due to recurring revenue.

I will spend money on anything that generates a positive ROI and is profitable.

You should, too. Putting artificial limits on your marketing spend as a percentage of revenue will limit your growth. It's better to diversify your marketing strategies to reach a broader audience. Consider a mix of digital marketing, content marketing, social media, paid advertising, and other tactics. Experiment with various channels to identify what works best for your business. Your goal should be to continually experiment with new channels and then double down on the profitable ones. As I mentioned earlier, when you find a profitable campaign, you should spend as much money as possible on it until it no longer meets your profitability target. You should do this for every channel you have.

This is yet another reason why cash-flow management is so important because, for money that you spend today on marketing that generates a sale, you can set up payment terms so you don't have to pay that marketing spend for up to thirty days until after you've gotten paid by your customer. This means you can pay your marketing expenses after your customer has already paid, freeing up more cash immediately for you to reinvest in marketing or allocate to other areas of your business. First, you need to make sure that your marketing campaigns are tracking correctly and are profitable.

LEVERAGE PAID MARKETING TO BOOST ORGANIC MARKETING

There are many ways to leverage your paid traffic to help grow your organic traffic. In this way, you can generate even more impact from your ad spend. When you run Google Ads, you get access to the "search terms report," which shows you exactly what keywords a searcher used before they clicked on your ad and what keywords they searched before purchasing your product.

Since you can see exactly what searchers were looking for that led to a sale, these reports are a gold mine for finding new topics to create content about. Look specifically for topics you haven't yet written about that are directly related to your product. You should also pay attention to the click-through rates of your different ad headlines to see what phrases drive the most engagement. You can then use this information to update your page titles and copy on your website to increase your organic click-through rates.

It's also valuable to run paid campaigns on both Google and social media platforms to test different marketing campaign messages. With a limited budget, you can test several different ideas to see which generates the most engagement and sales, and then you can roll out the winner across your website, email campaigns, and platform.

At MMG Media Group, we recently leveraged paid marketing to grow the organic reach of our website Financial Residency, which we acquired in 2022. By the time we acquired it, the brand had already established historical relevance and a solid reputation, but by using a combination of paid and organic marketing, within three months, we were able to take it from $2,000 of monthly revenue to over $50,000. First, we assessed how the brand was showing up in searches. We noticed it showed up in only 7 percent of searches for one of its core offerings: physician mortgages. We knew we could improve this number and that making the brand more visible to these searchers would lead to conversions and more revenue.

We started with organic marketing and hired writers to improve the SEO of existing content and create new content that was helpful for users. This helped us, but we knew it would take a long time to see the results we were aiming for—which was to get Financial Residency to show up in 90 percent of Google searches for mortgages. We decided to run a Google Ads campaign, but because we had no data on how many conversions we would get from paid ads, we decided to start small and test.

Within a few weeks, Financial Residency was earning a 30 percent profit margin on our ad spend. More spending led to more visibility for our ads, which led to more search-term data that we then used to make further edits to our existing content and create new content. We also used the profit from our ads to pay for more writers so we could scale even faster.

BUILD AN AFFILIATE PROGRAM
(AND PAY ONLY WHEN YOU GROW)

Now that you know your numbers so well, the next step is to expand your marketing through affiliate partnerships. This is one of my favorite marketing strategies because you pay only for the results you want. As I explained in chapter 3, affiliate marketing is a performance-based strategy in which businesses reward individuals or other companies (affiliates) for driving traffic or sales to their products or services. It works on a commission basis, where affiliates earn a flat fee or a percentage of revenue from sales they drive to your business.

The best thing about affiliate marketing is that you pay affiliates only for actual results, making it a cost-effective marketing strategy. You should spend as much money as possible within your target profit margin to affiliates generating sales. You get to set your target CAC and pay affiliates that fee only when they make a sale.

Affiliate sales are tracked through links customized for each partner, so it's easy to see which partner generated a particular sale. Many online sales platforms now have affiliate-program tracking-link capabilities, so you can easily set up and run your partner program through your sales platform. The nice thing is that your links will already be connected to your existing sales platform and checkout cart, so the need for technology setup should be limited.

You should seriously consider launching an affiliate program and building relationships with people who have platforms that would be interested in your product. Affiliates often have their own established audiences or niche markets. Partnering with them allows you to tap into these markets you might not reach otherwise.

To effectively use affiliate marketing, you must establish clear terms, provide affiliates with necessary promotional materials, track performance accurately, and maintain good relationships with your affiliates. To maximize the benefits of this strategy, identify the right affiliates who align with your brand and target audience.

Join Someone Else's Affiliate Program and Get Paid for Referrals

In addition to setting up your affiliate program, you should look for other products and services that resonate with your platform. Once you've built a community, there are likely great products or services you use or like that could be valuable to your audience. This can be very lucrative.

The personal finance tracking app I used, Personal Capital, was the best on the market, so it was easy to recommend to my audience.

Whenever someone signed up using my link and tracked at least $100,000 in assets using the tracker, I would get paid $200. I was also a user of QuickBooks, so I recommended them and got $75 for every new user who signed up through my link. The website hosting company I used paid me $225 for each new customer I sent them. By the time I sold Millennial Money in October 2020, I had worked with over 200 companies as an affiliate.

MANAGE TRADITIONAL MEDIA

Even as viewership across traditional media like newspapers, news websites, and TV is declining, these outlets can help you reach a broader audience for your product or platform when you can get exposure. The problem is these platforms often aren't targeted and need substantial exposure to move the needle on your business. However, there are many SEO benefits to being featured by traditional media outlets, especially if the outlet can link to your site on its socials or web pages. Traditional media can also be helpful when building an email list since it can help you reach so many new people.

The best way to get mentioned in the traditional media is to have a story or a product worth sharing. However, you can make it easier for journalists to find you by pitching them good and interesting stories and products. Writers are always looking for a good story idea, but they often have to wade through so many bad pitches that it can be hard to get them to pay attention to a good one. Building relationships helps. Reach out and try to provide value by sharing something relevant to them—don't just ask for something. If a journalist reviews products like yours, send them your product for free. Ask them if they can connect you to the person at their company who manages performance marketing.

As you build these relationships, you increase the chances that someone will write about you or share your story with someone else who will write about you. Then you need only a few mentions or inclusions to start getting others. Media generates more media. I've found that if one news outlet or platform writes about you, then there's a significantly higher chance someone else will. Stories travel fast and will reach the people who will write about them.

TV is different beast and can help you reach a broader audience, but the compounding effect is often low. My appearance on the *Rachael Ray* show sold a bunch of books the day the episode aired and then over the next few days, but I don't think it was instrumental in selling books over time or building my brand (except that it generated a nice clip that I can use in other promotions). No matter your business type, it's worth trying to build relationships with the media, but it should be a supplemental strategy, not your primary focus.

DIVERSIFY YOUR MARKETING AND LAUNCH NEW PRODUCTS

No matter how well your business is growing and how much money you're making, eventually something will stop working. At some point, the law of diminishing returns will come into play—even with the best marketing strategy. Your TikTok ads won't generate sales forever. Your organic traffic will plateau, or you'll get hit with Google algorithm updates. Instagram ad prices will get too expensive and you won't be able to make a profit. You'll know when your CAC starts increasing, shrinking your ROAs and profit. Yes, you can increase your prices to offset the increasing CAC and work hard to nurture your customers into repeat buyers, but eventually, your profit margin will start to decline. It's not an if but a when.

The only way to prepare is to remember Truth #5: Master one thing, then diversify for resilience. You need to diversify your marketing by experimenting with different types of organic marketing platforms and various paid marketing channels. But you should also consider launching new products that are relevant to your audience. There is almost always a natural limit to the market for any product. Once you've reached that limit, you need to offer something new by expanding your product or service line to attract new customers and keep existing ones coming back. Of course, you don't have to wait until you've exhausted your marketing efforts to start offering new products. You can start whenever you have an idea and sufficient resources to execute it. You might already have ideas for new products or services you want to create, but if you're looking for low-hanging fruit or inspiration, below are some ways to find new product ideas while simultaneously revealing your target market.

LOOK AT YOUR COMPETITORS AND
KEEP UP WITH THE MARKET

What types of products do your competitors offer that you don't? Are there any that you can easily add into your mix as an upsell to increase your average order value? If a lot of your competitors are selling something similar to you, there's a good chance that they're probably making money on it. Look at their most popular products and the ones people are talking about online. If you're selling an e-commerce product, I strongly recommend using a spy tool or plug-in like Helium10 or others to analyze Amazon sales volumes and profit for any particular product available on the site.

What's happening at the forefront of your industry? What are the cool brands building, and what are the influencers talking about? You should always pay close attention to your market—subscribe to all the best newsletters, set up Google Alerts, follow the key influencers and creators, and participate in the forums. You can quickly dive into Reddit forums, Facebook Groups, and search through tags on TikTok, Instagram, and X to see what people are discussing. Is there a new product that everyone is excited about? Even just paying attention will help you stumble onto new product ideas. Keep a running list. Think through what would resonate most with your existing audience, then ask them.

ASK YOUR COMMUNITY AND BUILD AN INNER CIRCLE

If you have a few new product ideas, ask your community what they think about them. Be open that you're thinking about building or creating and ask for their feedback. A simple Google Form or Typeform survey will work. In addition to asking them for feedback, ask them what other products they've been buying recently that are related to yours. For example, if you sell a baby bottle, ask your community: "What are some awesome products you've recently bought for your baby?" Look into each of the products they recommend and see if it makes sense for you to sell something similar.

If you have a large community, you can ask if any of them want to join your "New Product Group" or "Inner Circle," where you'll share new product ideas and have closer conversations. I have an "inner circle," a smaller group within my larger community, who give me feedback on everything from new book ideas to book edits to new digital product ideas. They love my work and are more than happy to share their honest feedback in exchange for being able to hop on calls with me.

Once you have any idea, you can use your audience to test—and potentially fund the creation of—your product. Send a survey or share a blog or social post with the details on what you are thinking of offering. Ask for more feedback. What features or functionalities would they like to see? How much would they be willing to pay?

If you're offering a service, use this feedback to launch it quickly and tweak it as you learn more about what your customers need. If you're providing a product, you can set up a preorder page and provide some incentive, like a limited number of products, for people to purchase the product before you produce it. You can then use this money to fund the production of the first version of the product. After that, you can use the profits from the first product to fund the production of the second, improved larger-run version. In this way, you can create an entirely new product without laying out any cash up front to make or market it.

CHAPTER 11

ALIGN YOUR INCENTIVES TO HIRE GREAT PEOPLE AND KEEP THEM HAPPY

"Hire for passion and intensity; there is training for everything else."
—Nolan Bushnell, cofounder of Atari and Chuck E. Cheese

Over the past fifteen years that I've been an entrepreneur, the companies and teams I've built have all looked different. I started as a Solopreneur working solely with contractors, which gave me flexibility. I was able to stay in the trenches and do the work I enjoyed and outsource everything else to contractors. But even though I paid them well, the contractors I worked with were never incentivized enough to help me build my business. They may have enjoyed working for me, but they had their own businesses to run, and it was difficult to keep good people around. Hiring and managing all these individuals on my own ended up burning me out.

When I built my digital marketing agency, I became a Growth Entrepreneur with business partners, full-time employees, and the traditional hierarchical structure. I was a boss, manager, and business partner. This took up a lot of time, and as the business grew, I spent a huge chunk of my time managing a team of full-time employees. They were all paid well and were extremely talented, but they were never really passionate about the work because, in hindsight, I wasn't passionate about the work. While I'd work to fire up the team and keep the morale high, deep down I didn't really believe in what I was selling. Somehow, my team could sense this. So they did their jobs, but nothing else. None of them cared about growing the business, which makes sense, because it wasn't their business.

As is pretty typical in digital marketing, there was a high amount of turnover at my agency, especially among people in their twenties. This meant I once again dedicated a lot of my time to filling roles. After six years I'd reached my limit. Honestly, I'd reached my limit well before this, but I didn't trust myself yet. I was still in the grind phase of my financial independence journey and completely focused on accumulating as much money as quickly as possible. Eventually, I realized I'd never build a company with 100, 500, or 1,000+ people. I'm sure I could probably do it if I wanted to, but I have little interest in spending my time this way.

Every entrepreneur faces this same decision: how many people to hire and when. At a certain stage of growth, you will no longer be able to manage all the core functions of your business on your own. The increased complexity that naturally occurs as you gain more customers, grow your product lines, and multiply the number of tasks you need to complete every day will begin to take your attention and energy away from more important pursuits—in your business and your life. You can't—and shouldn't—do it all yourself. You need to hire people.

Even if you work with contractors to complete basic tasks, you cannot outsource the management of these tasks to someone outside the company. You also can't outsource strategy. You need someone (or most likely a few people) who can act as extensions of yourself. They don't need to know everything about your business, but they do need to understand your goals and how everything functions together. They also need to be focused on *your* business, not working with several clients in equal capacity, to support your continued growth. When you reach a point where you can't effectively oversee all the core functions of your business (or you no longer want to) it's time to expand your team.

Before you do this, you need to think critically about exactly whom you want to hire and how. Becoming an employer adds one kind of complexity while removing another. Payroll is the biggest expense for most companies, and the number one thing on most stressed entrepreneurs' minds is "How am I going to make payroll this month?" Plus, there are legal and tax implications to hiring people that you'll have to consider (or pay someone else to consider for you).

Most important, you have to consider the human component of managing employees. How will you assess performance? What employment policies will you have, and will they apply equally to all team members? How will you keep your team motivated and growing? Managing people takes time and effort. How are you going to approach it?

Most experts on hiring and managing present a one-size-fits-all approach and assume a traditional model of employment where you hire people to complete a specific set of tasks for a certain amount of time per week in exchange for a negotiated salary and benefits package. But, as I've stated many times in this book, I prefer a more flexible model. One that allows you to decide whom and how to hire on a case-by-case basis while honoring your limits. Here's how.

ASSESS YOUR *TRUE* HIRING NEEDS

Many entrepreneurs struggle to determine the number of people they need to hire. While there's no magic formula to this, it's easy to over-hire or underhire, depending on your growth goals. Almost all the entrepreneurs I know overhire. They start growing and feel the only way to grow is to rapidly hire new people. Sure, this is one way to grow quickly—assuming you hire good people—but hiring people is expensive. If you're using your own money and don't fully think through the economics of each hire, you can easily burn a lot of cash and add unnecessary risk to your business.

This happens all the time at high-growth tech companies when they take on external funding. They feel pressure to grow quickly, so they hire a bunch of people without considering the roles each person would need to fill to justify their salary. Then, if they don't hit their growth targets or keep getting funding, they have to lay off people just as quickly.

Instead of this growth-at-all-costs approach, I use a simple framework to help me evaluate my business needs and be as sure as possible that I'm hiring the *right people* for the *right job* at the *right time* and for the *right amount of money*.

To do this, I ask myself the following questions:

1. Can technology solve this problem, or does it require a human being?

I always try to figure out how to use technology to solve my problems. It's much cheaper than hiring a person and is often easier to manage. That said, people are more creative and intuitive than technology, especially because people can manage and oversee areas of a business that require humans to help them grow. You can use the best email management platform in the world, but someone needs to oversee the management of the platform and optimize its performance. Quick-Books makes bookkeeping and tax preparation extremely efficient, but only an expert bookkeeper or accountant can spot discrepancies or help you strategize for the future.

2. Does this work require a full-time person to complete it?

To determine if the work you need done regularly requires a full-time hire, start by writing out a list of the tasks they would work on and their responsibilities. Then, track the rough number of hours you spend on similar tasks and use that number as a baseline. Then try to estimate how many hours above what you're spending someone who was hired specifically to do that work would need if their role is designed to grow some area of your business. Does it seem realistic that they could dedicate forty hours a week to fulfilling those responsibilities? If not, keep adding to the list of responsibilities from other areas where you need help in the business until you get there. You can stack their responsibilities for early employees until their primary role requires their full time.

Most full-time employees you hire will justifiably try to do as little as possible. Of course, you should try to hire people who aren't like this, but it's human nature. One way to minimize this happening and maximize your return on your investment in a full-time hire is to craft the role so they have enough work to do and can add as much value to your business as quickly as possible.

The most important thing you can do is write a detailed job description based on the responsibilities list you already created above.

This will help you organize the role and responsibilities so it outlines exactly what you need. It's a great tool for homing in on what you need and becomes essential for recruiting and managing others. One easy way to craft your job description is to look at your competitors' job descriptions. I regularly monitor our competitors' job descriptions to see what roles they are hiring for and how they structure them. I've learned a ton doing this, including what technologies my competitors use, because they often mention them in their job descriptions.

Also, once you hire someone, their job descriptions become your tool to measure their performance. Are they fulfilling the duties outlined in the job description? Are they going above and beyond?

HOW TO WRITE A COMPELLING JOB DESCRIPTION

- **Draft a Clear Title and Summary:** Use a clear and specific job title that accurately represents the role. Use a job title that people in your industry will be familiar with since job seekers often use such titles when searching for available positions. Follow it with a summary that describes the job's primary responsibilities and importance within the company. Add some personality by sharing your company's goals and story. Incorporate relevant keywords and phrases that candidates might use when searching for similar roles online. This can help your job posting rank higher in search results.

- **Detail Responsibilities:** Outline the specific day-to-day tasks and responsibilities expected of the candidate in more detail than you include in the summary. Be clear about what the role entails, its impact on the company, and the goals you expect the person who fills that role to achieve. A vague job description can lead the wrong people to apply, while a specific one forces you to determine exactly what you're looking for so you don't waste your time or anyone else's. You only want people who are excited about the opportunity to apply. The more detail you can provide, the better applicants you will get.

- **List Desired Qualifications and Skills:** Clearly state the qualifications, skills, and experience necessary for the role. Differentiate between "must-haves" and "nice-to-haves" to attract suitable candidates. Make sure you include any technologies you'd like them to have experience using, understanding that there are so many new technologies coming to market that even the best candidates might not yet be familiar with them. I see some descriptions that require people to have experience with ten or more technology platforms, which is unrealistic.

- **Highlight Your Company Culture and Values:** Be open about who you are and what you stand for. Highlight the company's culture, values, and unique benefits. Candidates often look for alignment with company culture when considering job opportunities. They want the right fit just like you do.

- **Be Transparent about Salary and Benefits:** When you include a salary range, you are more likely to attract qualified candidates excited about the salary. Some states legally require companies to list a salary range on all job descriptions, but I recommend including it. Transparency will not only help you weed out potential candidates who will demand more than you're willing to pay, but it will also set a ton of transparency and openness and, therefore, help you gain the trust of anyone who applies.

- **Provide a Clear Call to Action:** Encourage potential candidates to apply by including a clear call to action. Whether it's asking them to apply through a specific portal or directing them to contact someone, make it easy for them to take the next step. For almost all roles, I require a cover letter, asking candidates to explain why they're interested and why they think they'd be a good fit. It's so easy to apply to jobs online that creating this requirement can weed out less serious candidates. Quality candidates tend to stand out.

  Use language that is engaging, positive, and inclusive. Avoid jargon and use simple, descriptive language. You should also review and update job descriptions regularly to ensure they remain relevant and aligned with any changes in the role or company needs.

With a smaller company, your first hires should be flexible and curious enough to do multiple jobs that the business requires. You won't be able to afford someone for every single role, so you should look for someone with broader skills that your business can leverage. As you grow, you can move people into more specialized roles based on where you see them excelling and what they're interested in focusing on.

3. Does this role require a visionary, manager, or doer?

The number one goal of hiring is to hire the right person for the right role. If you hire the wrong person, they can easily get frustrated. Three different types of people can work within your company, so you must consider which one you need for your specific role. These three are:

VISIONARY

This is the person who comes up with ideas. They always have new ideas, but they can struggle with bringing them to life systematically.

Most entrepreneurs are visionaries, which is their biggest opportunity and challenge. It's common for visionaries to have "shiny object syndrome," where they jump from one idea or opportunity to another and can struggle to stay focused. This is one of my biggest challenges, but I'm always mindful and work hard to keep focused on moving my businesses forward because I'm aware of this weakness.

MANAGER

The managers are the systems organizers and overseers. They like managing processes and people. They keep things organized and ensure the systems run well. They can be proactive, but they need clear direction from the top, which can be challenging for visionaries who aren't natural managers. While it's very easy for a company to hire too many managers, you only need a few great ones to keep your entire company running smoothly.

DOER

These are people who like doing tasks and checking boxes. They get stuff done and love the satisfaction of checking something off a to-do list. They are the backbone of your company because they are the ones doing most of the work. Most of your contractors will be doers, and doers will likely be your first hires. However, if you're a visionary and hire doers, you need to make sure you have organized SOPs they can work from. You also need to closely monitor doers when you don't have managers in place. They can get frustrated without clear instructions and easy ways to benchmark their performance. You can't expect doers to be visionaries or managers.

While it's rare, some people can be two or even all three in one, but they are usually strongest in one area. However, it could vary by disciplines. For example, someone may be a visionary in one discipline but a doer or manager in another. I'm strongest as a visionary, but I'm also a doer because I can come up with ideas and execute them myself. But I'm not a good manager. This is my biggest weakness, so I always lean toward hiring managers and doers.

4. How much will it cost to hire this person?

People are expensive, especially when you add in the cost of benefits, bonuses, and other forms of compensation over several years. What is the market salary range for the person you're trying to hire? You can easily find this by looking at other job descriptions online and talking with recruiters in your industry. Consider not just the base compensation but the cost of any benefits you plan (or are required) to provide (e.g., health insurance, unemployment, disability, etc.).

You also need to factor in taxes since employers are responsible for paying half of each employee's Social Security and Medicare taxes. There are also administrative costs associated with being an employer. For instance, you will need to register as an employer in each state where you have employees, and you may need to take out specific insurance.

To make sure you can afford all the costs of hiring, add an extra 30 percent on top of the salary you expect to pay. As a general rule, you never want to spend more than 5 percent of your total revenue on any one person. Will you need a system to manage payroll and compliance? Thankfully, there are many good all-inclusive options that are relatively inexpensive and can help you do this, but don't forget to factor in those expenses as well. Consider paying an employment lawyer or CPA to walk through all the considerations and costs to budget your needs accurately.

5. How much money will this person need to generate for the company to justify their hiring?

Ideally, you want an employee to generate two to three times their annual salary in revenue each year. So if it costs $100,000 a year to hire someone (including administration costs), they should be earning the company at least $300,000 in gross revenue. One way to measure this is to look at the money you currently have coming in under that role. If your digital advertising campaigns bring in $15,000 a month ($180,000 a year) in revenue, you can hire someone for at least $60,000 to manage your ad campaigns.

If you want or expect that hire to grow revenue from digital ads, you could set a target for growth (say, from $15,000 to $20,000 a month) and increase the budget by a comparable amount. I always prefer to know I have the money coming in to cover someone's salary, though for certain functions it can be difficult to quantify exactly how much a particular person is bringing in. Either way, you should know what revenue you'll use to pay for that person.

HIRE HIGH-LEVEL PEOPLE FIRST

As a Solopreneur, you hired contractors to manage the tasks you couldn't or didn't want to do yourself. As a Growth Entrepreneur, as you're considering whether to employ someone full-time, you want to hire the people who will help your business grow. To do this, it's useful to think about potential hires as either A, B, or C players.

While visionaries, managers, and doers describe the type of role someone is best at, being an A, B, or C player measures how capable, proactive, and great at their job they are. Some people are just better at their jobs and for your company than others. A players give a company energy, whereas C players take away energy. B players fit somewhere in the middle.

C players are reactive as opposed to proactive. They require a lot of oversight and management time and generally do as little as possible. While they might do a decent job, they don't add any extra value to your business and tend to take up a lot of company energy and time. While they generally will be younger and less experienced, some people can stay C players forever. Your business might need C players to run efficiently, but you shouldn't focus on bringing on any C players full-time at this stage. Stick with hiring contractors and paying them to save you time.

In my experience, most people are B players. B players are generally reactive but can be proactive in areas they are passionate about. They'll do the job pretty well and can add real value to your company. They clock out when the day is done, but sometimes before the work is done. While they tend to be more advanced in their skill set and have a broader perspective on the work that goes into making a specific area of the business function, they don't go above and beyond much unless they have powerful incentives to do so. They take quite a bit of time to manage, but don't generally take an outsize amount of company time and resources.

A players are the people who can take your business to the next level. They are proactive and will go above and beyond to make your business successful. They take pride in their work. While they are generally highly skilled, experienced, ambitious, and creative, they don't have to be. Even an entry-level employee can be an A player if they continually push to improve your business. Many A players think like entrepreneurs, even if they're not business owners. They are highly motivated and on board with your mission and goals and derive a lot of fulfillment from their work. While they are motivated by incentives, they also just want to do a good job.

When you find the right A player for your business, they behave more like partners than employees. A players need little to no managing because they're much better at self-managing and taking responsibility. When hiring your first employees, you want to focus on A players or, at the very least B players who have the potential to become A players. One challenge with A players is they can get frustrated and quit if they aren't surrounded by very high-quality coworkers. You never want to surround A players with C players, and even working with B players can sometimes be challenging for them.

To figure out what kind of A players you should hire first, you need to consider the core functions of your business. Refer back to the SOPs you crafted in chapter 8. If necessary, update them to reflect all the domains and tasks within your business. Next, build out these essential functions into teams of discrete but related tasks. The size and structure of these teams can vary widely, based on the company's growth stage, industry, and specific business needs.

In smaller companies, you might be able to combine some roles into one large role, while larger organizations might have more specialized teams. Tailoring teams to suit your business's unique requirements is essential for optimal performance and growth.

For example, your teams might include:

Marketing: Tells potential and current customers about the company and its products. It also helps a company increase its visibility and makes it easy to capture leads.

Sales: Reaches out to potential or current customers who may be interested in buying from the company

Customer Service: Helps customers who have questions or problems

Product Development: Creates and improves the things the company sells

Operations: Ensures all the internal processes within the company function smoothly

Finance and Accounting: Oversees the company's finances and keeps track of revenue, profit, losses, debts, tax liabilities, and anything else that impacts the company's financial health

Human Resources (HR): Handles employee communications, benefits, recruiting and hiring, and any conflicts or concerns that arise internally

Information Technology (IT): Monitors and improves the company's technology infrastructure and networks

Legal and Compliance: Ensures the company is operating legally

Supply Chain and Logistics: Makes sure the company can source everything it needs to make its products and deliver them to consumers

Quality Control: Makes sure the company's products are free of defects

Data Analytics and Business Intelligence (BI): Analyzes the company's finances, industry trends, economic forecasts, and other data to help the company make good decisions

Strategic Planning: Strategizes what the company should do in the future to ensure success and continued relevance

I always start by hiring for roles that can help the company make money, e.g., marketing and sales. I handle customer service myself for as long as possible so I can remain close to the market and understand customers' questions, problems, and experiences. Then, I pass customer support to my assistant before hiring anyone else. But if a business is growing quickly, customer service will take up a lot of time and you should hire someone to handle it to ensure customers are having a great experience. I also recommend leaning into technology by setting up a simple customer-support ticketing system that allows you to track and respond to all queries.

For every other function, I prefer to outsource by relying on technology and contractors. Because I like to keep my businesses relatively small and lean, having dedicated staff to handle things like accounting, legal issues, and HR is unnecessary, especially since they don't generate revenue for our business.

To dive deeper into how to structure your team's functional areas, I encourage you to check out the Accountability Chart in Gino Wickman's great book *Traction* to learn more. The Accountability Chart is a visual tool that defines roles and responsibilities within your organization. It ensures that everyone knows their role and who they report to, reducing confusion and duplication of efforts. The chart is just one part of Gino's highly popular Entrepreneurial Operating System (EOS), which he expands on in the book. It's a must-read as you're building your team.

FIND AND VET THE RIGHT PEOPLE

I only hire passionate people who love what they do. I also only hire people with whom I want to work and create. One benefit of being an entrepreneur is that you get to choose who is on your team. There's something special about creating and collaborating with people you genuinely love working with.

Try to hire true believers who understand what you're trying to accomplish and are excited to help you get there. You might know the foremost digital marketing expert in the world, but if they don't see your vision and aren't excited to be part of your team, they're only going to take you so far because they'll probably leave the second a better opportunity comes along. You want to find someone with the perfect combination of attitude and skills—and, ideally, you want these qualities to be evident before you hire them. That's why it always makes sense to hire the people you know, preferably those you've worked with before.

The six people I work with at MMG Media Group previously worked with me as contractors before they came on full-time. They had already proven their value through their work, and I knew we worked well together. This de-risked the hiring proposition a thousandfold. As I write this, we've been working together for over two years and have increased the value of the business from $0 to over $10 million in that time.

Once you have a clear job description, I recommend looking for people within your existing network by posting the job on LinkedIn and emailing it to your contacts. The more you know about a person in advance, either because you already know them or they come highly recommended by someone you trust, the easier it will be to determine if they are right for the job. I also encourage you to reach out to people you think could be a good fit, either because they have worked for one of your competitors or they have a particularly impressive background. Even when I'm not actively looking to hire, I consistently monitor LinkedIn for people in my industry who have been laid off or are working at a company that has recently laid other people off.

If your network and firsthand outreach don't surface any good-quality candidates, you can post the job on industry forums or job sites, but the broader your reach, the more unqualified applicants you'll have to search through. If this fails to yield any great candidates, you can engage a recruiting firm to help you find someone, but these firms often charge 10 to 25 percent of the first-year salary of the person they place at your company. Still, the cost may be worth it.

Recruiters who specialize in your industry often have a more extensive network than you do, especially if you're new to hiring. I've used recruiting firms a few times when I was looking to fill a senior-level role quickly. If you're having trouble finding someone who is the perfect fit and need to fill the role quickly, consider hiring someone on a limited or contract basis for a few months before deciding if you want to make a full-time offer.

A quick word of caution: be careful about hiring family or friends. I've certainly become friends with people I've worked with, but I've never been able to turn an existing friendship into a business relationship unless I've worked with the person before. As an entrepreneur, you will be forced to make tough choices, which become even more difficult if they impact your personal life. That said, starting a business with a friend or family member can be fruitful since you will both have the same amount of skin in the game. Just be sure to set up the proper boundaries and limits and make sure you're on the same page about the strategy and vision.

HOW TO INTERVIEW

Once you've narrowed down your list of candidates, set up the first round of interviews. You can do them over video or in person, but not just over the phone. On more than one occasion, I interviewed someone over the phone only to have an entirely different person show up for the second, in-person interview. In the first interview, I usually spend an hour asking each candidate why they think they'd be a good fit, why they're interested in the role, and specific questions about their résumé to understand their experience better.

I'm looking for someone I'd be excited to work with, so I know pretty quickly (usually within the first fifteen minutes) if someone could be a good fit. If I don't see it working, I respectfully end the interview before the hour ends and am open with them about why. Otherwise, I always leave at least fifteen minutes at the end of the interview for the candidates to ask me questions. I am looking for someone naturally curious and interested in the job, so if they don't have any questions, they're probably not a good fit.

If the conversation goes well, I invite the candidate to a second interview, which I always conduct in person. At this interview, I come prepared with more specific questions to better understand how the person thinks and responds to an actual scenario. I ask them to explain certain projects they've worked on, problems they've solved, and their thoughts on the industry and role. I also ask them about their career goals, what they like to do in their free time, and what they are most passionate about. I never do a third round of interviews, so I'm trying to get as much information as possible at this stage to make a final decision. After the second round, if I'm not absolutely sure about someone, I don't hire them. When someone is right for a position, you'll know.

It's taken me years to get good at interviewing, but I encourage you to be yourself, be transparent, and try to have a good, free-flowing conversation. Especially when you have a relatively small team, you want to hire people you can get along and work with easily.

There are three questions I ask myself before I hire anyone.

1. Would I like to work with this person?

Whether I enjoy the company of someone is more important to me than how talented or experienced they are. When hiring someone at this level, you have to ensure you're on the same page and that communication and collaboration are as frictionless as possible. Do you trust them? Even if you work in different physical locations, you'll spend a lot of time talking to and engaging with this person.

If you don't enjoy something, you will naturally try and avoid it. That's going to impact your business and your quality of life. You're not going to change someone's toxic personality, and having an unpleasant person on the payroll will make it more difficult to hire good people in the future or to keep good people at the company for long. Pay attention to any red flags, even if it's just your gut telling you it's not a good fit.

2. Is this person currently succeeding in a similar role?

In most cases, the best people are currently performing at a high level in a similar role at another company. When people are doing well at work, they're usually not desperate to leave, so you will probably have to be more proactive to tell them about the opportunity you offer and convince them to give you a chance.

Based on the laws of simple probability, it's also not likely that the person you most want to hire will actively seek the job while you're seeking a candidate, but that doesn't mean they're not open to the right offer. Seek out people already doing the work you want them to do for you and reach out directly.

3. Is this person fulfilled by the work?

The woman who manages SEO for our MMG Media Group websites is passionate about SEO. She loves it. Yes, she gets compensated well for her work and has a vested interest in helping us grow since she shares equity in the company (more on this below), but she also takes great pride and satisfaction from increasing our Google rankings for different search terms. She's not a workaholic. She's just really good at her job, and because she loves the work so much, she stays on top of things and spots trends and issues the rest of us might never see.

Competence is essential, but this passion and positive intensity can make a huge difference for a small, growing company. When someone is fulfilled by their work, they feel grateful to be able to do it and will stick with you because you've created an environment in which they can do what they love and be rewarded for it. You also don't have to manage or convince them to go the extra mile—they want to do it anyway. And passion is infectious. It creates a culture of excitement and energy and signals to everyone that this is a place where they can let their talents and gifts shine.

BE HONEST

Employers will often oversell a company or a position by failing to disclose important details, to convince people to work for them. Don't do this. Hiring people and then losing them because you have to fire them or they quit is expensive, stressful, and creates risk for everyone involved. If you're trying to hire someone great, it's tempting to oversell your company by saying it's growing faster than it is or by suggesting future plans you do not intend to pursue, just to get a person on board. This is especially true for small companies without a ton of brand recognition.

Companies also frequently lie about the scope of a role, suggesting it's bigger than it is, that there's unrealistic room for growth, or that the candidate won't have to take on duties that, in reality, are a core function of the job. Before you start these conversations, figure out exactly what you need from the person filling this role and what you're willing to give them in return—and what you're not.

For example, when I approach candidates about coming on as partners in MMG Media Group (meaning that, in addition to a salary, they receive equity in the company), I'm clear that their share doesn't come with any voting power. I'm happy to share my profits with my employees, but I'm not willing to cede control over how my company grows, because by doing so, I'm potentially giving up control of my life. I'm also up front about my strengths and weaknesses and what I want to spend my time doing (and not doing).

I tell them I don't like managing and I'm not good at it. If they need or want a lot of feedback and direction, I'm probably not the right person to work with. I tell them exactly how I will assess their performance and what I expect them to accomplish, and they tell me whether that's realistic. The partners I have today are fine with this arrangement and are happy to be left alone to do their jobs and share in the fruits of their labor.

If you're unsure what the role should entail, you can cocreate it with the person you hire. This can also be a good way for you to assess their vision for the role because they may have a better sense than you of how they can use their particular skill set to grow the company.

Regardless of how you determine the job description, be sure to formalize it in writing so that you have something to refer back to when assessing performance.

CREATE THE RIGHT INCENTIVES

Great people are rare, so when you find them, you should do whatever you can to hold on to them and make them happy. As I write this, I know that my business partners are working on building our company. I don't have to monitor their actions, because I trust them. Why? Because I've worked with them for many years, we respect each other, have complementary skill sets, and align our incentives. While I'm the majority shareholder, we all own the business. While feeling valued, fitting in with a company's culture, and believing in the core mission are important for hiring, retaining, and keeping your employees/team members happy, there is one thing that is more important than anything else: *incentives*.

Incentives motivate people to work hard, add value to your company, and build your business. But your incentives need to actually incentivize! People need to want what you're offering them, whether it's a salary, more flexibility, opportunities to learn and grow, a growth path for their career, connection, or all of the above.

The best way to align incentives is to personalize them to each person. People are unique and have different desires, needs, and goals. While most people want things like more money, flexibility, a clearly defined growth trajectory, to be a part of a team, to feel valued, etc., the ratio for everyone is a bit different, depending on who they are and where they are in their life. A young twentysomething with few commitments might be willing to invest more time in your business, require fewer trade-offs, and be motivated more by money than someone in their forties with a partner, three kids, and many commitments.

If one thing has made me a successful entrepreneur, it's figuring out what people want and then doing everything I can to give it to them. If you can align the incentive structure in your business with what your team wants, you'll foster unlimited potential for growth, you'll be able to keep your team happy, and you'll be able to retain great talent. It costs the average company 40 to 60 percent of an employee's first-year salary to replace them—and that's just the monetary trade-off. It doesn't account for all the lost company knowledge, experience, and potential compounding impact of that team member on your business over time.

Under the traditional hiring model, each employee trades a certain skill set and time for a base compensation package. This may increase over time or grow larger, thanks to commissions or bonuses, but the employee gets what is agreed to up front and has to renegotiate their contract for more money. There's a certain amount of efficiency to this because the employer can calculate how much each person costs them, and the employee knows how much money they'll earn at any given time.

However, the biggest downside to this model is that it pits employees and employers against one another. The employee always wants to make more and the employer always wants to pay less to keep more profit. If the employee thinks they aren't being compensated fairly, they will not be invested in the work or the company and will leave at the first opportunity. This, ultimately, costs employers money. And if the company ever has a cash-flow problem and can't cover payroll, they will be forced to lay people off.

If you don't want to give up equity in your company, the full-time employment model might be best for you, at least to start. This is also a good idea if you're hiring someone you haven't worked with before or don't know well. When you make someone a partner in your business, you are entering into a legal and financial relationship. You need to make sure you trust the person before taking on that risk.

PARTNERSHIP MODEL—WHY I BRING ON PARTNERS INSTEAD OF EMPLOYEES

I own 60 percent of MMG Media Group and my four partners own the other 40 percent, which entitles them to 40 percent of the profit at the end of each year in addition to their base compensation package. This equity model benefits my employees because they are rewarded directly for the value they bring to the company, and their potential income is essentially unlimited. It helps me because I know my partners are incentivized to work hard, and the bulk of their compensation kicks in only if the company does well.

This model also reduces my payroll expenses because my partners take a lower base salary in exchange for a bigger potential commission on the back end. It indirectly reduces other expenses because everyone is equally committed to maximizing profit and, therefore, thinks critically about how to spend a dollar. The lower base compensation also means I can hire people I might not be able to afford if I needed to pay them a higher guaranteed salary to match their market rate.

When planning a partnership model, consider the needs of each individual. Let them tell you what they need, then work backward from there. When it comes to equity, I always try to be generous. You want your partners to be excited and feel valued, not to feel as if you are trying to give them as little as possible. Don't be greedy. People can tell, and it won't make them feel good or excited. Most entrepreneurs give away too little equity, and it can be difficult for potential partners to evaluate the value of equity unless you make it very clear to them.

Look for a middle ground that makes you both happy. The best way to do this is to use questions like the following to guide your conversations:

What do you want to get out of this business?
How do they see the business fitting into their life? How much money do they want to make? How can you use the business to keep them challenged, engaged, and growing? Most people are happiest when they feel a sense of progress, of forward momentum in their lives.

How long are you willing to commit to this?
One of the biggest worries in a partnership is that your partner will leave the business early. Life changes and people move on, but it can be a big challenge when partners who are essential to the business leave. Try and get an honest understanding of how long they are willing to commit to the business. Set a time-based goal together, such as wanting to sell your business in five years.

What does success look like to you?
Success often means something different to different people. Listen to what it means to them so you can build this into your planning and communication.

What are your worries and fears?
I always ask this question because I want to know what people are worried about so I can think about how to build the business and communicate to mitigate those fears.

THE NINETY-DAY TEST

Whether hiring a full-time employee or a contractor for a larger role, I'm always open about having a ninety-day test period to assess their performance and overall fit within the company. This helps me structure how I manage these first ninety days, as I am not a natural manager. Then, at the thirty-, sixty-, and ninety-day marks, I conduct performance reviews, in person or over a video call, and follow up with an email that documents what we discussed. In these reviews, I'll often walk them through their job description and provide feedback on how well I think they are doing with their responsibilities.

I also solicit feedback on how well they think the position is working out for them and answer any questions they have. These reviews are meant to be transparent conversations to assess fit, impact, and performance. I want everyone to understand exactly where they stand and what they can improve. Within ninety days, you should be able to tell whether someone will work out for the long term. Many people over-promise and underdeliver, and some won't be great fits with your team. If the person stays with the team after ninety days, I conduct a performance review at the six-month and one-year anniversaries for the first year. After the first year, I try to do performance reviews once a year.

LET PEOPLE MANAGE THEMSELVES

As the CEO of my company, I largely stay out of the day-to-day inner workings of the business and focus my energy on identifying new acquisition opportunities and managing the economics of the business. I provide some high-level oversight to ensure everyone focuses on the right priorities, feels fulfilled, and is on the same page, and I'll occasionally recommend we move in a certain strategic direction.

However, I rarely push unless I feel very strongly about a particular idea. When I do, I share my rationale with the team to get their buy-in. Otherwise, I let my team manage themselves as much as possible. This works because we have a culture of transparency, mutual respect, and a shared goal. Our incentives are aligned, so we are motivated by the same things: growing our profit, working with people and on projects we enjoy, and keeping distractions to a minimum.

We have one team call per week and otherwise reach out to one other when needed over Slack or email. We all have access to the complete dataset for our websites, partners, and revenue, so anyone can log into any tool to analyze data or get the information they need without asking anyone else. This level of transparency saves us time and naturally builds accountability. We occasionally get on calls when necessary or agree it would be valuable to connect. This significantly frees us up to work when we want to work without constantly being interrupted.

While this works well for us, you need to find your own rhythm. Your team will grow around you, so you should be intentional about the culture you want to build. Be open, transparent, kind, respectful, and empathetic, and you'll thrive. Most important, be authentic. Successful entrepreneurs love to talk about how the culture they built has helped them succeed, but what works for them may not work for you. If it doesn't feel right, it isn't right, and you and your team will suffer from it.

As you build your team, I encourage you to read *The Five Dysfunctions of a Team* by Patrick Lencioni, who identifies the five root causes of team failure. You can avoid these dysfunctions by paying attention and building a culture that makes them less likely to occur.

1. **Absence of Trust**—Trust comes from the top and starts with you as the leader. The easiest way to earn trust is to do what you say you'll do and be open and honest about your mistakes, decisions, and motivations.

2. **Fear of Conflict**—Your team will watch how you handle conflict and then interpret that as the standard. Create an open culture that promotes constructive conflict, in which people feel comfortable disagreeing with one another and questioning or criticizing the choices of others. Doing so will make people feel at ease while simultaneously improving individual and company performance by holding each team member to the highest standard.

3. **Lack of Commitment**—If someone isn't committed to their role and your team, let them go. It's almost impossible to get these types of people to change, and as long as they are on the payroll, they will do more damage to your business than good.

4. **Avoidance of Accountability**—Be accountable for your mistakes, and others will follow. Keep everyone accountable by building a transparent culture where everyone has access to everything. This includes sharing the financial performance of your company. You can keep specific financial data confidential, but you should share as much data as you feel comfortable with in order to make it clear that everyone is in this together.

5. **Inattention to Results**—Prioritize reporting results during each communication with your team. Everything revolves around the results, so everyone should know what those are and be held accountable for delivering on them.

CALCULATE EACH EMPLOYEE'S ROI

When you start to hire people, you go from managing the twenty-four hours in your day to managing the number of hours your employees work for you. If you have ten employees who work for you eight hours a day, that's eighty extra hours you have to account for. The better you can leverage these hours, the more efficiently your business will run and the faster it will grow. The higher your profit per hour per employee, the more money you have to invest in other areas of your business. On the flip side, if you're not leveraging this time well, you're wasting money on payroll that could be invested more efficiently in another area of your business.

Just as you calculate the return on your spending using CAC and net profit margin, you can calculate the return on your employees' time for roles tied to revenue, cost savings, productivity gains, or any other tangible outcomes attributable to their work. You can evaluate your profit per hour per team, per project, per employee, and across your whole company. Setting up a way to regularly track this data will help you ensure that you're getting the highest ROI on your employees' time and help you determine the ideal cost economics of your business.

While there is no specific mathematical formula for calculating your employees' ROI, here is a simple way to do so for several scenarios:

(Revenue / Time) — Employee Rate or Team Rate = Employee ROI

Revenue: This is the total revenue for a particular project, service line, or entire business. You can use the revenue amount of anything to calculate the ROI of your employee's time related to it.

Time: This is the number of hours worked. You can use the total number of hours for a project or a time frame (e.g., monthly, quarterly, or annually).

Employee Rate: This is how much your business spends to employ a single employee for one hour. To calculate, add all the costs associated with hiring and maintaining the employee. This includes salary, benefits, training expenses, taxes, and any other overhead directly attributed to that employee. I usually estimate that it costs me an additional 35 percent of an individual's salary to hire them for one year. You can then divide that number by the number of hours the employee works per year.

To illustrate, let's say one of your employees earns a $150,000 salary each year; 35 percent of $150,000 is $52,500, so it costs roughly $202,500 ($150,000 + $52,500) to employ this person for one year. If this person works an average of 40 hours a week for 50 weeks of the year, that's 2,000 hours a year. So their employee rate would be:

$202,500 total cost to employ / 2,000 hours = $101.50 per hour

Blended Rate: You can also calculate your costs per employee for an entire team or your whole company by calculating what's known as a blended rate. I calculate this by totaling the salaries of the entire team, adding 35 percent of that amount to account for overhead, and then dividing that total amount by the total number of employees. Next, I divide that total by the average number of hours employees worked in a year. At my agency, we came up with a blended average of $112.50 per hour per team member, using the formula below:

$1,000,000 in total salaries + 35% of $1,000,000 = $1,350,000 total annual cost to employ all employees / 6 employees = $225,000 annual cost of each employee / 2,000 hours worked = $112.50 per hour

Using this information, let's revisit the original equation to determine the ROI on a $100,000 consulting product the team completed in 100 hours at the blended rate:

(Revenue / Time) — Employee Rate or Team Rate = Employee ROI per hour

($100,000/100 hours) = $1,000 per hour — $112.50 per hour Blended Team Rate = $887.50 Employee ROI per hour

To calculate the total profit earned on this project, you multiply the blended hourly Employee ROI by the total number of hours worked:

100 hours x $887.50 = $88,750 in Profit

$88,750 / $100,000 = 88.75% Profit Margin

In this scenario, both the ROI and profit margin are 88.75 percent. This means that 88.75 percent of the sales revenue is realized as profit after deducting all costs associated with making the sale. This is an exceptional profit margin I'll take any day!

You can also use this metric before you hire someone to calculate whether the position is worth hiring for, whether you can afford it, and how much you should be willing to compensate that person for their time. This will involve a certain amount of guesswork since you won't know exactly how much revenue a specific person will generate or how many hours it will take them to complete a project, but it will become easier the more you track ROI and make assessments.

Hiring and managing people are equal parts art and science. The more you work with people—either on a contract basis or as employees—the better you'll get at assessing what roles you need to fill and who will best fit your company. When you have a team of top performers whose incentives align with those of the business, you'll create a self-sustaining system that will allow you to grow exponentially with little oversight. This is how you create a sustainable business—one that can thrive without your having to micromanage the details of the day-to-day. These businesses are stronger, more likely to last for the long haul, and most attractive to potential buyers.

CHAPTER 12

SET YOURSELF UP TO SELL
(EVEN IF YOU DON'T WANT TO SELL)

"I have never cared what something costs; I care what it's worth."
—Ari Emanuel

The air was cold that October morning in 2020, but I was burning up, so I stepped onto my front porch to take the call from the finance manager at the Motley Fool. "We sent the wire about thirty minutes ago," they said. "You should see it hit your account within the next few hours." I put the phone on speaker and opened up my banking app. There it was. Millions of dollars sitting in my checking account. Millennial Money had just been acquired—a little over five years after I started it—and had made me more money than I could have ever imagined.

When I started Millennial Money, I had no idea I could sell a website. I didn't know what buyers would be looking for or how to build a business to be attractive to a potential buyer. It wasn't until I was invited to join an entrepreneur group of successful website owners, a handful of whom had sold their websites for millions of dollars, that I understood the potential.

As soon as I learned what was possible, I immediately started changing how I did things, to make my business attractive to a buyer. I did this even though I had no idea if I'd ever want to sell—or even if I'd have the opportunity to sell. This is key: even if you don't intend to sell your business anytime soon, you need to operate as if you might. If you don't operate this way, you risk losing all the value you've created if you're forced to sell or missing out on a big opportunity if you're not prepared for it when it comes along.

THE MEANING AND THE MATH OF SELLING A BUSINESS

Before we dive into how to build a business you can sell, let's talk about whether you *should* sell. If your company has been doing well and growing for at least the past two years, you'll eventually have to decide whether to keep or sell it. Either choice can be the right one. If you choose to keep the business, you can continue to grow it, live off its income, and eventually cash out on your terms. If you're interested in selling, and you've created enough value for someone who wants to acquire it, you can sell it and live off the money you earn from the sale, or reinvest that money in another venture. In most industries, there are more buyers than sellers for high-quality businesses, which gives you immense leverage as you work to find the right buyer with the best deal for your business.

Cashing out and selling your business can be life-changing, but it's not always a great idea if you're not ready to sell, either because you love your business or you haven't gotten the right offer. Selling a business also takes a ton of time and can get complex, so you should pursue it only when you're ready. There are many reasons to sell, but they all fall into two categories—math or meaning. The math is the amount of money you'll get from the sale. The meaning is how a sale will impact your purpose, identity, and all the nonfinancial pieces of your life.

The Meaning

Meaning is often more difficult to determine than the math because you need to go deep inside to figure out why you want to sell, what selling means to you, and what you'll do after you sell the business. There are many reasons to sell your business. You might be burned out, want to do something else, or see the perfect opportunity based on trends in the market. For me, with website valuations at historic highs, I thought we might be near the top of the market in July 2020 and that I'd likely never have another opportunity like that one. I knew the money would give me a level of security that was too compelling to gamble. I took the deal.

Some people have a clear idea of what they'll do after they sell their business: take a few years off, launch another business, buy a new car or vacation home or boat. I had no idea what I wanted to do, but the sale gave me almost unlimited opportunities. You don't need to have everything figured out, but before you pursue any deal, you'll want to do some soul-searching to make sure a sale fits in with the larger vision for your life.

When I was getting ready to sell, I found it helpful to talk to other entrepreneurs who had gone through the experience. I also gave myself some grace and approached it openly, knowing it would take me some time to figure it all out. It was probably going to be uncomfortable for a little while, but I'd need to remind myself that it was part of the process. I've found that when you remain open to life, opportunities eventually start showing up.

I also worried about what a new owner would do with the company I had spent so much of my life energy trying to build. While the buyer hired most of my team, they let go of a few, and I worried whether those who stayed would all fare well in their new roles. While I stayed on as a consultant for the year after the acquisition to make sure everything went smoothly and I was there to answer any questions, I was surprised by how little outreach I got and how little the buyer engaged with me. There had been a lot of exciting discussions about how we would work together after the sale and how they would use their resources to expand the reach of the website and my mission significantly. But little of this happened.

While I had the money, which changed my life, watching the Millennial Money website traffic decline under the new ownership was still a letdown. The reality is that it's tough to acquire a business and keep it growing, even under the best conditions. Most acquisitions fail. It was still sad to watch and messed with me as I wrestled with who I was without my business. Thankfully, this experience helped me expand my life and grow in other ways. Not having to work on the business, day in and day out, gave me more time to work out, catch up on all the books I'd wanted to read, and start a family.

Also, as you already know, I was able to reacquire Millennial Money less than two years later at a significant discount to what I sold it for, giving me a new opportunity to build the platform and expand the mission.

The Math

A profitable business can generate returns that might be difficult, if not impossible, for other asset classes to beat. For example, let's say you have a business generating $1,000,000 in revenue and a 30 percent profit margin. That means you have $300,000 in profit per year to use however you want. If you sell the business, you can invest the proceeds in a total stock market index fund that averages a 7 percent annual return, or in real estate, which averages a 5 percent annual return; but at those rates, it's going to be difficult to match the returns you could get by holding on to your asset. Let's look at the math.

Say that you sell the business for $5,000,000 (because the sale price is usually calculated as a multiple of current revenues) and then, after paying capital gains taxes, you have $4,000,000 in cash to invest. If you invest in a total stock market index fund with the expectation of 7 percent annual returns, you would generate $280,000 a year in income ($4,000,000 x 0.07).

By contrast, if you invest in real estate, you'd have roughly $200,000 in annual income ($4,000,000 x 0.05). Neither of these matches the $300,000 a year in profit you get from your business that you could also work to keep growing.

Yes, running a business is a much more active investment than simply putting your money in the stock market, but if you don't sell the company, you can continue to maximize revenue and profit and take advantage of tax optimization to increase your returns further.

This is all to say, if you have a durable business that is relatively immune to risk and generates consistent returns, it might not make much sense to sell, even if you can earn a multimillion-dollar payout. With the right systems and people, you may not need to spend much time running or managing your business. Rihanna probably won't sell her beauty or fashion labels anytime soon, because she makes piles of money from owning the assets and has systems and other people that run the businesses for her.

On the other hand, someone like me, who owns and runs websites for a living, might be more inclined to sell because our business is full of risk. Just one Google update could eliminate most of our traffic overnight, so I'm excited about the opportunity to build and sell quickly. This is why my company, MMG Media Group, exists.

When I sold Millennial Money, I earned more than the industry standard for personal finance websites because the Motley Fool wanted to use it to expand the reach of their core stock-picking sub-scription service to a younger audience. They didn't care about how much money the website made through my affiliate partnerships. They wanted the traffic and access to the audience. I calculated that it would take me seventeen years of consistent revenue to make the money they offered to acquire the website. With that math, selling was a no-brainer. I'd rather have the cash up front and invest it in some-thing else than take the risk of owning the website while hoping it would continue to generate meaningful revenue.

HOW TO BUILD YOUR BUSINESS TO SELL

Potential buyers will be more likely to make you an offer—and you'll be more likely to get the offer you want—if your business is profitable, organized, and respected in your industry. More specifically, you are more attractive to a potential buyer if you have:

1. **Strong Financial Performance:** A track record of consis-tent and growing revenues, healthy profit margins, and positive cash flow all signal financial stability and poten-tial returns for the buyer. You'll be much more likely to sell if you've generated consistent revenue for two years or more.

2. **Growth Potential:** Companies with a solid market position, a strong customer base, and potential for future growth in their industry are often appealing. This includes factors like a unique market niche, innovative products or services, or expansion opportunities. If you're growing, you can command a premium; if you're shrinking, it will be hard to sell or you'll be discounted.

3. **Competitive Advantage:** Companies with valuable intellectual property, patents, proprietary technology, or unique assets that offer a competitive advantage are often sought after. The more an advantage your company has, the higher value it will demand on the open market.

4. **Diversified Customer Base:** Buyers seek stability and potential for continued revenue streams from diverse sources. If all your revenue is from a few customers or clients, the business could be perceived as too risky to acquire. The more diverse your revenue is, the less risky the business will be perceived to be.

5. **Replicable Systems:** If you have replicable systems that make the business efficient and easier for a potential buyer to run, it will be more attractive to a buyer. These systems should be documented thoroughly through your SOPs.

6. **Operational Efficiency and Synergies:** Buyers look for opportunities to reduce costs or increase revenue through integration. Efficiency in operations, cost-effective production processes, and potential synergies with the buyer's existing operations are attractive.

7. **Flexibility and Resilience:** Flexibility to adjust to industry shifts or changing consumer demands is valuable, as is built-in resilience of your core business. It's even better if your business is recession- and climate-resilient. Asset-

light businesses are also attractive because of their flexibility and low overhead.

8. **Strong Brand:** A strong brand with a positive reputation in the market can significantly enhance the value of a company. It isn't easy to build a trusted brand, but it is essential if you want to get the maximum value for your company.

9. **Strong Team:** Buyers value a skilled and experienced management team capable of driving the company forward post-acquisition. Strong leadership, industry expertise, and a clear vision for growth are attractive traits.

10. **Not Dependent on You:** Far too many businesses depend on their founder to succeed, making them a less attractive acquisition target. Use systems, technology, and other people to remove yourself from the business.

Of course, buyers want profitable companies that are likely to keep growing, but they also want ones that will be *easy* to acquire. Seventy to 90 percent of acquisitions fail—and buyers know this. If your books are in order, your systems are well documented, your customers are happy, and you can demonstrate the value they will derive from an acquisition, you remove much of the uncertainty and headaches that come with the process.

Many entrepreneurs don't think about positioning themselves to sell their businesses while they build them because they don't fully believe they can build a business that someone will want to buy. But if you've created a business generating value and making money, someone out there will want to buy it. Trust me. It is significantly more difficult to start a business from scratch and grow it than to buy and grow a business that is already profitable. Eighty percent of businesses fail within the first five years. If a buyer acquires a business that has proven it can survive, they've significantly de-risked entrepreneurship.

There are three main things buyers look for when considering an acquisition: demonstrated profit, consistent historical growth, and a potential for continued growth in the future. Timing is important here. If an owner tries to sell too early, they won't have had time to prove themselves in the market. But if they wait too long, the market for their product may have already peaked. Maybe consumer demand has dried up, or the sector has become so oversaturated with competitors that their business is losing market share. Either way, it will become more challenging to sell in this environment.

For many online businesses, like the ones I've run, the sweet spot is two to five years. Once you have two or three years of consistent growth, you should start thinking about selling and getting your documents in order to be ready when the time is right. It can take three to twelve months to finalize a deal with a buyer, and any delays dragging this process out further can lead the deal to a slow death. It's much harder to close a deal than it is to find interested buyers. The second you lose momentum, potential buyers will start to focus on other things. Do as much as you can in advance to plan for a fast sale. As the saying goes, time kills all deals.

DOCUMENT KEY METRICS AND PROCESSES

The number one thing you can do to speed up a sale is to keep your books, financial records, and key financial and performance metrics organized and up-to-date. Buyers need to know how much money you're making, how quickly you're growing, what your expenses are, and how many liabilities you have (among other data points) in order to calculate their offer. Buyers also want to know they'll be able to grow your business efficiently, so it's also important to document key business functions and processes and keep them updated as the business grows and evolves. Documentation is worth doing even if you're years away from selling because it forces you to understand how your company makes money, what's working, and where there is room for improvement. All of this will make your business stronger and more resilient.

Analyze Your Long-Term P&L

The first documents any potential buyer will ask you for are your P&Ls and business tax returns. If your business has been around for a while, they'll want to see these documents for the last five years. The reason they want to see your business tax returns is so they can reconcile what you're reporting on your P&Ls with the information that you filed with the IRS to ensure there aren't any discrepancies. If you haven't been in business that long, they'll want to assess your P&Ls for however many years you've been in business. Buyers almost always require at least two years of P&Ls. If you have your books in order and have been monitoring your P&L regularly, this should be easy to do.

Potential buyers are evaluating the performance and calculating the value of your business by analyzing trends in revenue, expenses, and profitability over time. They are trying to use historical data to estimate future performance. On your P&L, they are looking at the following:

1. **Gross Revenue or Total Income**: Gross revenue is the total revenue before deducting any expenses. While gross revenue shows the overall income, it doesn't consider operational costs or other deductions. Understanding the business's scale is useful but might not accurately reflect its profitability.

2. **Gross Profit**: This is the difference between a company's revenue and the cost of goods sold (COGS). It represents a company's profit from its core business activities before deducting other expenses such as operating expenses, taxes, and interest. Gross profit helps assess a company's ability to generate income solely from its products or services.

3. **Operating Expenses**: These are the costs incurred in running the business's day-to-day operations. They include salaries, rent, utilities, marketing expenses, and other

costs essential for running the business. Evaluating operating expenses helps assess the efficiency of your business operations.

4. **Net Income or Profit:** This is what's left after deducting all expenses from your revenue. Net income represents the bottom line—the actual profit the business generates. Potential buyers often heavily consider this figure when evaluating the business's profitability and its ability to generate returns.

Make a point of running your full P&L annually, at the same time you usually look back on the previous year to see how close you are to where you would need to be to sell. The offer you can expect to receive depends on several factors but is usually calculated as a multiple (typically two to seven times) of your annual income (the amount you, as the owner, take home each year) or annual gross revenue. Buyers can usually justify paying more than what you're worth on paper today because they can project cost savings and revenue growth based on their model, processes, and scale.

As I write this, I'm working to grow four different companies: Millennial Money, which I reacquired after selling it a few years ago, and three others I've acquired in the past year and a half. My goal is to sell off each of these properties within five years of acquiring them for two to three times more than I paid for them. If you're unsure what number you should strive for, you can find out by examining acquisitions within your industry. What is the going rate for a company like yours and how close or far are you from being able to sell for that number?

Update Your SOPs

Remember the standard operating procedures you put together in chapter 8? You and your team should revisit these periodically to make sure they're up-to-date, thorough, and easy to understand. Someone should be able to read these and understand exactly what needs to be done to keep the business running—even if they've never worked in the business before. Efficient systems make it easier for an acquiring company to get up to speed and start making money, and if you have these processes documented, you make it easier for potential buyers to feel comfortable getting your playbook when they acquire your business. The easier it is for a buyer to see how they can integrate your business into theirs, the more valuable your business will be.

Documenting the systems and processes for your core revenue generators and the things only you know how to do is essential. These processes are your intellectual property. At MMG Media Group, we document how we write and optimize content for SEO, how we manage our websites, how we utilize all the plug-ins, and pretty much everything else that has to do with running and optimizing the websites to increase revenue. Because all of this is unique to us and is our intellectual property, we document it to train new team members, to keep improving it, and to prepare our websites for an acquisition.

We don't document how we do our bookkeeping, manage our payroll, or anything that's pretty standard for most businesses to do because any potential acquirer will either have their own way of doing these things or will be able to learn it elsewhere.

Know Your Key Performance Metrics

The more familiar you are with your numbers and the more information you can provide to potential buyers, the easier it will be for you to make your case to sell. While buyers won't necessarily need to examine all your performance metrics, the more you optimize your key growth drivers, the easier it will be for you to grow your company in a way that will naturally make you more attractive to buyers.

We've already discussed key metrics like Net Profit Margin, Customer Acquisition Cost, Customer Lifetime Value, and Churn Rate. It's worth revisiting these quarterly and having them available to show a potential buyer if the conversation progresses. If you have a performance dashboard, keep it updated and have it available during acquisition discussions.

Get Your Business in Order

After a buyer expresses interest in your company, they will perform several weeks, if not months, of due diligence to make sure no surprises are lurking beyond your P&L and balance sheet. Think of this like the inspection stage of buying a house. On its surface, a house may look great: it's the right size and in the right location and price range for your budget. But before you move in, you hire an expert to ensure there is no hidden damage you'd be responsible for.

Performing your own due diligence will allow you to identify and correct any problems before they can ruin your business or kill any potential deals. Here are some things to consider:

COMPLIANCE

This should go without saying, but no one wants to buy a company that is in trouble with the law. Pay your taxes on time, keep your filings and insurance current, and solve any legal trouble as quickly and cleanly as possible. If there is anything you believe would concern a buyer, be up front about it. Don't hide anything, because any secrets will eventually be revealed. If that happens during due diligence, it could kill the deal.

If it happens after the acquisition, you could be liable for not disclosing it. There are always weak points in any business. While you want to always present your business in the best light to make it attractive to a buyer, being up front about any potential legal or compliance issues will build trust and help the seller understand what they are acquiring.

REPUTATION

If no one wants to work with you, you can only be so successful. Eventually, someone else will offer what you offer, and any vendors, customers, employees, partners, or associates you've offended will leave you for a better option. Keep your customers happy by delivering great products and services. Pay your vendors in full and on time. Cooperate with your competitors instead of trying to undermine them.

Treat your employees fairly and create a supportive working environment. People talk, and having a good reputation will attract more buyers. Potential buyers are likely already paying attention to your business and what you're doing. They might be listening to your podcast interviews and reading your newsletter. You never know who is paying attention, so you should always be yourself and treat others well.

CREATE A CULTURE OF INDEPENDENCE

One of the biggest challenges with combining companies is aligning disparate cultures to work together or alongside one another. One of the biggest problems with small companies and start-ups is that the culture centers too much around the founder's personality and whims. This makes it difficult to imagine how the company would function without the founder in charge or how their opinions and preferences would square with the new owners if the founder stayed on after the acquisition. One of the ways to avoid this is by systemizing and automating your business so that it doesn't depend on you to function—a process we discussed in chapter 8, on productizing your business.

Another way to do this is to foster a culture of independence and autonomy in which employees can work and think freely, and management doesn't get in the way of effective decision-making. This is good for you because it makes your life easier. It's good for employees because it gives them a sense of ownership. And it's good for buyers because they can trust that your team is competent and accountable if they stay post-acquisition.

Over the past decade, there has been a popular trend of working to create a great and unique company culture as a way to attract talent, but when it comes to selling, a super-specific culture that works only because of a few key people can hurt your chances of being acquired—or at the very least not help—because a potential buyer could view it as too difficult to integrate with their own culture.

USE UNIVERSAL SYSTEMS

When deciding which software, programs, or technology to use, stick with widely available ones with established reputations and histories as opposed to start-ups or novelties. This makes it easier for the buyer to onboard your company because they will likely be familiar with your tools. Avoid niche products that have not gained widespread use and newer products that may go out of business anytime.

At my company, we use Amazon Web Services (the world's most widely used cloud-computing service), open-source code for our site development, Google Suite for email and document sharing, and other popular tools that would make it easy for a buyer to integrate with their systems. Since we are building our websites and businesses to sell, we engineer everything from the beginning to make it easy for almost any company to take over the operation and integrate it with their systems.

HOW TO FIND POTENTIAL BUYERS

Most buyers interested in your company will have an existing relationship with you before they start discussing an acquisition. They either already do business with you or work in a similar field and are familiar with your brand. You may also know them personally. Given this, fostering relationships with people you consider potential buyers is important.

You can make educated guesses about who will be interested in buying, but a great offer can come from anywhere. Keep your options open and remain agile while staying strategic about how you want to grow your business and honor your limits. You don't want to make a decision *just* because it might appeal to a potential buyer, but the more you understand who those buyers are and what they're looking for, the more information you have to help your company grow.

Acquirer companies will have a few things in common. They are usually established companies that have been around for several years. They are either already actively acquiring in your industry or looking to move into it. Buyers could be private equity firms, holding companies, or one of your competitors. Many companies dedicate a portion of their annual revenue to mergers and acquisitions (M&A) activities. This means there are a lot of companies out there that have a ton of money they need to spend each year on acquisitions. This is great news for you as an owner.

As you become more visible in your industry, you will inevitably get outreach from potential buyers and brokers. However, while this outreach can be extremely exciting, it can also waste a lot of time or be a distraction. A word of caution—it's very common for competitors to reach out to companies while posing as potential buyers or to hire a broker to act as a potential buyer so that they can use your excitement to get competitive intelligence about your business. They act as though they are interested in your company and try to learn as much as possible through conversation about how you run your business.

Some will even take it all the way to writing a letter of intent and acting like they want to buy your company, only to bow out after conducting due diligence and combing through your entire operation. Ask around and do some digging on the company and broker to get a sense of their reputation before disclosing too much. Be cautious and protect your intellectual property as much as possible when engaging with potential buyers. If you don't trust them, run the other way. Even if you all sign NDAs, you should still be very cautious, as it will be difficult to prove they stole your intellectual property even with an NDA.

To identify quality brokers and companies, pay attention to recent acquisitions within your industry. You can do this as part of your regular industry research or set aside dedicated time once a quarter or every six months to do research. You don't need to do this right away, but you should make it a habit when you're two or three years into your business so you can start laying the groundwork to sell if necessary. There is a ton of free information online specific to various industries.

Check out reports from reputable industry associations, publications, or brokers specializing in mergers and acquisitions within your industry. If you're not sure where to start, even a simple Google search of "[current year] acquisitions in the [industry name] industry" or "biggest business sales in [industry name] this year" or "business broker in [industry name]" should help you compile a list of brokers who work in your industry. Since brokers are in the business of selling companies, they should be pretty visible. Follow these brokers on LinkedIn and X, and subscribe to their newsletters, as they will sometimes announce deals once they're finalized.

Once you've identified potential buyers, start following them if you haven't already so you can stay on top of other acquisitions they make. Another smart strategy is to attend conferences, meet-ups, and industry events where there will be buyers. Just being visible in the industry can go a long way.

As you read industry reports, gather information to help you strategize your growth and potential future sale. What type of companies are selling? What are the company's competitive advantages? Who is buying companies and who is being bought? How much are these companies selling for? Why are buyers buying and what plans do they have for the acquisition going forward? How is the deal structured? Do you notice any trends?

CONSIDER YOUR PERCEIVED VALUE

Numbers don't lie, but they also don't tell the whole story about how valuable a company is. In many cases, the true value lies in the eye of the beholder. What might be a great bet for one buyer might be a liability for another, and a buyer's reasons for being interested in a company might be unknowable or even illogical.

For example, I recently opened Clintonville Books, an independent bookstore in Columbus, Ohio. Bookstores are notoriously low-profit businesses and the model represents everything I've cautioned against so far in this book. Bookstores are asset-heavy, geographically limited, and usually require several employees and a lot of consistent manual work to generate revenue.

They also have nothing to do with personal finance or investing, aside from selling some books on those subjects. But I am an avid reader and love being surrounded by physical books. I even collect antiquarian books. Without books, I never would have become a millionaire by thirty, if at all, and I am constantly buying new books and recommending my favorites to friends. Independent bookstores provide tremendous value to their communities.

The only reason I'm starting a bookstore from scratch is that the only other bookstore in my area that I was interested in acquiring had no interest in selling. But if they were, how I would calculate an offer to buy a bookstore would probably vary greatly from how another local bookstore owner would. I would have paid over market rate for their stores because of their locations and the time they could have saved me.

There are many reasons one company may want to acquire another company, beyond the numbers reflected on their P&L. They might buy a company because doing so allows them to:

- Expand into a new but related sector
- Expand into a new territory
- Save money on customer acquisition costs
- Save money on production or sourcing costs
- Attract a new customer demographic
- Acquire proprietary technology or intellectual property
- Eliminate a competitor

I set up Millennial Money as an affiliate business that earned revenue by referring our website's visitors to other vendors who paid us a commission whenever someone purchased from them through one of our affiliate links. This helped us grow, but when the Motley Fool acquired Millennial Money in 2020, they completely revamped the business model. For them, using the site to promote their products was much more lucrative than earning a commission from a competitor.

The value was not in the affiliate model but in the traffic we had built to our site. Instead of buying advertising or building their own millennial-focused content platform, they used their money to acquire us because they believed it would be more efficient to build on what we already had. If another affiliate-based media business had acquired us instead, they no doubt would have kept our model intact.

Your job as an owner looking to sell is to position yourself in the eyes of each particular buyer. Often, the companies interested in acquiring you are looking at several companies and comparing their value. That means the burden is on you to make the case for why your company is the best investment. You want to have that story ready early on, so the more you know about what they're looking for and where your value lies, the easier it will be. You want to determine their needs and opportunities and explain how you can fulfill them.

For example, one of the companies I own, BankBonus.com, helps users choose bank accounts and credit cards depending on their needs. Like all our businesses, it earns revenue through affiliate commissions, primarily through banks. The most obvious buyer for a website like this is a large bank like Chase, which is already a bank we recommend and get affiliate revenue from. Currently, Chase has to pay for all the traffic we send to their site—and they're still competing with the other affiliates we work with. If Chase bought BankBonus.com, they could eliminate the other affiliate partnerships and convert all the traffic to their products. They could also use their resources to scale it and drive more traffic, which means they'd be increasing their revenues while simultaneously reducing expenses. By identifying this potential upside, I've made it incredibly easy for them to make me an offer.

You can also use the needs of potential buyers as a filter to make better business decisions. This is especially important when expanding your product or service line because it can help you limit your choices. For example, a potential buyer like Chase would be interested in a tool that matches website visitors to mortgage loan officers. So I built one. Meanwhile, they likely wouldn't get much use out of a YouTube channel, which I'm sure would offer a lot of value to my target audience. Even if you're growing rapidly, you still have limited resources. Having another barometer to help you make decisions makes you more agile and efficient.

HOW TO GET THE BEST DEAL AND THE BEST TERMS

The best way to get the best deal is to find multiple companies that want to acquire your business and have them bid against each other. Three companies wanted to acquire Millennial Money, and two went head-to-head to present the highest offer. The Motley Fool had the highest offer and I also believed they would be the best buyer because our missions were similar and they had many resources to grow the business.

You might assume that the best deal is the one that pays you the most money, but there are an infinite number of ways to structure deals. While some sellers are looking for the biggest payout, others are willing to take less money and sell to a company more aligned with their values or future plans. Others might sell to a company they believe will keep building it and preserve its legacy over time.

You might be more interested in getting as much cash up front as possible. Or you might want to forgo a huge up-front cash payment in exchange for equity in the buyer's business to minimize your immediate tax burden and maximize the upside. Some deals involve a combination of cash, equity, and other forms of compensation.

While there are many valuation models that you can use, the reality is that someone will pay you whatever they think the business is worth to them. Business valuation methods can vary depending on the industry, the company's size, profitability, and other factors. However, buyers typically use one of several traditional approaches:

1. **Market Valuation:** Look at how much similar businesses in your industry have sold for recently. You can find this information in press releases or SEC filings. Sometimes brokers can also help you find this information or you can uncover it in industry reports. In my industry, I maintain close relationships with different brokers, who often fill me in on the information they know about recent sales.

2. **Multiples Valuation:** Use ratios or multiples from similar businesses to estimate your business's value. This includes

looking at things like revenue. I sold Millennial Money based on a multiple of 7.2 times the past twelve months of total revenue. In my industry, businesses typically sell for 2 to 5 times, so I made above industry averages. It's also common to use a multiple of earnings before interest, taxes, depreciation, and amortization (EBITDA) instead of revenue for larger businesses. EBIDTA shows how much profit the company is making from its main operations before taking out certain expenses like taxes and loan payments. Critics of EBITA-based valuations believe they can be misleading because there's no standard way to calculate it, making it easy to manipulate.

3. **Income-Based Valuation:** Estimate your business's value based on its ability to generate income for the owner or cash flows in the future. This includes looking at things like projected future earnings or discounted cash flow. Some common income-based valuation methods include:

    Seller's Discretionary Earnings (SDE) or Owner's Discretionary Income (ODI): This looks at the income a buyer could expect to receive from the business. It's typically used to value small businesses, especially those with a single owner-operator, closely held family businesses, and businesses with less than $1 million in annual revenue. It's also a common valuation method in cases where the business's financial records may only partially reflect its true earning potential or when there are significant owner-related expenses. It's referred to as SDE when you're a seller and ODI when you're a buyer.

    Discounted Cash Flow (DCF): This estimates the present value of a business's future cash flows by considering the time value of money. The "time value of money" refers to the concept that money available today is worth more than the same amount of money in the future, due to its potential earning capacity. This principle reflects the opportunity cost of not having the money now, which you could invest to earn interest or other returns.

Imagine you want to buy a lemonade stand. You know it will earn you $100 yearly for the next five years. However, money today is more valuable than money in the future because you can invest it and earn interest. You want to determine how much the lemonade stand is worth today. You apply a discount rate, say 10 percent per year, to account for the time value of money. Using a DCF calculator, you find that the present value of all those future earnings is approximately $379 in today's money. So, you might be willing to pay up to $379 for today's lemonade stand.

Capitalization of Earnings: This approach determines the value of a business by dividing its expected annual earnings by a capitalization rate. Just as you might expect a 7 percent average return per year for investing in a stock index fund, your capitalization rate is the return on investment you expect from owning the business. Most business owners want at least a 10 percent return or more per year for owning a business.

To calculate a business's expected value using the capitalization of earnings approach, business owners first need to determine its expected annual earnings. This involves calculating or estimating the business's expected annual earnings based on historical earnings and adjusting for any known future changes or trends. Next, they need to decide on a capitalization rate, which is the rate of return an investor expects to earn from the business. This rate is often expressed as a percentage. For example, if an investor expects a 10 percent return, the capitalization rate would be 10 percent. Finally, the business owner can apply the capitalization of earnings formula to determine the value of the business, which is:

Business Value = Expected Annual Earnings / Capitalization Rate

For instance, if a business expects to earn $100,000 annually and the desired capitalization rate is 10 percent, the value of the business would be calculated as:

Business Value = $100,000 / 10% = $1,000,000

Using this approach, the business owner can determine that the business is worth $1,000,000 if they expect to earn $100,000 per year and desire a 10 percent return on investment.

Asset-Based Valuation: Figure out how much your business is worth based on what it owns, like buildings or equipment. Industries like manufacturing, real estate, or transportation, where assets comprise a huge portion, if not most, of the value, usually use this method.

For many businesses, especially those with strong customer relationships or unique intellectual property, valuation methods like the income-based approach or market approach may provide the most accurate reflection of their value. Valuing a business is industry-specific and often involves professional expertise from accountants, attorneys, business appraisers, financial advisers, or brokers to determine its worth accurately. You need to get familiar with the standards in your industry.

Once you have a sense of how much your company is potentially worth in dollars, you have a benchmark from which to negotiate. When discussing deal terms with a potential buyer, here are the key elements you want to consider and potentially negotiate.

TOTAL PURCHASE PRICE

The total purchase price is the agreed-upon purchase price for the business. This price is typically based on one or a collection of the valuation metrics we've discussed in this chapter. It's often agreed upon in early communication and then first formalized in the letter of intent (LOI). When you sign the LOI, you agree to work together to move the acquisition process forward and won't entertain other offers for a specified period—usually ninety days. However, it's unfortunately common practice for a buyer to present one offer in an LOI and then reduce the offer after the due diligence process, to try and get a better deal.

As the seller, you should be prepared for this to happen and have the lowest number in mind that you'd sell for. If the buyer's offer is still above that number, you should sell, or consider declining the offer if it's below what you want. You can also counter their offer and be clear that you'd be willing to call off the deal if they can't meet it. This is why you should trust whomever you move into due diligence with and be confident that you'll be able to get a deal done.

Next, you and the buyer must agree on how and when the total purchase price will be paid. There are several ways to do this:

Cash Up Front

This is the amount of cash that's paid up front for the business. For the seller, it is risk-free compared to other options because it is a guaranteed lump sum that doesn't rely on the business's future performance. I recommend getting as much cash up front as you can.

Earnout

An earnout is a way to buy or sell a company when the buyer and the seller can't agree on the value of the business. It's an agreement in which the buyer agrees to pay more money in the future if the company meets certain goals or targets after the sale. These targets can be things like making a certain amount of money, growing the business, or developing new products.

An earnout reduces the purchase risk for the buyer by tying some of the payment to the company's future performance. However, the seller takes on most of the risk because they don't have as much (if any) control over the company's performance after it's sold.

Earnouts can lead to disagreements if there are misunderstandings about how to measure the company's performance or if something unexpected happens that affects the company's ability to meet the targets. To avoid problems, it's important to have clear and specific terms in place.

Seller Financing

Seller financing is when the person selling a business helps the buyer pay for it by lending them money. This means the buyer doesn't have to rely only on banks or their own money to finance the purchase. The buyer and seller can negotiate the loan terms, such as how much interest the buyer will pay, how often they make payments, and what happens if they don't pay.

This is more flexible than getting a loan from a bank, so both sides can make an agreement that works for them. Seller financing can be helpful for buyers who don't have enough money to buy the business or who can't get a loan from a bank. When a seller offers financing, it shows they believe the company will be successful in the future. By lending money, they are saying they think the business will make enough money to pay back the loan.

For sellers, offering financing can attract buyers who couldn't buy the business otherwise. It can also make the seller more money because they can charge interest on the loan. But seller financing has risks, because if the business doesn't do well, the buyer might be unable to pay you. If they default, you'd get the business back, but you might not want it back or would rather have the money. Both the buyer and seller need to make sure they agree on the terms and understand what could go wrong.

Equity

In a business acquisition, the buyer can offer equity to the seller in several ways. One way is by giving the seller shares or stock in their existing business. This means the seller becomes a part owner of the buyer's business. Another way is through stock options or warrants, which give the seller the right to buy the buyer's stock at a set price within a specific time. The buyer might also issue convertible securities, which the seller can convert into the buyer's common stock later on, usually under specific conditions or at a certain time. Sometimes, an equity deal involves an earnout agreement wherein the seller might receive more shares or equity in the buyer's company based on how well the business performs after the sale. The buyer might also offer the seller a chance to invest in their company directly by buying shares or equity using cash or other assets from the sale.

Any equity compensation comes with risks because the value of the equity could go down over time if the business doesn't do well. This means you could get compensated with equity that ends up being worth very little or even nothing in the future. But on the flip side, if the company does well and its value goes up, then any form of equity compensation could be valuable.

All the forms of equity listed above are similar but may be taxed differently, so you should always discuss the options with your accountant, attorney, and broker if you're working with one, to fully understand how the equity would be given and your tax responsibility over time. Sometimes, you have to pay taxes immediately after getting equity grants, which can be very expensive. In other cases, you can defer tax into the future. Every situation will be unique and can have profound implications for the final amount you get for your business, so I recommend paying an expert for advice.

The best way to decide if equity compensation is worth it is to decide if you believe in the company's future prospects. Do they have good leadership in a growing industry? Do they have a unique competitive advantage? How well has their stock done in the past? Would you invest in this business otherwise? If you believe in the future potential of the business, then it's worth considering equity as part of your seller's compensation.

Consulting, Employment, and Noncompete Agreements

As part of the sale, the seller might enter into a consulting agreement in which the seller agrees to provide advisory services or guidance to the buyer for a specified period after the acquisition. The terms could include compensation for the seller's expertise, knowledge transfer, or assistance in the transition phase to ensure a smooth handover of operations.

In cases where the seller is a key figure in the business, the buyer might offer an employment contract or a job offer to retain the seller's services post-acquisition. This could involve the seller continuing in a leadership role within the acquired company or taking on a specific position that utilizes their expertise.

As part of the acquisition, the seller might agree not to compete with the buyer's business for a specified duration within a defined geographical area or industry. This agreement can be included to protect the buyer's interests and prevent the seller from starting a similar business that could compete with the acquired company. This is common practice, but doesn't prevent the seller from starting a new, noncompetitive business.

TIME YOUR EXIT ACCORDING TO THE MARKET

While it's impossible to predict the future, trends can be great indicators of where your market is heading. As you study the trends, look for different cycles in the market. There are always better times to buy and sell depending on what's happening. When interest rates are high and borrowing money is expensive, acquisition activity often slows down. When interest rates are low and money is cheap to borrow, acquisition activity often increases.

Also, industries can evolve rapidly; it may be a perfect time to sell if your market gets hot, or nearly impossible to sell if demand for your type of business has declined. Paying attention will help you take better advantage of those cycles. In my experience and from watching so many companies in my industry, most businesses wait too long to sell and miss the opportunity.

Selling a business is similar to selling a house: timing is everything. You want to time your sale when demand is high to command the highest price and most favorable terms possible. If you start noticing certain trends, it's time to consider selling:

- **A flurry of acquisitions within your industry:** Sometimes, rapid acquisitions mark a bubble—like the dot-com boom of the early 2000s. Other times it may mark the beginning of a longer-term trend. Either way, you can capitalize on the positive attention.
- **Increasing valuations:** If the sale price for companies in your industry trends upward, it's a sign that the sector is becoming increasingly valuable. This could be a gradual trend, but it's important to note so you can know what to expect when your time comes—and spot the market peak.
- **A strong economy:** When macroeconomic growth is strong, interest rates are usually low, so it's cheaper to borrow money to make investments. When interest rates increase, would-be buyers typically slow down their activity until a more favorable environment comes along. If you are ready to sell and notice talk of a recession or market downturn, consider selling before it's too late.
- **Shifting consumer behavior:** This may mark a temporary trend similar to a fad diet, fashion trend, food craze, or a major market disruption—like how the rise of streaming decimated the home video and DVD industry. You want to be on the lookout for things that will affect how you do business—new technologies, new safety concerns, new social, economic, or political priorities. As I write this, AI is poised to transform most industries in ways we are only beginning to predict. Savvy entrepreneurs are already looking for ways to adopt and adapt so they're not left behind.

If you don't want to sell or can't sell, you should keep growing your company at the pace and in the way you'd like. You can wait to try to sell when your business is more attractive to potential buyers or the timing is better. While selling your business might not always be possible, I encourage you to take each offer and opportunity seriously. If a company is interested in acquiring yours, and you're also interested in selling your business, you should move quickly to get the deal done. There are many moving pieces to any deal, and the sooner you can get going, the better. Most deals will take at least three to six months, if not longer, to go through and a lot can happen in that time frame.

Make sure you work with an accountant if you are planning to sell your business in the future, as there are many things an intelligent accountant can set up early on to minimize the complexity and tax implications of a business sale.

The world is moving faster than ever and opportunities are changing rapidly, so even if your business is doing well and you enjoy running it, you might want to sell it whenever you can. This is what I did, and I'm happy with my decision. I know a few of my friends and competitors weren't as lucky and declined very strong offers to acquire their businesses or they didn't move quickly enough, so they missed the opportunity. One had a $50 million offer that got rescinded because the company's board fired the CEO and pulled the acquisition, which had been in the works for months. Another declined an offer for $12 million, hoping to wait until he could get $15 million and a few months later lost over half his traffic in a Google algorithm update. This stuff happens all the time.

Yes, there are stories of entrepreneurs like Mark Zuckerberg declining a $1 billion offer from Yahoo for Facebook in 2006, and now he's one of the top ten richest people in the world with a personal net worth of $117 billion, but the reality is that most businesses fail. Anytime someone offers you a lot of money for your business, you should take it seriously. And even if you have no plans to sell your business, you should build it so it will be easier to sell if you one day have an offer you can't refuse.

LEVEL 4
THE EMPIRE ENTREPRENEUR

It didn't feel real. As I lay by the pool at the house I'd rented in Palm Springs, I refreshed my net-worth tracking app every few hours to make sure. Yes, it was true. It was December of 2020 and I was a few days shy of my thirty-fifth birthday. Two months earlier, I'd sold Millennial Money for a life-changing amount of money. It was one of those rare life moments that surpasses the hype. I'd sold my business, and I had no idea what I would do next. I thought seriously about retiring early and spending the next decades hanging out doing whatever I wanted.

I spent the next year and a half taking it easy. My wife and I bought our first house, one with enough rooms to each have an office, accommodate a few kids, and have space left over for guests. I mowed the lawn every Saturday, bought a grill, and tinkered with my old moped in my garage. I worked on my VW camper, watched the sunsets, and walked my dog through the park. I slept in every day. I worked through the mountain of books I'd built over the years. Many days were spent just lying around reading. I spent a lot of time deepening my meditation practice.

It's amazing how you expand into the space and time you open for yourself.

I enjoyed it, but eventually, I started to get the itch to create something new. I'm happiest when I'm creating and growing. When I don't create anything new and I'm not getting enough high-quality inputs and stimulation, and when I'm not expanding as a person, I start to get down. After a year and a half of living a simple, minimal life, I was ready to build again.

First, I created a list of the things I didn't want to do. Because I know that freedom exists only within limits, I started writing down my limits. I didn't want to trade my time for money, have an office, be tied to a physical location, have employees, have clients, travel much, take on outside investors, have any physical assets to manage, or add any unnecessary stress to my life. I didn't want to work on a set schedule, and I wanted to take extended time off whenever I felt like it. I also didn't want to do anything that was too easy because I knew it wouldn't keep me engaged.

After I'd outlined my limits, deciding what I wanted to do was easier. I decided to do two things I love: keep writing books and building a new business.

But this time, I would do it a little differently. I wanted to write this book, but I didn't want the aggressive timeline I had with the first book or to dedicate all my time to writing. I wanted to take more time and write it at a more leisurely pace, so I could have time to start a new company and, hopefully, also have a kid.

I also didn't want to build the same type of business I'd previously built, so I decided to build a different kind of company that didn't limit what I could create and invest in. I started a holding company. This is the future of entrepreneurship. Instead of having one company and putting all your eggs in one basket, you can build a company that holds many companies and invests in other types of assets. You can create a holding company with adaptability and resilience at its core.

I'd go so far as to argue that holding companies provide the perfect structure to maximize your financial returns and happiness amid an increasingly uncertain future. There's a reason why Jay-Z, Adele, Pharrell, and pretty much any savvy creator, investor, or entrepreneur at the upper echelons diversify their investments through holding companies. They own and invest in multiple businesses. They don't build one business. They build empires.

Now that you've grown your business to a certain size—or have decided to sell your business—you need to figure out what's next. At this stage, even if you haven't sold, it might not make sense to keep reinvesting money in the same business if there's no smart way to do so. I see far too many entrepreneurs who keep throwing money back into a business that doesn't need it or waste money by reinvesting in tactics or strategies that aren't good uses of money. If you don't have a good use for each dollar your business makes, then it's smart to look at what you can invest in outside of the business.

While there are many legal structures and entities you can set up to do this efficiently, I'm a big fan of doing it within a holding company—think of Warren Buffett and Charlie Munger's Berkshire Hathaway. But you don't need to build a multibillion-dollar company with this structure. A holding company is similar to an LLC in its structure and can be infinitely customized to support your business goals. It can also easily evolve and grow as you change.

We'll spend the next few chapters discussing how to set up and build a holding company, with particular emphasis on assessing and acquiring existing companies to add to it. I'll share exactly how I'm finding companies to acquire and the process to acquire them.

Even if you're starting out in your entrepreneurial journey or aren't ready to start a holding company yet, knowing what they are and how they work is useful because it allows you to think big and see what's possible.

CHAPTER 13

ESTABLISH A HOLDING COMPANY TO GROW YOUR EMPIRE

"The only way you survive is you continuously transform into something else."
—Ginni Rometty, former CEO of IBM

Between now, as I'm writing this, and 2030, more than $7 trillion worth of businesses will be sold as baby boomer business owners move into retirement. This once-in-a-generation buying opportunity is open to anyone interested in buying a business and leveraging entrepreneurship to create more freedom.

While you can buy a business and run it, the future of entrepreneurship is creating and running a diversified holding company that is recession- and climate-change resistant, with adaptability and resilience built into its core. Amid increasing uncertainty, the holding company structure allows one business to pick up the slack if another in your portfolio struggles. It also allows you to leverage centralized teams and economies of scale that reduce expenses, increase revenue, and increase profit. Once used only by the superrich to build massive empires, holding companies are now easier to create than ever before.

A holding company is an entity that is created to manage and/or invest in other companies and assets. You can use your holding company to buy companies or invest in stocks, real estate, nonprofits, patents, and pretty much any other asset class. You can also use a holding company to separate the divisions of your existing company into different entities, protecting each one legally and financially. Setting up a holding company is pretty simple, but it's worth paying for professional legal, financial, and tax support so you can make sure it's structured for your specific goals and to maximize the benefits.

If you currently own a company, you can start a separate holding company as a "parent" company and then place your existing company underneath it without impacting the current operations, finances, or taxes of your existing business. If you don't currently own a business or you're starting from scratch, you can easily set up a holding company and start building or acquiring companies or assets underneath it. Any company you own underneath your holding company is known as a "subsidiary company," and any business owned entirely by your holding company is known as a "wholly owned subsidiary."

This hierarchy helps separate all your businesses so they have additional financial, legal, and tax protection and can be managed as subsidiaries. The most significant financial advantage is that you can use the cash flow from one or many of the businesses to invest in the companies that need the cash the most to grow or to buy new companies.

You can also stash the cash in a safe asset class like a high-yield savings or money market account or certificates of deposit while you wait for a good use for it. There's a reason Warren Buffett is sitting on over $130 billion in cash as I write this. He has so much money coming in from Berkshire Hathaway's holdings that it would be irresponsible to reinvest it in most of his businesses. It's better for him to hold the money and let it earn interest or returns while he waits for a worthwhile investment.

In addition to managing cash flow, you can use your holding company to create immense tax efficiency in several ways, depending on how the holding company is set up. Within a holding company, there are two levels of taxes—the corporate taxes the subsidiary companies pay on the profit they generate and the tax that the holding company pays based on the percentage dividend they receive from their subsidiary companies. The real tax advantage comes because holding companies can deduct the losses of one company from the gains of another company across their subsidiaries, minimizing the tax burden at the holding company level. As a majority owner of the holding company, you can keep the tax burden within the holding company by not selling any of your stock or ownership stake in your holding company.

It's worthwhile to pay for good professional help when setting up your holding company because the money you will save in taxes from ensuring you have the right structure should more than cover the initial setup fees. Tax laws change frequently, so it's worth retaining or hiring a full-time, experienced accountant specializing in your industry to continue optimizing your portfolio and minimizing your tax burden.

Another significant advantage of a holding company is that it offers substantial legal protection, so if one company gets sued, the assets of the holding company and its subsidiaries are protected. You can also protect your other businesses if you need to deal with creditors.

THE FOUR TYPES OF HOLDING COMPANIES

The type of holding company you'll want to set up depends on how similar the businesses in your portfolio are and your business goals. There are four types, none of which are mutually exclusive. It's common to have a Type 4 holding company that includes a Type 1 company within its holdings.

1. **Type 1: The Roll-Up**—This is when you have a holding company that owns companies with a lot of overlap and similar businesses. For example, if you buy all the dog-washing companies in your city, combine them into one company and consolidate the customer service, accounting, and marketing teams for all of them, this is a roll-up holding company. Within a roll-up holding company, you'll typically still own more than one company—some will be roll-ups, while others can be related but still separate companies (e.g., a dog-washing business, a dog-walking business, and a local pet store chain). Roll-ups are particularly useful structures for commodity products or services with a lot of scalability potential.

2. **Type 2: Platform Holding Company**—As with a roll-up, the platform holding company holds several companies within the same industry, all of which leverage the same operational teams. The difference is that platform companies aren't all rolled into one entity; they are treated as separate and are individually known as "platform companies." This is the type of holding company MMG Media Group currently is, but I plan to evolve it into a Type 3 soon and potentially into a Type 4 one day.

3. **Type 3: Aggregator**—This is when your holding company holds companies in multiple industries, but they leverage the same teams and operational economies of scale. If I buy my local tree-trimming company and put it under MMG Media Group, I would own personal finance websites and a tree-trimming company. The economies of scale would be limited to my using the same bookkeeper for both, as well as the same technology, systems, and processes to manage lead volume across my businesses.

4. **Type 4: HoldCo**—This is a traditional holding company where you own different types of businesses that don't have much, if any, overlap, so there aren't many synergies. Each business is operated as its own company with redundant functions across your holding company. Each company has its own customer service, marketing, and other independent teams. This has unlimited scaling potential. Berkshire Hathaway is a great example: it owns Dairy Queen and Geico, two entirely different companies that function independently, but the cash generated by each can be used to buy or invest in other companies at the holding company level.

Let's dig into Type 4 and Berkshire Hathaway more specifically. Berkshire Hathaway is the most successful holding company of all time. It has been managed by CEO and cochair Warren Buffett since 1965 and cochair Charlie Munger since 1978 until his death in 2023.

Today, Berkshire Hathaway owns all or part of more than 100 companies, employs more than 380,000 people, and generates an annual revenue of more than $300 billion.

While it derives most of its operating income through its portfolio of more than seventy insurance companies (including Geico), it also invests in diverse areas such as automotive dealerships, utilities, restaurants, retail, media, air travel, and manufacturing. Among the brands it owns outright or has voting stock in are Dairy Queen, See's Candies, the Pampered Chef, Fruit of the Loom, BNSF, Duracell, and Apple. But you don't have to operate at nearly this scale to take lessons from its example.

The Berkshire Hathaway blueprint has been written about extensively, and if you're interested in the idea of creating a holding company or investing, I strongly recommend that you go straight to the source and read Warren Buffett's annual Berkshire Hathaway shareholder letters, which you can easily find online. They are chock-full of wisdom, and Buffett is transparent about how he runs his holding company. There's no better place to learn than from the masters. Two great books you should read are *Buffett: The Making of an American Capitalist* by Roger Lowenstein and *Poor Charlie's Almanack* by Charles T. Munger.

Here are a few of Buffet and Munger's insights about holding companies and investing that have most impacted me:

- Stay within your "circle of competence," meaning invest only in things you understand. It's often less risky to invest in a business you know as opposed to a business you have to learn.
- You only need to pick one really good investment every five years. This one is tough for me because I want to invest in so many things, but I'm getting better at being patient and looking for better opportunities.
- You will make several lousy investments, but one great one will more than make up for all the rest. Don't let a few mistakes discourage you from continuing to build and diversify.
- Work with people you trust who have complementary skill sets. The only way to manage a bunch of companies at one

time is by having good people who work at your holding company level and good people who manage your companies. You should focus on your strengths and have other people do everything else. This also removes you from the day-to-day and gives you the opportunity to be in control of your time.

FIVE SIGNS IT'S TIME TO START A HOLDING COMPANY

You'll know it's time to consider starting a holding company when you reach certain milestones.

1. You're Generating Too Much Cash to Invest Back in Your Business Responsibly

When the marginal rate of return on your investments within your current business starts to decline, it's time to look elsewhere for opportunities. You can always find something to spend money on—and those things may grow your business. But you need to consider the best use of a dollar. Is the number of sales generated from spending an additional dollar on ads worth as much as the return you could get investing that dollar in the stock market? Or investing in another company that is growing rapidly?

You'll likely recognize when you can't reinvest any more money in your business efficiently, but the simplest way to recognize it is that your profit margin, return on ad spend, or total sales volume has plateaued despite your increased investments. Of course, these slumps can happen for many reasons, and you don't want to simply stop your marketing efforts if sales have plateaued. But they are a sign that you need to do something different, and different doesn't have to mean dumping more of your cash back into the business. There's often a limit to how much you can reinvest in the company before you end up seeing diminishing returns.

Many companies and entrepreneurs I've worked with throw money down the drain by constantly testing new marketing channels and competitive tactics or continuing to spend large sums of money on tactics that are no longer profitable. As we've discussed, with paid-marketing channels specifically, you often need to pivot or take advantage of a limited window of opportunity before your competitors copy what you're doing and costs increase.

You might be able to keep reinvesting money in your business with diminishing returns, but you need to determine a floor. My personal target profit margin is consistently above 40 percent, and I never go below 20 percent, because it's simply not worth the overhead and risk in my business.

Remember, not all value is monetary. Is investing money in your company bringing your life as much value as it would if you spent that money to help a local nonprofit you support or hire a new full-time staff member? Does the idea of entering a new industry or buying into your friend's start-up excite you more than the idea of opening a second location or expanding the product line of your current business? You can't quantify some things through your profit and loss statement.

2. You Identify a Potential Risk to Your Core Business

If you've built your business around a trend or technology at risk of becoming obsolete, you must protect your assets if your business becomes unviable or needs to adapt quickly. If you run a pool-cleaning business in an area on the verge of being massively impacted by climate change, the chances of your remaining profitable as your customers are displaced might be small. In the meantime, there is still a need for your services, but it doesn't make sense to continue trying to grow as you perceive an increasing amount of risk. You're better off investing excess profit in another venture or pivoting your business.

As I write this, there is an impending threat in my industry of AI disrupting content writers, websites, and Google search results. Because of this, I'm already starting to invest in websites that I think are less likely to be impacted as heavily by AI. For example, will Google's AI be able to give you finance advice? That seems risky for Google and legally challenging, although I'm not saying it won't happen. The future is uncertain, but the more attuned you are to the changing forces and their *actual* threat to your business, not just the hype, the easier it will be for you to pivot.

Home-service companies are so attractive because AI can't come out and fix your plumbing. Meanwhile, online business moves much faster and requires you to adapt and evolve more quickly than many traditional industries as consumer preferences change.

3. It's a Buyer's Market

Market forces in most industries are constantly shifting, so it's essential to pay attention to the market dynamics in your industry and industries in which you're interested in acquiring a company. You can do this by following industry research, paying attention to conversations online, and connecting with brokers, who are often willing to share tons of free information about the market to build a relationship with you in the hope that you will one day work with them.

I have consistent ongoing conversations with five different brokers in my industry every few months, and we openly share market insights. They ask me what's happening on the ground floor of my finance-content portfolio, and I ask them what's happening in the buyer and seller's market. These relationships are incredibly fruitful, and I encourage you to seek out and build relationships with brokers in your industry.

Have you noticed another business in your community or industry that is doing well and has captivated your interest? Or a company that used to be thriving but is now struggling? Is there some disruption going on in your market that has left owners freaking out about how to adapt? Whenever Google announces another algorithm update that will impact search rankings, some affiliate-based website owners experience a big decline in revenue because customers stop being able to find their site.

Because of my knowledge of digital marketing and SEO, I know how to navigate many of these changes and use the uncertainty of others as an opportunity. I keep a list of companies I'm interested in and continually look for opportunities to expand and strengthen my portfolio of sites. Not only do I reach out, but as our reputation at MMG

Media Group has grown, more website owners looking to sell or partner up are reaching out to us. My market is going through an immense shift and more owners are looking to sell. Because of these market shifts, my industry has gone from being a seller's market, where websites were regularly being sold for record multiples, to a buyer's market, where valuations have come down considerably, and there are many deals for buyers like me who are looking to add to their portfolio. This could radically shift back to a seller's market at any time, so I'm trying to take advantage of it now.

4. You Spot a Market Opportunity

The more experience you gain as an entrepreneur, the better you get at spotting opportunities to make money. I see new business opportunities everywhere—from sectors like media and financial services, where I have historically owned companies, to industries where I have no experience but can spot shifting trends, to markets I'd never previously paid attention to except as a hobby.

You don't necessarily need direct experience in an industry to succeed in it. Most entrepreneurial skills are transferable, and there are probably tools and systems you can use from your current or previous experiences to grow a business within a completely different sector. As I'm writing this, I'm in the middle of setting up Clintonville Books, my brick-and-mortar bookstore. While I frequent bookstores and collect books, I've never owned a bookstore or a retail store or even worked in retail. But I'm finding the skills I've gained as an entrepreneur to be invaluable in rapidly learning the industry. The fresh perspective, coupled with experience and curiosity, helps me see opportunities that others don't.

In the past few years, I've considered buying a gas station, an HVAC company, a literary agency, a community arts center, a warehouse, and many other things. One of my favorite things to do in my free time is search for businesses that are up for sale on websites like https://buybizsell.com, https://loopnet.com, and https://acquire .com. However, I don't recommend buying physical businesses through websites, as brokers often list them only as a last resort when they can't sell them through their networks. It will be harder to find a good deal.

It's better to establish relationships with brokers who can provide you with a constant stream of new deals, also known as "deal flow." But these websites are great for learning, and you can get a good sense of the economics of many types of businesses. Then, you can watch a few YouTube videos to identify the risks and challenges of these business models more specifically. Just yesterday, I watched a video on the pros and cons of buying a FedEx delivery route and quickly determined it was not a great business, as prices are set by corporate, and contract delivery labor is hard to manage.

No matter the industry, I'm confident I could use my digital marketing and financial management expertise to grow pretty much any business if there is an opportunity, which makes the bigger question of whether or not to focus my time there right now. Just because I *can* buy and grow a business doesn't mean I *should*. I now actively convince myself to not get into new businesses and industries when I see opportunities—and there are always opportunities.

If you're paying attention, the opportunities will show up. It's like the energy you put into the world returning to you tenfold. It's not that difficult when you're curious.

5. You're Ready for a New Challenge

If you want to grow as a person and an entrepreneur, there's a limit to what a single business can teach you. At a certain point, you'll need to expand your horizons to satisfy your entrepreneurial spirit. There is nothing wrong with cashing out from your business and using your investments to fund your lifestyle for the rest of your life. And if your goal with growing your business has been to officially retire early and spend your life doing things that do not generate a financial return, then who am I to tell you not to follow your bliss?

But humans are wired to create. We get bored if we're not busy and solving problems. Once you understand how money grows and how you can leverage your resources, talents, and systems to create more value for yourself and others, it can be tough to walk away forever. You can add a lot of value to the world that cannot be quantified in dollars, but because money is such a powerful tool, you will often find that some of the best ways you can have an impact are by leveraging your skills and resources to make money.

Money becomes a by-product of your creation, which you can reinvest in the world as you see fit. Exploring other companies and industries is one way to add another level of richness, excitement, and expansion to your life as your entrepreneurial journey unfolds.

HOW TO SET UP A HOLDING COMPANY

You can set up your holding company as a limited partnership, LLC, or corporation and incorporate your existing company underneath it. All you need to do is pick a name for the holding company and register your company in the state where you'll operate or where you want to be registered (Delaware is one favorite because of its anonymity, its tax treatment, and its laws that tend to favor LLCs); submit the state filling fee (typically between $100 and $500); get any licenses or permits that might be required to be a business in your state; register your business online with the IRS and get a FEIN (federal employer identification number) that you will use to file your taxes and fill out W-9 forms; and then draft an operating agreement for the company that states all the rules and bylaws.

The operating agreement outlines in detail the structure of how your business works and operates. Depending on how you want your holding company to work and function, it can vary in complexity. Pretty much anything is possible, so this is why working with an expert is so important. While you don't file your operating agreement with the IRS, it's important to be thorough in order to guide your operation and any agreements with partners and investors. The total cost to set up the holding company with expert advice will vary but should be no more than $2,500 to $10,000, depending on your operation's complexity level.

Now that you know the signs and how to set up your holding company, the next question is:

What Do You Want to Invest In?

As I've noted, under a holding company, you can invest and grow your money through pretty much anything, but there are some tried-and-true asset classes that are easier to invest in and have more predictable or manageable returns. There are also many ways to invest in these asset classes. Let's dig into them.

Real Estate Is Durable and Has Exceptional Tax Advantages

I once heard a great quote (unfortunately, I can't remember who said it): "Eventually every successful business becomes a real estate business." The reason is that real estate has so many tax advantages, and as businesses grow, it becomes a no-brainer opportunity.

The benefit of owning real estate within a holding company is that you can generate consistent cash flow through rental income. You can also leverage a bank's money by taking out a loan or mortgage to buy the property, giving you the ability to add assets to your portfolio that increase in value as you pay down the mortgage and the property appreciates in value—without having to put much of your own money in up front. Investing in real estate also has incredible tax advantages that you can use across your holding company since rental income and appreciation can be kept within the company and reinvested in something else.

There are additional tax advantages to owning real estate within your holding company instead of holding it personally. When real estate is in a corporation, you can take a deduction for depreciation over the expected life of the asset, reducing your tax bill every year based on a percentage of the original asset purchase. You can also deduct mortgage interest and principal payments if the real estate is being used to make a profit. You can also deduct legal fees and other expenses incurred while managing the property.

A real estate business is different from other types of businesses, so some entrepreneurs advise you to stay in your lane. But whether you're a pro real estate investor or not, it's worth considering whether you should own the physical building your business is in, own an office building where you have an office, or simply start investing in residential or commercial real estate, either directly by owning them through your holding company or indirectly by investing in them through REITs (real estate investment trusts).

Owning the building your business is in is one way to de-risk your business by diversifying into another asset class. You can also get the added benefit of using the money you'd spend on rent to pay down your mortgage, all while the property appreciates. You also don't have to worry about your rent increasing, because you own the building.

Stocks in Public Companies as Passive Investments

Whenever you buy stock in a company, you are buying a piece of ownership. If you own Apple stock, every time someone buys a new iPhone, they are buying it, in part, from you. The great thing about stock ownership is you're a passive owner. You buy the stock, sit back, and make or lose money as the value of the company and its stock grows or declines. You don't have to make any decisions about how Apple is managed.

As a holding company, you can buy and sell stock within your holding company and get greater tax advantages than you could by buying and selling that stock within your personal brokerage or retirement account. Buying stock within a holding company has many tax, financial, and legal advantages, including the ability to offset gains or losses of selling your holdings across your subsidiary companies. You can structure your holding company so you can divide the gains or losses among your subsidiary companies, and they are not typically reflected on one consolidated balance sheet for the entire group. Instead, each subsidiary company maintains its separate financial statements, including its own balance sheet, income statement, and cash-flow statement.

Berkshire Hathaway started investing in Apple in 2016 and now owns 5.8 percent of Apple through its stock holdings. Warren Buffett uses the cash flow from his other companies, like Geico, to buy stock ownership across various companies within his holding company. Within the past few years, Berkshire Hathaway has generated many billions of dollars of profit from simply owning this stock within its holding company. In 2022, the company received approximately $823.5 million in dividends from Apple alone, and they didn't sell a single share, so the value of their holdings also continued to grow.

Direct Investment in Private Companies

In addition to buying stock of an established company in the public markets, you can also use excess cash flow within your holding company to invest directly in private companies that are raising money or looking to grow. There are many ways to do this. You could invest through special purchasing vehicles (SPVs) where you invest directly in a company alongside a venture or investment fund, or you could go even further and create your own fund, venture capital, or investment company to invest in start-ups looking for capital. It is increasingly common to see "venture" divisions or companies within holding companies that invest in new start-ups and make riskier investments in newer private companies.

Over the past few years I've have the opportunity to invest in over twenty-five private companies and start-ups alongside OpenAI, Jeff Bezos, Samsung, Nvidia, and other investors. While direct investments in private companies are historically risky, they present incredible upside opportunities as investments. It's also increasingly common for entrepreneurs with extensive experience, or those who own companies within a particular industry, to start a venture firm. Harry Campbell (aka the Rideshare Guy) is so well known in the rideshare space, he recently created an investment fund backed by Bloomberg to invest in seed-stage rideshare start-ups because he has so many connections and access to so many deals.

Buy a Business That Is Already Profitable

Buying a profitable business can be extremely lucrative because you can buy a business for two to three times an owner's annual profit and then earn and grow the profit for the next ten, twenty, or even forty-plus years. Additionally, you can increase that income by growing the business, and you only have to pay the first two to three years of current income to do so. That's an insane upside.

Whether you're selling or buying, the way you value a business is typically the same. In the previous chapter, I covered the four most popular valuation methods (market valuation, multiples valuation, income-based valuation, and asset-based valuation). To illustrate how to calculate a potential return on investment, I'm going to use the income-based valuation method for the owner's discretionary income (ODI), which is the income a buyer could expect to receive from the business. It's referred to as seller's discretionary earnings (SDE) when you're a seller and as ODI when you're a buyer.

You can easily calculate your return on investment for buying a company:

Using the hypothetical example of buying a business for $200,000 without a loan and an ODI of $100,000 per year, the rate of return would be ($100,000 − $0) / $200,000 = .5x or 50 percent return on your investment in year one. The returns can add up significantly if you push this out over ten years.

To calculate the return over a multiple-year period, you add a multiplier for the holding period as follows:

Return on Investment (ROI) = ((ODI − loan repayment) x Holding Period) / Initial Investment

Here's a simplified example to illustrate the calculation using the same numbers above over a ten-year hold period:

ROI = ($100,000 x 10) / $200,000

ROI = $1,000,000 / $200,000

ROI = 5x or 500%

In this example, the company is expected to generate a return of five times the current ODI over the next ten years. That's a 500 percent return! And that's if the ODI stays the same. Just imagine the return if you increase your ODI substantially by growing the business.

At this stage, you've established yourself as a legitimate, profitable company, which means you should either have the cash to buy a company outright or you would qualify for a low-interest loan from a bank, the government via an SBA loan, a private investor, seller financing, or a mixture of a few of these options.

Realistically, you'll need to put down 10 to 25 percent of the purchase price, but you can finance the rest. The nice thing about a loan, if you need one, is that it allows you to keep 100 percent ownership of the business. It's also easier to get a loan when you're buying a business that's already profitable and you might be able to buy a business that generates a much higher ODI because you're using a loan. Buying a profitable business also reduces your risk since you're investing in a proven business model and can potentially grow the business beyond its current revenue by reducing inefficiencies, launching new products, expanding into new markets, and more.

Buying a business at 2 to 3 times its earnings is significantly cheaper and potentially a much better value than buying publicly traded tech stocks like Apple, Google, and Amazon that routinely sell for 30 times their earnings. Or real estate development stocks that sell for 43 times on average. You can see what any stock is selling for relative to earnings by looking up its P/E (price to earnings) ratio.

Let's look at the potential returns of buying a business compared to other asset classes, using a hypothetical company with $100,000 a year in (ODI) and an acquisition price of $200,000 (2x ODI).

ASSET CLASS/ INVESTMENT VEHICLE	EXPECTED ANNUAL RATE OF RETURN ON INVESTMENT (ROI)	ANNUAL RETURN ON $200K INVESTMENT
High Yield Savings Account	5%	$8,000
Total Stock Market Index Fund	7%	$14,000

Investment in Private Company via Private Equity	10.48%	$20,960
Residential Real Estate	10.6%	$21,200
Buying a Business	50%+	$100,000

Buying an existing business that's already profitable can be a low-risk investment to expand your empire. When you buy a profitable business, you're acquiring not only profit and cash flow but an existing customer base, a brand, internal processes, competitive advantage, and more. Not only can you buy a profitable business without needing to take all the risks of starting a business from scratch, but you can also buy businesses for a much smaller amount of money than you might think. However, you do have to run the business after you buy it!

I'll dive deeper into the acquisition process in the next chapter.

CHAPTER 14

HOW TO IDENTIFY ACQUISITION OPPORTUNITIES

"The investor's chief problem—and even his worst enemy—is likely to be himself."

—Benjamin Graham

A few months ago, I considered buying a warehouse near my home in Columbus, Ohio. It was in a great location and priced as a bargain in an off-market deal. My friend knew the seller and introduced us. As I've gotten used to buying, growing, and selling digital businesses, I've become curious about physical ones. Even though the profit margins of physical businesses are lower than digital ones, there's still a large profit potential. I'm also interested in investing in old-school, tried-and-true recession-proof businesses to diversify my assets.

I looked at this property's finances and realized there was a ton of inefficiency I could fix to reduce expenses and increase revenue. It seemed like a great deal and I was excited about it. I got very close to making an offer, but then I got an expert to interpret the soil-testing and level-two environmental-testing results previously conducted on the building site.

Unfortunately, the warehouse was built on an old railroad coal yard, and the soil was highly toxic and full of carcinogenic chemicals that would not only be potentially very harmful to me and any tenants but would also expose me to an immense amount of legal liability. It was so bad that the company couldn't even estimate how much it would have cost to remediate the toxic soil, only saying it could cost into the millions and take over five years. I knew immediately I was in over my head.

It's not that I realized the deal was bad; I realized it was bad for me. I have no experience with soil remediation or zoning laws and am not interested in learning about it now. Someone else will buy that warehouse—and they will probably make money on it by hopefully fixing the issue before rezoning it for condos—but I wasn't willing to trade my time and energy for the profit it could realize.

There are tens of thousands of companies for sale on any given day, and there are always deals to be had. But just because you *can* buy a company and make it profitable doesn't mean you *should*. I encourage you to read that sentence again. This is something I constantly remind myself. What makes sense for one owner might not make sense for you. With so many opportunities available, you must create your own criteria to narrow down your choices. Remember that your freedom comes from your limits.

Here are some of my recommendations for good businesses to buy:

1. A BUSINESS WITH STRONG CASH FLOW AND HIGH GROSS PROFIT

The most significant advantage of buying an existing business instead of starting one from scratch is that you can start generating profit from day one. No one is forcing you to buy a business, and you can spend as much time as you need evaluating companies to buy until you find one that is a great fit, has a great model, generates the target profit you want, and has room for improvement.

Running a business amid increasing uncertainty is challenging enough. You don't need to make it more difficult by acquiring a company that will be a ton of work to turn around and isn't already successful. Yes, you can work extremely hard to turn around a struggling business, but why risk it when you can buy a sure thing?

I don't recommend buying a struggling business or what's also commonly known as a "distressed asset" unless you have significant experience turning around struggling businesses. Most are harder to turn around than you think. While you can find deals on distressed businesses, why add additional risk to your investment and increase the odds that it won't work out?

You want to buy a business with high gross profit margins, not just net profit, since net profit can be easily manipulated, often by presenting lower expenses than are realistic.

Here's the difference between gross profit and net profit:

Gross Profit = Revenue — Cost of Goods Sold

Gross Profit Margin = (Gross Profit / Revenue) x 100%

Net Profit = Revenue — Cost of Goods Sold — Operating Expenses — Taxes

Net Profit Margin = (Net Profit / Revenue) x 100%

Since, as an acquirer, you will be working to quickly reduce operating expenses through optimization and merging with your other teams, net profit is a less useful metric than gross profit.

You should look for a business with a minimum of 40 percent gross profit. A range of 40 to 60 percent is great, and anything over 60 percent is exceptional. The more cash flow the business has, the more you can use it to grow the business and invest in other companies within your portfolio. For example, I recently acquired a website with strong cash flow just so I could use that cash flow to cover the costs of developing all the new content for an existing website within my portfolio.

2. A BUSINESS WITH PASSIVE-INCOME POTENTIAL

Are you buying a business or buying a job? Some businesses will require more owner time than others. A passive-income business is a business where you can hire people and use technology to manage it so you don't have to trade much, if any, of your own time for money. You're leveraging someone else, selling their time for money, and paying them. This is why Warren Buffett doesn't manage Berkshire Hathaway companies—they all have their own managers. Warren makes the money, but he's not in the weeds.

3. A RECESSION-RESISTANT BUSINESS

The economy will go up and down over the many decades you're an investor, but some industries withstand recessions better than others. For example, no matter what the state of the economy, people still need their heating and air-conditioning to work. Here are some good recession-resistant business categories.

- **Home Services:** Homeowners (and, in some cases, even renters) always need professionals to help them maintain their properties. Some of the most resilient and sustainable home-services businesses include plumbing; electrical installation and repair; and heating, ventilation, and air-conditioning companies (HVAC). These have a large market, are recession-proof, and have strong repeat and subscription potential. You can also charge more for these services because they require those who provide the services to have professional licenses, which reduces overall competition. Other viable home-service businesses include pest control, locksmiths, landscapers, contractors, solar-panel installers, cleaning services, and many others.
- **Health Care and Medical Services:** Businesses related to health care, including medical clinics, urgent care centers, and pharmaceutical companies, often see steady demand during economic downturns as people prioritize health and medical needs.
- **Education and Training:** Businesses offering education and job training services can be recession-resistant, as individuals often seek to improve their skills or retrain during economic downturns to enhance their employment prospects.
- **Health and Wellness:** Wellness-related businesses, including gyms, fitness centers, and health food stores, may continue

to generate income as consumers prioritize their well-being during stressful times.

- **Information Technology and Software:** Businesses offering software solutions, cybersecurity services, and IT consulting often remain in demand as companies rely on technology to maintain operations and security.
- **Childcare Services:** Childcare centers, particularly those offering affordable and reliable services, often have consistent demand as working parents require childcare regardless of economic conditions.

Unfortunately, acquiring in these spaces is getting more competitive as more private equity money moves into them, but there are still deals to be had, and like most markets, they will ebb and flow.

4. A BUSINESS THAT'S CLIMATE-CHANGE RESISTANT

While it's difficult to comprehend the full impact of climate change, it's worth evaluating the impact that climate can have on any business you're looking to acquire. The climate will also impact many supply chains, so it might be difficult for you to get products that your business requires. This is one of the many reasons I favor online content-driven businesses, as they have significantly fewer climate risks (though they do have other risks).

HVAC is an excellent business because as most places in the U.S. get warmer, the demand for functional air-conditioning will increase. Another category of climate-change-resistant businesses includes those involved in renewable energy production. These companies, encompassing solar, wind, and hydropower sectors, are well positioned to thrive as the world transitions from fossil fuels to clean energy sources. This category includes businesses like solar-panel manufacturers, wind farm operators, and renewable energy technology providers.

Another resilient sector comprises businesses specializing in energy efficiency and conservation solutions. These companies offer products and services such as LED lighting, insulation, smart-building technologies, and energy-efficient appliances. Their offerings align with the increasing demand for reducing energy consumption and minimizing carbon footprints.

Sustainable agriculture businesses focusing on climate-resilient, precision, and organic-farming practices are less susceptible to climate-related disruptions and market volatility. Additionally, businesses specializing in green building materials, sustainable construction practices, and eco-friendly building designs are well positioned in the construction industry as environmental regulations become stricter.

5. A BUSINESS THAT'S NOT DEPENDENT ON ONE TRAFFIC SOURCE OR MARKETING CHANNEL

Marketing channels and tactics come and go. Buying a company with diverse traffic and marketing channels and a business that works well with an email or text list insulates the business as consumers' platform preferences change. Shift to platforms you own, e.g., your website, newsletter list, text list, etc.

6. A BUSINESS WITH A COMPETITIVE ADVANTAGE

There is always a risk that once you acquire a business, it will become less competitive, especially if its success has largely depended on a founder or owner who is the face of the brand. There is also a risk that your competitors will see the sale as an opportunity to poach your employees and customers. This is why it's essential to buy a business with a competitive advantage that is transferable to the new owner.

Maybe it's been around a long time and is a trusted brand. It's extremely difficult to compete with a decades-old brand that is highly regarded in its community. Or maybe the industry requires licensure, which is a barrier to new competition entering the market. It's well known, for example, that trade businesses like plumbers and electricians can grow much larger because practitioners require specific licensing and training.

7. AN ASSET-LIGHT BUSINESS

You know that I'm partial to asset-light businesses. I don't want a company with a warehouse full of inventory or many repairman vehicles. I like running my business from anywhere and minimizing the headaches. Buying a business with a ton of trucks or equipment that needs to be maintained can add a lot of headaches and management to the operations. This can be particularly challenging if you've never run an asset-heavy business.

8. A BUSINESS WITH IMMEDIATE PRICE-INCREASE OPPORTUNITIES

With every business I've acquired, I knew how quickly I could increase revenue and prices before I bought it. In most cases, this means I have a relationship with an advertiser who pays me more money per lead than they were paying the previous owner of the website I'm acquiring. This means that on day one, after acquiring the website, I can add my affiliate partner links to the new website and make 20 to 30 percent more revenue per lead or sale—just from swapping out the links. This helps me recoup my investment a lot faster. Many businesses have this same opportunity. Can you increase prices on the services, products, partnerships, or subscriptions the business currently has? This is where having prior experience in a market really helps, but many industries have price elasticity.

9. A BUSINESS WHERE YOU CAN LEVERAGE YOUR EXISTING TEAM AND TECHNOLOGY TO REDUCE EXPENSES

In addition to increasing your revenue quickly, you should look for opportunities to decrease expenses by using your existing team and technology. This is where having some existing economies of scale can be helpful. When I acquire a new website, I can often reduce the expenses by 90+ percent because I already have editors, writers, a website-hosting account, designers, and programmers in-house that I can use. This is commonly known as a roll-up, which I defined in chapter 13.

10. A BUSINESS WITH BUILT-IN TAX EFFICIENCY OR WHERE YOU CAN OPTIMIZE THE TAXES

You've already learned that the U.S. tax code favors entrepreneurs and small businesses, and you can use that to your advantage when looking for a business to buy. Some companies are more tax-efficient than others, but you can often quickly lower taxes with many business acquisitions through more effective financial and tax-management strategies. You can also take depreciation deductions on many types of asset purchases. Taxes are likely the lowest they will ever be, due to the increasing need for local, state, and federal government to fund infrastructure projects. Optimize while you can.

Considering these criteria, let's examine the process of assessing whether a particular deal is right *for you*.

STEP 1: ASK YOURSELF, "DO I *REALLY* WANT TO DO THIS?"

Acquiring a new company can help you build your empire quickly and make you very rich, but even the best acquisition adds a new level of complexity to your life. You are still the owner even if you hire people to manage day-to-day operations. You still need to oversee everything for as long as you own the company, and you will need to be extremely hands-on for at least three to six months as you assess, negotiate, and finalize the deal and onboard the new company.

Be honest with yourself: Do you *really* want to be involved in this process? What trade-offs are you willing—and unwilling—to make? What kind of—and how much—value does this venture need to create to be worth it? What excites you about this opportunity?

STEP 2: WHAT KIND OF ACQUISITION
DO YOU WANT TO MAKE?

You need to consider how you can leverage your existing skills, resources, processes, systems, and expertise to receive a return on your investment. How does this acquisition in your portfolio add value to your business and life? Broadly speaking, you can make two types of investments or acquisitions in a holding company: vertical or horizontal.

Vertical integration occurs when you buy a company that relates very closely to and is within the same industry as one you already own. Vertical integration helps you establish economies of scale, which means you can do things more efficiently since you control multiple aspects of your business, which you would otherwise have to outsource. A key example is when a company buys one of the other companies within its supply chain—for example, if Apple buys a factory in China, it can reduce the cost of manufacturing iPhones. Look for vertical integration opportunities by assessing your largest expenses.

For me, our largest expense is writers. Currently, we spend a lot of money every month hiring freelance writers to produce pieces for our various websites. We get a pretty good rate since we have so much work for these writers and have built up goodwill with them after several years of keeping our promises and paying on time. But if I could find a reputable copywriting agency to buy, I could help grow that business while simultaneously reducing the costs of my other businesses. We also spend a lot on web hosting, so I could buy a hosting company. I haven't done this yet because web hosting requires having and managing clients, which I don't want to do.

Horizontal integration occurs when you expand into other industries where you can leverage economies of scale. This is how our current MMG Media Group holdings work. While the holdings are all independent of one another from an editorial perspective, we can employ the same network of writers we use for one site to write for others because the topics are similar. We can also apply many of our SOPs—for ad campaigns or accounting—so everything runs more efficiently.

As a hypothetical example, let's say you owned a home-cleaning company and you've created a proprietary system for booking, tracking, scheduling, and following up with clients. You could buy a lawn care company that provides a service your existing clients would likely be interested in and use the customer service platform for both businesses. This allows you to schedule multiple services simultaneously and cross-promote services and promotions with both clientele. If this acquisition works, you could then buy a plumbing company, a home repair service, an HVAC company, or a contracting company, all of which could serve the homeowners you already work with.

STEP 3: RESEARCH THE CURRENT MARKET

Before you start actively looking to acquire, you want to acquaint yourself with how potential acquisitions in that industry are being positioned and valued. You should spend at least three to six months doing this before you spend too much time exploring one company. This will allow you to explore different industries, sectors, and locations, spot trends, and understand financing basics.

The best opportunities will likely arise within your network and communities. These will be the ones with the most complements to your existing businesses or skill sets and the ones you will best be able to assess because you're working closely with them already. In my industry, I study my competitors closely and my competitors know that I buy websites, so when they want to sell, they reach out to ask if I'm interested in buying their site. Sometimes, they reach out before putting the website on the market, so I get an opportunity at an "off-market" deal, and other times they reach out after they've already listed the website with a broker. Either way, I can make an offer if I'm interested.

Since I've been watching their websites closely, I know which ones I'd be interested in acquiring and which are easy to pass on. There are also smaller, up-and-coming websites that I'm tracking. When they get the right amount of traction, I might reach out and ask if they're open to an acquisition. I find the best deals by being intensely focused, connected, and knowing my market. This isn't easy for an introvert like me, but I actively work on cultivating and growing my network because I'm interested in the market.

You should also use online resources to investigate companies currently for sale, especially if you're interested in acquiring outside your current sector. The websites BizBuySell.com, EmpireFlippers .com, and many others allow you to easily search for companies currently for sale. As I write this, there are also new websites popping up, like the Website Flip (an aggregator of websites for sale) and Kumo (an aggregator and sorter for business listed on BizBuySell.com), which make it even easier to search for a business based on a variety of search criteria.

While business-listing profiles vary depending on the website you're on, each listing always includes an overview of the company, the listing price, annual revenue, expenses, profit, and often other metrics like the owner's take-home pay, the business's competitive advantage, growth opportunities, and more. The listings make it easy to filter through opportunities and, if you're interested, reach out to the owner or broker in charge of the sale.

Remember that brokers commonly inflate the earnings of the business in these listings. So, just because the "sticker price" might be high doesn't mean that's what you'll need to pay to acquire the business. When evaluating how much a business is worth, you'll want to do the same math we walked through in chapter 12 when discussing how to set up your business to sell. Pay particular attention to the owner's compensation and cost of goods sold (this is often underreported). If you do end up moving into the due diligence phase of evaluating a business, then you'll have to dig deeper into these numbers to determine how much cash you can realistically harvest from the business each year.

Even if you don't buy a company through one of these sites, they give you a sense of asking prices and which industries are ripe for investment. How are companies valued in a particular industry, sector, or location? What trends are you seeing? Which markets are particularly competitive and could indicate a buyer's market? Which companies excite you? How would a particular acquisition help you scale your empire? Would it be a vertical or horizontal integration?

I'm also a big fan of joining communities to learn what other entrepreneurs are doing and get advice on structuring deals. As with pretty much everything else, there is probably a Reddit thread dedicated to holding company owners in your area or industry and even in-person events for entrepreneurs nearby. I attend a conference for small holding company owners every year. I also belong to an online community with over 1,000 high-net-worth entrepreneurs, and I've built my own community for entrepreneurs. Just spending time among people doing what I'm doing for a few days returns twenty times the amount I pay for flights, hotels, and expenses in the information I can use to grow my businesses. I know hundreds of people I can turn to for advice on everything from hiring lawyers to tax optimization techniques.

HOW BIG A COMPANY SHOULD YOU BUY?

The more revenue a company makes, the more expensive it will be to acquire. However, it may also take more work to manage and integrate it with your existing operations. Here are some common challenges of acquiring a company depending on its revenue.

Up to $1.5 million in revenue

This is a tiny business, likely run by the founder and a group of contractors or a few employees. This revenue level has a fair amount of risk because so much of the business's success likely depended on the founder or CEO. This is commonly known as the "key man" risk. Businesses at this revenue level often don't have enough profit or strong enough cash flow for the owner to take home much or for the business to grow quickly because there's not enough cash to reinvest in the business to scale.

Businesses at this level can be inexpensive to acquire and a great value if you have an infrastructure already set up to grow the business or if you've already been successful in the industry. However, they can be a higher risk if you haven't acquired a business before.

$1.5–$5 million in revenue

This is the sweet spot for most first acquisitions. These are good companies to buy within a new holding company because the business has a structure that can easily be optimized without being too large, having too many employees, or having an immense amount of complexity. It's also generating decent revenue, but there is still a big opportunity to quickly scale revenue and profit through better management and more effective marketing and sales.

This company likely has five to twenty full-time employees, a decent management structure, a stable customer base, and a good reputation. The traditional sales, HR, and accounting roles will likely already function. Some of the internal processes have been fine-tuned, and the business runs with oversight from its CEO or founder but likely can work well without them.

$5–$10 million in revenue

This is a medium-size company. You should have some solid operational experience before acquiring it. In a business of this size, there are typically a lot of moving pieces, with multiple layers of management and all the core business areas established. The business will likely have an executive team, sales team, customer service team, HR team, and more. This is the perfect size company to leverage for a roll-up because it has all the centralized operational teams in place. To accelerate growth, you can grow the cash flow and reinvest it in acquiring competitors with smaller revenue.

$10 million+ in revenue

This is a large company with a lot of complexity and is a real player in its industry. Acquiring companies of this size requires significant financial, operational, and strategic resources. If you're operating at this level, you'll have a substantial team in place and experience in the industry. At this scale, you want to acquire companies that already have a high-performance management team in place. You'll also want to hang on to and leverage the vast amount of institutional knowledge within the teams.

While larger companies are more difficult to integrate within your existing operation, they can quickly help you acquire a competitive advantage and a significant market share. Companies of this size are sometimes called platform companies because they are a way to establish market position and acquire smaller businesses underneath. These platform companies are also attractive acquisition targets for huge companies. Many large companies acquire only businesses doing $10 million+ a year in revenue.

STEP 4: UNDERSTAND AND BECOME THE CUSTOMER

Once you identify a company that seems like a decent deal, you can dig a little deeper to learn more about how the business operates. You can learn a lot from financial statements, but one of the most efficient and effective ways to determine whether a company is run well is to find out what it's like to be a customer. Visit the website. Buy the product or sign up for the service yourself. Join the email list. Read the customer reviews online. Dig deep into the Google search results, not just the first page. Spend a few hours experiencing the brand as a customer and through customers' eyes. What you're looking for are happy customers and also room for improvement. Make a list of the things you uncover that could be improved.

While you're playing the customer role, don't disclose your interest in buying, to ensure you get the same experience as everyone else. How does the product compare to others like it? Does the brand offer something its competitors don't? What is their customer service like? How do they treat repeat customers?

One of the reasons See's Candies has been so profitable for Berkshire Hathaway—earning the company an 8,000 percent return since its initial investment of $25 million in 1972—is because its customers have always loved the brand. Warren Buffett knew this because he talked directly to customers of what was then a regional business. They raved about the candy and the customer service, and Buffett knew he could capitalize on that loyalty and expand to other regions.

STEP 5: LOOK FOR INEFFICIENCIES AND ANOMALIES

The next chapter will cover how to perform full due diligence on a company you're serious about acquiring. Still, as you're considering your options and narrowing your criteria, you can use publicly available information to dive deeper into a company's finances to determine if a deal is as good as it seems. You want to look for both inefficiencies and anomalies. The more inefficiency, the more opportunity you have to improve the company's operations and grow it for profit. On the other hand, anomalies may indicate red flags you want to avoid.

Leverage your experience reading your own P&Ls and financial statements to look for inaccuracies and inefficiencies. While you won't have access to this data during the initial business evaluation phase, during due diligence, you first want to check that the total business revenue is correct by reconciling/confirming the P&L with the company's bank statements and tax returns. Revenue can be manipulated, inflated, or deflated in a P&L, but the bank statements and tax returns will confirm if the revenue was actually received. Business owners who are hiding something might report less revenue on their tax returns than the bank deposits show, so they have less of a tax burden, or report more on their P&L to inflate the value of the business.

With some experience, you'll be able to spot inefficiencies as quickly as inaccuracies. You're looking for areas where you could quickly (1) reduce expenses and (2) increase revenue. I can quickly look at a P&L and see where I can do both things in my industry. The number one expense, outside of salaries, for content companies is hiring contract writers or creators. I've been able to negotiate a much lower per-word rate than many of my competitors, leading to an average of 80 percent savings on our content costs. I can look at a website's P&L to see how much it spends on content and know I can immediately reduce those costs by 70 to 80 percent.

It's often easiest to spot opportunities to reduce expenses when looking at the P&L because you can potentially leverage your existing team to take on some of the work and reduce head count. Or you can use your experience to negotiate lower recurring vendor or partner costs. While it's never easy, one of the first steps new business owners often take when acquiring a business is to lay off contractors and employees to reduce expenses quickly. Over time, many companies get bloated and have too many people working for them, or they've signed up for too many services. Bringing a fresh set of eyes to the P&L, you can find these opportunities to cut expenses quickly and thus increase profit.

The next thing to look for are opportunities to increase revenue. The fastest way to increase revenue is to increase prices once you acquire the business—assuming the customer base can support it. You will know if this is possible by studying the industry, the company, and its products. If they are priced lower than their competitors, then there is an opportunity to increase prices. If they have a competitive advantage, there is an opportunity to raise prices. If demand is rising faster than supply, there is an opportunity to increase prices. If the business has a lot of loyal customers who can't live without its product or service, there's an opportunity to raise prices. Also, if you work in a similar industry, have a large customer email list, or are better at digital marketing than the current business owner, you will know from looking at the P&L, customer pricing lists, and marketing efforts that you could quickly increase revenue.

If you spot anomalies, you'll need to gather more information to determine their seriousness. You're looking for things that indicate bad (or dishonest) bookkeeping, legal liabilities, bad debt, shady business practices, or anything else that isn't normal for that business. For example, if you're considering buying your favorite local barbecue joint but they report a 60 percent profit margin when the industry average for restaurants is closer to 5 percent, you need to question how they report those numbers. Ask the broker—or, if possible, the owner—about it and see how they respond. If their answer checks out and they can back it up—or if it points to an inefficiency that you can improve—then you may decide to continue the conversation. You'll need to recalculate the deal's value if they're cagey.

STEP 6: HOW ARE YOU GOING TO PAY FOR IT?

While I have never taken out a loan or gone into any debt to buy a business, there are several options to consider when deciding how to finance a deal. You can pay all cash, of course, but financing part of the deal generally makes the most financial sense so that you don't have to commit so much cash. Almost all deals involve some amount of cash up front and then financing for the rest of the amount.

The biggest reason I don't use any debt is the same reason I don't take on any outside investment—I don't want my business decisions limited by responsibility to anyone else or any form of debt I need to pay back. Not having any debt allows me to make more strategic decisions when growing my business and protects the business from cash-flow fluctuations because I'm not on the hook for an interest-bearing monthly debt repayment. Not having debt also allows me to grow at my own pace. However, this does limit the size of businesses I can acquire.

If you don't have the money to acquire a business or you want to acquire a larger business, you can use some form of financing. However, it's important to be cautious and not jeopardize your financial health. Make sure you understand the terms of the financing deal and your obligations.

If you're buying a business from a seller who has a broker, then the financing options the seller is open to will typically be in the sales listing or business packet. If the seller wants to sell quickly, they will likely be open to multiple payment scenarios. You can get pretty creative in structuring how you pay for deals, and it's a big part of the negotiation process. An M&A attorney or an experienced broker can help you propose a deal structure that works with your business goals and start negotiating with the seller. Ultimately, the deal structure can significantly impact how much you end up paying for the business and over what time frame.

Here are some of the most common financing methods and the advantages of each:

Seller Financing

This is when the seller agrees to let the buyer pay part of the sale price directly to them over an agreed-upon period at an agreed-upon interest rate. This is a popular method of financing and many sellers are open to it as long as you're willing to pay a large percentage up front in cash. Usually, seller financing will make up 25 percent or less of the total deal price. For example, if you were to purchase a business for $2.4 million, you might pay $1.9 million in cash up front and finance the remaining $500,000 through seller financing at a 5 percent annual interest rate over three years. The advantage here is that you can put less cash down, and the seller gets the deal done and earns a bit of interest on the loan amount.

Earnout

An earnout is when you agree to pay a portion of the sale price up front in cash but the rest as a percentage of your revenue from the business over a defined period. You typically make monthly or quarterly payments to the seller based on a percentage of the revenue the business generated. There are two types of earnouts: guaranteed and performance-based. A guaranteed earnout means you guarantee the total amount no matter how well the business performs. This is a better guarantee to the seller that they will get their money.

As the name implies, a performance-based earnout is based on the business's performance and can be for either a defined amount or an uncapped amount with more upside. With a performance-based earn-out, the seller is paid only if the business does well enough to pay the earnout. Still, if the amount is uncapped or has a higher cap and the company performs well, then the seller could have the opportunity to make a lot more money. With non-guaranteed earnouts, there is typically more risk for the seller.

For example, with a $2.4 million website sale, you could pay $1.4 million cash and then negotiate the additional $1 million to be paid as an earnout as 20 percent of the revenue is paid out each quarter. If the earnout is guaranteed, there would typically be a set time frame for it to be paid, such as three to five years. If, at the end of the time period, the 20 percent of revenue hasn't been enough to cover the full balance of the earnout, then it would be the buyer's responsibility to pay the rest regardless of the performance.

If the earnout was performance-based without a time cap, then the buyer would pay it off as 20 percent of annual revenue for as long as it takes to repay the full loan amount. If the business eventually shuts down and there is no more revenue, the buyer wouldn't be liable for the balance of the earnout. This is, of course, risky for the seller. But if the business exploded and the earnout period was five years, that 20 percent could be worth substantially more to the seller than $1 million. As expected, sellers generally prefer guaranteed earnouts but might be open to performance-based ones if they are bullish on the prospects of the business under new ownership.

SBA Government Loan

The Small Business Administration grants certain business owners low-interest loans for various uses, including acquiring other small businesses, through its 7(a) loan program. These ten-year, low-interest loans are worth up to $5 million and can finance up to 80 percent of the cost of buying a business. SBA loans are granted and administered through SBA partner banks.

You might come across a business listed for sale that says it's SBA prequalified, which means a third party has evaluated the company to determine the likelihood that the business is eligible for an SBA loan. You can also submit business deals to an SBA-preferred lending partner bank or an SBA-qualified evaluator to evaluate the likelihood of being approved for an SBA loan.

Just like taking out any loan, there are SBA lending partners who conduct due diligence on both the business and your personal finances before approving you. This is good news for you because these experienced lending partners will often approve a loan only for a business that has a proven track record of revenue, profit, and positive cash flow. They evaluate the business closely and require borrowers to have sufficient cash flow and liquidity to cover the loan payments.

To get approved, you are often required to use your business and personal assets as collateral for the loan, which could be risky if you don't have confidence in your ability to run the business. You don't want to lose your house, for example, if you can't repay the loan. However, if you're just starting out in your career and don't have any assets, this might not be risky at all. And even if you do have assets, because of solid due diligence and the SBA loan process, SBA loan default rates are under 10 percent every year and some years in the 2 to 3 percent range—meaning most buyers who get approved for an SBA loan go on to pay off their loans.

The SBA evaluator will typically require you to submit:

- Three years of historical tax returns (personal and business)
- Your current and prior year complete financials, including your P&L, accounts receivable, and accounts payable aging summaries
- A current inventory list with the approximate valuation
- A list of your existing business and personal assets
- Current personal financial statements
- Personal credit history
- W-2, 1099, and other verifiable and reported income documentation
- Review of personal collateral availability
- Strategic growth plans for the business

In addition to doing your due diligence, one way to de-risk your acquisition is to buy a business that generates a higher amount of SDE, make a larger down payment so you have more equity, and have a larger cash buffer or cash reserves. Like any loan, the less leverage you use, the less risky it tends to be.

Bank Loan

If your business or the business you are interested in acquiring is local, then it's worth considering working with a local bank to secure a loan. Many local and regional banks and credit unions would be happy to loan you part of the money to acquire a business if you meet the terms and have good credit.

While having an existing relationship with a local banker can make this process easier and your bank might give you more favorable terms to keep your business, you can start shopping for local loans as soon as you have the business in mind. As with the SBA loan, you might need to put up your business and personal assets as collateral, so some risk is involved. As noted, if the business is located within or near the community where the bank is, you might have a better chance of getting the loan because community banks want to support their communities.

Private Lender Loans

Investors, fellow business owners, and people with deep pockets interested in or familiar with a particular industry may offer loans to entrepreneurs looking to acquire a business as their own form of investment. Often, a private lender's loan interest rates are higher than SBA and bank loan rates because you're dealing with one person or a smaller lending office, but they can often get you money faster so you can buy a business quickly. Most private lenders want zero equity in a company. They want to earn a solid interest rate on the money they loan you. Loans are typically secured by your existing business and, occasionally, your personal assets.

Syndication

Syndication is a good option if you want to acquire a larger company than you can afford. You can pull together a bunch of investors, all of whom contribute a percentage of the purchase price in exchange for a relative stake in the company. You can make a lot of money and grow your business more quickly by taking this approach, but managing other peoples' money (on top of managing the purchase of a massive company) adds a lot of complexity to your life. I've had billionaire-family investing offices offer me $50 million to acquire and manage networks of affiliate websites, but I don't want to be a billionaire or oversee other people's wealth. Remember your limits.

STEP 7: ASK YOURSELF AGAIN, "DO I WANT TO DO THIS?"

You've gathered all this information on an opportunity. The numbers check out and you can see the growth potential. But before you initiate a deal conversation, I encourage you to check in with yourself again and remember that time is more valuable than money. Just because you can buy something doesn't mean you should. Here are a few questions that help me at this step:

- Are you acquiring a business or a job?
- Do you *really* want to be in this business?
- How well does this fit within your portfolio?
- What is the real upside here?
- Is your money more useful somewhere else?
- Do you see yourself running it for the next one to three years until you've fully automated it to run within your holding company?
- Do you really want to be in this business knowing everything you know?
- How big will your commitment be?
- How much risk will you be exposed to?

There are plenty of opportunities to make money—and more are arising daily. Don't settle for ones that won't enrich your life.

STEP 8: ASSEMBLE YOUR TEAM

Remember that according to the *Harvard Business Review*, 70 to 90 percent of acquisitions fail. This can happen for myriad reasons—cultural differences, inability to integrate systems efficiently, market forces, and so on—and there's no way you can fully predict how an acquisition will go until after it happens. That said, you can mitigate that risk as much as possible by performing due diligence on your target asset before you finalize a deal.

This stage can get complicated and technical very quickly, so it's best to hire experts to do this work for you rather than manage it yourself. Still, you'll want to know what to look out for so you can ask the right questions and assess the information that comes back to you. Think of this like the home inspection phase of the process: you're confident you want this property, but you need to ensure that no surprises are lurking behind the walls before you sign the dotted line.

If you're going to buy a company for more than $250,000, it's worth hiring the following experts to help:

An M&A Attorney

Even if you already work with a lawyer, you want to find someone specializing in mergers and acquisitions. This person will help you craft your letter of intent, the NDA, and the purchase agreement on the company in question. There are a lot of intricacies that come with merging two companies. Something as simple as filing the wrong paperwork (or filing it late) or failing to secure the correct licenses or insurance can cost you thousands, if not millions, of dollars in legal fees and fines. With so much on the line, it's worth hiring the right person to do the job for you.

Finding great M&A lawyers can be challenging, so start by asking your network or reaching out to people who have bought or sold companies to learn about their experience. Put some effort in. If you find the right person, they can help you through the acquisition process and become an adviser who can give you perspective on deals before you spend too much time looking into them. If you build trust with that person, they will eventually learn your business enough to recommend courses of action that align with your overall strategy.

An Accountant

Similar to legal issues, you don't want to skimp on making sure your finances are in order and your taxes are up-to-date. Start by talking to your accountant, but you may want to hire someone with an M&A background to ensure the deal is set up correctly and in the most tax-efficient way from the beginning.

A Broker

As in real estate, a broker facilitates introductions and meetings between interested buyers and sellers. If you already have a relationship with the company you want to buy, you may not need a broker, but they can offer advantages in certain circumstances. Many acquisitions are overseen by brokers representing the seller, so you probably won't need an additional one unless you'd prefer to outsource the communication. A good broker will play the long game. Even if a particular deal falls through or the broker is representing the seller, not you, they will continue to send you opportunities because they know you're a serious buyer.

Now let's walk through the deal-making process.

CHAPTER 15

GET THE DEAL DONE

"The world doesn't pay you for what you know; it pays you for what you do."
—Jack Canfield

If you're ready to buy a business, I encourage you to stay organized, maintain clear, consistent communication, be transparent, and move quickly. Even in the best-case scenario, you're looking at a six-to-twelve-month timeline from the initial interest call to closing the deal. While you can do it in less than six months, if the business is small, that's very rare. Remember that time kills deals, so the longer you spend evaluating the deal, the more likely the seller could change their mind, another buyer could show up, and the market dynamics could change to make the business more or less valuable.

There are infinite variables outside your control when buying a business. But there is a lot that you can control, so you need to understand the process going in and manage what you can. The business-buying process is pretty standardized for most industries, but the time it takes to complete each step can vary depending on the business's complexity or nuance. For this chapter, I will use the example of buying a website or digital business to showcase the framework.

THE TEN STEPS TO BUYING A BUSINESS

1. Reach out to the business owner or broker

After you've identified the business you want to acquire, reach out to the business owner directly or their broker if they are using one. There are three types of outreach: cold, warm, and hot. Cold outreach is when you don't know the business owner, have no connections to them, and don't know if they want to sell their business. Warm outreach is when you get word from a friend, connection, or social media that an owner might be interested or is definitely interested in selling their business. Hot outreach is when the business owner is ready to sell and announces they're open to receiving offers directly or through a broker.

If a business isn't listed for sale on a website or through a brokerage, you should contact the owner directly and express interest in buying their business. I get two to three emails a week from someone interested in buying one of my websites. From experience, I know these buyers are looking for a great deal, and many want to buy and flip websites quickly for a profit. Others are looking for a great off-market deal.

Other buyers who reach out are just fishing for information since the very nature of the business buying and selling process requires some level of disclosure. The owners of good businesses frequently get approached by potential buyers, so they likely aren't going to be very receptive or responsive to cold outreach because they're skeptical or have no interest in selling.

The best way to approach cold outreach is to be direct and transparent. Explain who you are, why you're interested in the business, why you are qualified to buy it, what a realistic timeline looks like, and what you are willing to pay up front. You can play the whole "What do you want for it?" game before sharing what you're willing to pay, but sellers are in a position of power here, so they will want to hear your offer first. The goal of the cold outreach is to showcase your credibility, build some trust with the potential seller, and make it easy for them to gauge the seriousness of your offer. Most of the outreach I get are simple emails like: "Are you interested in selling your business?" This puts too much onus on me to ask follow-up questions. Even if I am interested in selling, I don't take these buyers seriously.

Selling a business can be a challenging and emotional process, especially for someone who hasn't done it before. From the start, you want to make it clear that you're legitimate, easy to work with, and highly motivated. In addition to reaching out via email or phone, you can message the owner directly on LinkedIn or X, two platforms business owners often use. Direct messaging through social media can be particularly effective because the potential seller can quickly evaluate who you are from your profiles.

If you're emailing, include a link to your website or business website and make it easy for the business owner to evaluate and confirm who you are. Unfortunately, it's easy to impersonate someone on social media. If you're interested in a business with a physical location, you should also show up and ask to speak to the owner in person, even if you've already reached out by phone, email, or social media. The cold outreach can be challenging but very fruitful in snagging an off-market deal.

Warm outreach is easier because, whether or not the business owner is interested in selling, you already have a mutual connection or a way to start the conversation. This is how I get most of my leads. People know I'm interested in acquiring personal finance websites, so they share my information with those interested in selling their websites. If I know someone who knows the business owner I'm looking to connect with, I may ask them to make an introduction or I'll mention our mutual connection in my initial outreach to the owner.

Many business owners are potentially interested in selling their business, but they aren't actively seeking buyers. The idea of selling your business is in the back of most business owners' minds. Any hesitation is often a matter of timing, not knowing how the selling process works, or not wanting to take the time to find a buyer. When you know someone in common, a business owner is more likely to trust you, which makes it easier for you to get an off-market deal.

With hot outreach, the business has been listed "for sale" by the owner or broker. In either scenario, there is often a limited window of two to eight weeks during which the owner or broker collects offers. If the owner is genuinely serious about selling, they will want to close the deal relatively quickly. In this case, the best strategy for reaching out is to be forward and direct in your communication.

Reach out, expressing who you are and why you're interested in the business. Showcase that you're a serious and qualified buyer and ask for more information about the business. Sometimes, but not always, the business owner or broker will ask what your offer is before sharing any information about the business. If you are serious, sharing an offer is often useful. For-sale listings usually include an asking price, so your response should be a reasonable counter based on that number. The business owner naturally wants to get as much as they can for their business, so the asking price might be inflated and they might be open to negotiation.

If they are not open to negotiation, they will list the price as "firm" or "nonnegotiable" in the listing. Other times, sellers price a business reasonably because they want it to sell quickly for personal or market-driven reasons. As I write this, several websites are priced reasonably because the owners either need the money or are worried about the threat of AI disrupting their businesses.

2. Both parties sign a nondisclosure agreement

The NDA is a simple agreement that forbids the seller and buyer from sharing any information the other discloses as part of the sales process. NDAs include a confidentiality clause stipulating that any information discussed is to be used only to evaluate buying the business and can't be disclosed to anyone outside the agreed-upon parties. Usually, an NDA only permits you to discuss the business details with your immediate team or partners within your company, but no one outside the company.

Most NDAs also stipulate that you can't disclose that you are considering buying or selling to anyone outside the company. Additionally, NDAs often require you to destroy or delete any copies of data or reports that the seller sends you once the negotiation process is over. NDAs also often restrict the buyer's and seller's ability to hire anyone from the other's teams that they hadn't previously engaged with, for two to three years.

3. Review the business packet or information compiled by the business owner or broker

After the NDA is signed, it's safer for the business owner to disclose information about their business through discussions and supporting documentation. They are likely doing this with several potential buyers at the same time, so you should move quickly but diligently if you're interested in the business.

Typically, if a broker represents the business, they will create a PDF summary of the business for interested buyers. This summary often includes an asking price, an overview of the business, a history of the business, revenue and profit data, traffic and sales-performance data, information on why the owners want to sell the business, as well as write-ups about the future opportunities and challenges for the business, and insights on key competitors. Almost always, the owner has outlined growth recommendations to highlight what they believe are the best opportunities for growing the business and the potential threats. These opportunities and threats are often generic, but some are helpful starting points for deeper analysis.

Sometimes, this packet will include the P&L, statement of cash flows, balance sheet, and screenshots of Google Analytics data. Other times, buyers will receive this information only after they submit an offer or proof of funds. The latter can be as simple as a bank screenshot, statement, or letter outlining that you've been approved for financing and showing you have the necessary funds to acquire the business.

Often, a broker will interview a business owner about their business and include the interview transcript and a video or audio recording. In this interview, the broker will ask the business owner a set of frequently asked questions that potential buyers have. In my experience, they'll ask questions like: How do you monetize your website? How have you grown your website traffic? What are the three biggest opportunities you see for the business? What happens if you lose your biggest affiliate partnerships?

Many of these business packets are compiled by the business owners and aren't audited by a CPA. This means you are trusting that the information is accurate, but you will need to verify this during due diligence through your own analysis or by working with a CPA. Most "sell-side brokers" will help a business owner compile the packet and do very light due diligence to ensure, for example, that the business is generating the approximate amount of revenue it's stating or that its website traffic is what's reported. But they usually won't go any deeper than that. I also tend to find that brokers will do everything they can to make the earnings and profit seem as strong as possible since they are incentivized to sell the business at the highest price. I'm always skeptical when the expenses are much lower than a typical business of its type. Thankfully, for online businesses I buy, it's relatively easy to log in and look at the sales data through the business owner's digital cart and credit card transaction data. As a buyer, you can also hire a "buy-side broker" to manage this due diligence process, but you must also understand it yourself.

If you're dealing with a business owner who isn't working with a broker or hasn't compiled any of the information above, the deal will be a bit more challenging, and you'll likely have to do a bit of the digging up front. Some business owners will be organized and can assemble the information you request in a few days or weeks. Unfortunately, many business owners are great at running their businesses but not great at managing the books or staying organized. It's common for some business owners to commingle their personal and business finances and not keep their books up-to-date or work with a bookkeeper. Some business owners don't even know their own numbers—they rely on a COO or third-party whom they keep on retainer to manage the accounting and day-to-day operations.

If the business owner is disorganized, you may need to spend more up-front time digging into what is available. This makes it more difficult to evaluate the business or uncover issues that could become problems. However, there could also be opportunity in inefficiency, since you're likely much more efficient and could easily turn the business around with better internal organization.

This is another reason why it's so important to be organized in your business if you want to sell one day. Having everything organized makes your business a more attractive acquisition prospect than a disorganized business. Thankfully, because of technology, staying on top of this stuff has never been easier.

4. Compile initial questions

After you've reviewed all the data provided by the broker or business owner, you should compile a list of questions, and be as specific as possible. The broker's FAQ included with the sales packet will be helpful but not thorough enough for your evaluation purposes, though some of the FAQ answers can help you come up with follow-up questions. Don't hold back. This is your chance to poke holes in the data and learn as much as possible about the business. Many industries have templates of questions you can reference when compiling your questions. I've found my M&A attorney to be valuable at this stage in helping me evaluate the sales packet and develop a list of detailed questions. If you're working with a buy-side business broker, they can also be helpful.

The less data the broker or business owner has presented as part of their packet, the longer your list of questions will likely be. Often, it's best to write down and then email all these questions to the broker or business owner so they can spend some time hunting down the answers before taking the next step and scheduling a call.

5. Have a call with the seller, broker, and your team (including your attorney and accountant)

Some owners or brokers will answer your questions directly in an email response to save time, but it's still always a smart idea to hop on a conference call with the seller, broker, and any members of your team to dig further into their answers. While this call can consist of just you and the seller, it can also involve any team members you'd like to include. I always try to have my M&A attorney and possibly another team member, to get a different perspective.

This call is designed to get your questions answered and to get to know the seller. It can be as long or as short as needed to address your questions about the business. You might need a few calls to get all your questions answered, but one call is customary for most deals. It's important to note that, on this call, you shouldn't make offers or talk about any deal terms. This will happen later when making a formal offer.

The goal of your calls and your continued analysis is to get to the place where you feel comfortable enough to make an offer. While this can extend over several weeks or longer, once you've bought and sold a few businesses, you can—and should—move quickly if you're interested. A few days ago, a broker representing a competing website contacted me and asked if I'd be interested in acquiring the website. I said possibly, so he sent me a PDF overview of the business, which was about fifty pages long. I spent thirty minutes reading through it and compiled a list of questions I sent to the broker later that day.

By the following day, the broker had emailed me the answers to all my questions and given me access to the website's Google Analytics account to take a deeper look. The answers in the email opened up a few additional questions, and I requested a call with the broker and the website owner. I was on the phone three hours later and we talked for about an hour. During this call, I determined the website wasn't a great fit for my portfolio because too much of its revenue was concentrated on two different affiliate partnerships. I wouldn't have known this without having the call and asking this question. It took me about three hours over three days to evaluate the deal before I moved on.

You're looking for a business you're excited about buying and see fitting in well within your portfolio. After having a call and analyzing the data, it should be pretty obvious what your strategy will be—how you can quickly increase revenue, decrease expenses, or leverage the economies of scale of your existing portfolio. You should already have thought through what your rough game plan will be after acquiring the site. You should walk away if you feel unsure, confused, or overwhelmed. If you spot any red flags, walk away. If the owner gives you a bad vibe, walk away. There's always a fair amount of risk in acquiring any business. Don't walk into a higher-risk situation because you don't know if the owner is truthful or you suspect something fishy is happening. Remember: trust what you feel.

Even when I'm evaluating websites and have access to analytics and revenue data, there are things I can't see—for example, how the website owner built links to the website in the past. If I spend a lot of time looking, I can uncover some of this, but I can't see it all. If the website owner engaged in any shady link-building schemes or was guest posting on a ton of websites or buying links, then there is a high risk that traffic could decline significantly after Google updates its core algorithm. If I sense that something shady could have been going on, I pass on the deal. The risk is just too great.

While feeling nervous is normal, there's a big difference between excited and fearful. Your decision should be a clear yes or no. Any "I don't know"s or "maybe"s are a sign to pass on the deal. As with anything, experience over time will sharpen your instincts.

6. Make an initial offer and outline your terms

After the call, if you're interested in buying the business, the next step is to put together a formal offer, commonly known as an indication of interest (IOI). You can deliver this as bullet points in an email or a short memo, or skip directly to presenting a letter of intent (LOI), which is legally binding. At this phase, if a broker is involved, they will usually collect offers from multiple parties to present to the seller all at once. If this is the case, an email LOI is probably sufficient. Ask the broker, to be sure it is. The bullet points should include your monetary offer, any payment terms you're suggesting, information on if and how long you want the seller to stay on board for the transition, and any other terms of the deal you want to include. Most of my offers are four or five bullet points.

If you work directly with the seller, an email might also suffice. I prefer to keep offers informal and share as much in an email as possible. I always ask the seller if they're okay with simply negotiating the large points of the deal over email (things like price, amount of cash up front, any earnouts, etc.) before formalizing the offer in an LOI.

While the LOI is also pretty simple to put together, it's a legally binding agreement that I want to send only after we've already agreed on most of the big terms of the deal. I don't want to lock myself into any agreement before both parties agree. However, on some occasions, a broker or seller will accept an offer only in the form of an LOI, in which case I'll send my offer in that form. Also, on rare occasions, if I'm interested in moving the deal quickly, I'll send an LOI instead of an email, making it as easy as possible for a seller to sign and for us to move into due diligence.

After you submit your formal offer, the broker or seller might have some follow-up questions or want to talk again on a call. If the seller is working with a broker, the broker will always handle this back-and-forth communication. If the seller works alone, you'll talk directly to them. Alternatively, your attorney could speak with their attorney while keeping you both in the loop.

7. Submit a letter of intent and proof of funds

The LOI is a legally binding agreement stating your intent to buy the business or asset under specific terms. The LOI includes the offer price, the structure of the payment terms (percent of cash up front, any guaranteed or performance-based earnouts, etc.), a detailed description of the assets you're acquiring, information on any debts you're taking on, a timeline to conduct due diligence, a confidentiality agreement, terms of a noncompete if you require that the seller not work in a role or competitive capacity for a specific period (usually two to three years), and a guaranteed period of exclusivity when the seller agrees to not engage in sales discussions or take any other offers for a limited period of time (usually ninety days) while you conduct due diligence. Unless the seller requires you to submit an initial offer as an LOI, this step usually happens *after* both parties have agreed on the major deal points.

While the LOI doesn't legally require you to buy the business and you can still back out of the deal, it's a firm commitment to buy the business and is designed to lock the seller into an agreement with the potential buyer under certain terms. This is a bigger commitment for the seller than the buyer, because the buyer can keep looking at other deals in addition to this one, but the seller can't accept any other offers during the defined period of time. Meanwhile, the buyer isn't committing to buying the business or asset, just confirming their intent to do so pending more comprehensive due diligence.

In reality, the buyer can conduct the due diligence and learn everything about the business and then simply decide not to move forward with the acquisition, for any number of reasons. This is why it's always a risk for a seller to get locked into a ninety-day exclusive period with a nonserious buyer and why it's so important to vet your potential acquirer and trust them before getting into this process.

It's an unfortunate yet common practice for larger companies like

Apple or Amazon to pursue an acquisition and even sign an LOI with a company, but only use the process as a fact-finding mission to get proprietary intelligence on someone else's business. There are countless stories of entrepreneurs getting excited by acquisition talks with large companies, only to be blindsided when the company doesn't move forward at the eleventh hour.

Once you send the LOI, brokers and often buyers will also require you to submit what is known as "proof of funds," which is visual and verifiable proof that you have the assets to buy the business. Sometimes, a broker or buyer might request proof of funds earlier in the process, but it's most often sent with the LOI. If you're a massive company, you likely don't need to submit proof of funds, but you'll need to provide it as a first-time or unknown buyer. Acceptable formats include screenshots of bank accounts, bank statements, a letter approving your financing if applicable, or other proof of assets.

Even though, by this point, the high-level terms of the deal have been agreed on, you might still need to negotiate some finer points. Once that's done, both parties sign the LOI. After that, the next step is to conduct thorough due diligence and dig into the business data to ensure that the business you want to purchase has been represented accurately and no unwelcome surprises are hiding in the walls.

8. Perform your due diligence checklist

Once you have a signed LOI, it's common for a buyer to send a seller a due diligence (DD) checklist, which outlines all the documents, information, and access they would like to receive from the seller to examine the business.

The buyer or seller will also set up a cloud-based folder on a platform such as Dropbox or Google Drive for the seller to upload all the requested information and documentation. This becomes the working folder to keep the DD process organized.

As outlined in the LOI, you've got a limited amount of time to complete the DD process, so you want to get moving quickly. If you run out of time, you may extend the LOI by another month or two if needed and the seller agrees. But there's no reason to delay and you should try to be as thorough and efficient as possible.

If you're a detail-oriented person who loves numbers, you might enjoy managing the DD process and doing most of the work yourself (with the occasional help from your professional team). I enjoy digging into P&Ls, Google Analytics data, and the inner workings of businesses. I love to learn more about the company and uncover opportunities to improve it. Leading the DD helps me move faster once I've acquired the business because I already know so much about it. I actively keep a list of the next steps and strategies I'll implement and even make rough timelines for getting started.

But if you're not into numbers or you'd rather spend your time doing something else, you can outsource the DD to an experienced broker, consultant, attorney, or accountant, or some collection of all four. Even if you're leading the DD yourself, you'll still want to consult your team members, but you can outsource almost all of it to your team. Depending on the complexity of the business and the experience of your team members, the fees for these types of services can vary widely from a percentage of the deal (1 to 5 percent) to $500 per hour plus. There are all different tiers of options, but this is where it's worth paying for experience.

Whether you're leading the way or working with a broker or consultant, every DD checklist should be customized based on the industry and type of business or asset you plan on acquiring. Below, I've condensed the most important documents, information, and access you should request when evaluating almost any business.

FINANCIAL REQUESTS

The goal of this request and analysis is to ensure that the profit and loss statements are accurate. You do this by reconciling the revenue and expenses on the P&L with bank statements, credit card statements, and tax returns. The P&L should show the actual revenue the business received or generated, based on the money received into the bank accounts.

Also, the tax returns should show the total revenue, expenses, and profit, and these numbers should line up. If the owner says they've mostly paid in cash and, therefore, you can't track revenue through deposits or tax records, then you can't count that revenue as part of the valuation of the business. Only verifiable revenue should be counted. You should ask to see:

- The last three years of P&Ls, balance sheets, and statements of cash flow
- Bank and credit card statements for the past three years
- Accounts payable (A/P) and accounts receivable (A/R) aging reports
- Payment processor statements for the past three years (if the company takes payments using a service like Stripe or PayPal, or credit cards)
- Copies of the past three years of corporate tax returns, including asset depreciation schedules
- Loan agreements for any outstanding debt, as well as accompanying statements for the past three years (if the company has taken on debt of any kind)
- Payroll summaries for the owner and all employees, from the company's payroll provider
- Seller financing note if they are financing any of the deal
- CPA audits of financial records (if available)
- Any letters from the IRS, payment agreements with the IRS, or information on any back taxes that are owed
- Detail of any liens on the business (if relevant)

OPERATIONS AND HR REQUESTS

The goal of this request is to ensure that the seller owns the business and has the right to sell the business. It's also to understand their contracts with their partners, employees, vendors, and customers to ensure those can be reassigned to you, the buyers. You should ask to see:

- Operating agreement of the LLC or corporation with amendments
- Articles of formation with the state

- Statement of good standing from the state where the LLC is registered
- Information about any previous or ongoing lawsuits or worker's compensation injury claims in the past. (You should also get your attorney to search for these.)
- Patent, trademark, and intellectual property ownership proof, including registrations
- Organizational chart of total staff
- List of staff, with salaries, benefits, date of hire, as well as employment contracts, and any copies of performance reviews
- Employment manual
- Copies of business registrations, licenses, and certifications. Make sure these are current.
- Copies of business insurance policies
- Real estate leases or contracts
- Equipment rental agreements or maintenance contracts
- Client list with all contact information, as well as select client references
- Copies of client, partnership, and affiliate agreements. Sometimes partnership or vendor agreements are nontransferable, meaning they don't transfer with the sale and you'd have to renegotiate them yourself, possibly with less favorable terms. I've run into this issue multiple times.
- Supplier, distributor, and vendor contracts
- Customer contracts for any large customers, deals, or recurring services
- An inventory list with an associated value of inventory
- List of equipment, fixtures, and furnishings of a physical business location

EMPLOYEE, KEY MANAGEMENT, AND CUSTOMER INTERVIEWS

Once you've progressed in the DD process and verified all the information about the business to your satisfaction, you'll want to make an offer. After submitting the offer, you'll request that the seller set up interviews between you and key employees and customers. In these interviews, you'll want to ask about the company's culture, what it's like working there, what works and what doesn't, and where they see room for growth and improvement.

This is a delicate situation because employees you speak with might share the information, and you don't usually want customers and employees to know the owner is looking to sell before the deal is done. You are using these interviews to get a behind-the-scenes look at the business. You're also trying to assess whether the management will be easy to work with and how competent they are, while also trying to identify opportunities to improve the business (which can come from the employees, management, or current customers).

PRODUCT AND MARKETING REQUESTS

The goal of these is to fully understand the products and services of the business, as well as how they've been sold and marketed in the past. It's also to understand where the business's website traffic comes from, how website visitors engage with the brand, and any online sales data. What you should ask to see:

- Detailed list of all products and services with the associated pricing details
- Copies of all marketing materials and campaigns from the past three years
- Access to Google Analytics, Google Search Console, and other digital performance data
- Marketing performance reports (if available)
- Contracts with advertising, marketing, or PR agencies

9. Asset purchase agreement

If you know you want to move forward with the deal as you finish your due diligence, you should start drafting your asset purchase agreement (APA). Where the LOI states your intent to buy the business, the APA is the actual agreement to buy the company. This document should be comprehensive and should fully outline in detail all the assets that are being included as part of the sale of the business, the complete payment terms, a full list of the transfer steps that need to be undertaken by the seller before the buyer releases the money that will be held in escrow.

It's also common to require that the seller include documented standard operating procedures (SOPs) for running different business areas. When I sold Millennial Money, I included SOPs for running the entire website, optimizing SEO content, sending the weekly newsletter, and many other core components of the day-to-day business operations.

If the seller plans to stay involved in the business, then the APA can also include the terms of their future involvement. Creating a separate services agreement outside of the APA that dictates those terms is also customary. When I signed a one-year contract to continue working on Millennial Money after selling it, the payment terms and work expectations were all outlined in a separate agreement.

I recommend you work with an experienced M&A attorney or broker to craft your APA. It's worth the money to ensure you're protected. The APAs that my attorney put together, whether I'm buying or selling a website, have all been incredibly comprehensive. They've protected many potential scenarios I never would have considered before.

It's typical for the buyer to draft the APA and send it to the seller for their legal review and edits. While you can let the seller review and comment on the APA themselves, it's a good idea to encourage them to work with an attorney if they aren't already. This will save you time and headaches because it's essential for the seller to understand what they are selling and the terms of the deal you've proposed. It's common for there to be some back-and-forth between the buyer and seller before everyone agrees on all points of the deal. Once everyone agrees on the terms of the APA, the next step is to schedule the closing.

10. Close the deal

Congratulations, you're ready to buy a business. You and the seller will now schedule a specific closing date on which you will each sign the APA, when all the assets will be transferred, and the money will be released from escrow to the seller. So, as soon as the closing date is set, the buyer will send the money for the deal to an escrow holder, a third-party attorney, or a company like escrow.com. The asset transfer can typically take place in one business day. It could take longer, but the seller is incentivized to move quickly so they can get paid.

Once the buyer and seller agree that the steps have been completed, the money is then released from escrow to the seller. The transfer is officially complete, but there is still a lot of work to be done post-sale.

AFTER THE SALE

Now it's time to get to work. The post-sale period involves intense work, reflection, and decision-making. While every business is different and I don't know what industry you're acquiring in, below are some of my overarching thoughts on how to effectively merge the business, transition the teams, and make sure you're able to make the most of the first ninety days as the new owner.

You'll want to spend the first thirty days working through the opportunity checklist you created while conducting your due diligence. But don't make any huge decisions for the first one to three months. Focus, instead, on the low-hanging fruit opportunities that are quick wins and improve the business. You don't want to make drastic changes without first spending some time getting to know the business better.

Take advantage of the consulting agreement you negotiated with the previous owner to help you with the transition, getting all the value of their time and expertise. They will likely be thrilled with their big payday, want to celebrate, and probably check out. Be organized and clearly communicate how you want to utilize their time. Set up scheduled weekly calls and be prepared with questions. Dig into the SOPs they shared and work through each step, ensuring you understand it, and compile any questions you have about why they do something a certain way. While you're working through the SOPs, note opportunities you see to improve the existing processes.

This first ninety days is a period of intense learning. Dive into all areas of the business and be as hands-on as possible. Spend time with as many employees as you can and ask them what they would like to see improved or changed in the business. Go out and meet your biggest customers and ask how you can improve their experience. Are there any products or services they wish you offered? What would help them be more successful or happier? Take the time to experience the product and service yourself. Dig into every aspect of it: the design, marketing, sales, delivery, account management, customer service—all of it. You need to know the ins and outs of everything you're selling and how the business functions. Based on your experience, you'll see many things that need to be improved. Some will be quick fixes. Others will be larger and take more time. You won't be able to do everything at once, nor should you.

Unlocking value comes from prioritizing all the opportunities in front of you and being strategic about your choices. You'll want to build simple systems that help you document and monitor the impact of your decisions. If you make too many large decisions at once, it can be difficult to measure the cause and effect of your choices. For instance, I don't recommend shifting the entire marketing, sales, and product strategy simultaneously. There's too much risk in dramatic changes early in the business unless they are really needed.

Keep the finances organized. This will make it easier to see revenue and profit growth and ensure you can adequately manage any earnout or financing you took on as part of the sale. Being responsible for any debt or earnout payments will limit the amount of available cash you have to reinvest in the business, so you need to be smart with your money. Make sure you pay your earnout or make your loan payments on time.

The first few months—and even a few years—of owning a new business are exhilarating, especially if it's your first acquisition. Still, you want to keep all the lessons you've learned to this point at front of mind, specifically the 7 Truths. Growing your empire invites complexity into your life, so take time to return to the basics. Know your limits, stay engaged, and trust your intuition.

CHAPTER 16

WE EXPAND INTO THE SPACE WE CREATE

"If you spend time building a beautiful garden, the butterflies will come to you."
—Mário Quintana

It's a cold January day, but I'm at peace and full of warmth. I live in a beautiful house surrounded by trees. I feel full and alive. I can feel myself expanding in ways that I never would have imagined. The biggest change in the past year was having my daughter. She softens life as it passes. Being a dad has grounded me. It gets me out of my head. I love watching my daughter uncover new things and hearing her laugh. That laugh. The last ten years have gone so fast. It feels like I've lived a few lifetimes in that time.

My beard is almost all gray. I feel like I'm in the prime of my life—in those years that I'll look back on as the good old days. I don't take it for granted. I'm starting to think more about maximizing the impact of my time and how to leave a legacy. Sure, we'll probably all be forgotten in a few hundred years, but the energy we put into the world and each decision we make ripples into eternity. I didn't think about legacy in my twenties and thirties, but now I have a daughter, multiple properties, books I've written, more money than I expected to have, and growing businesses. I just recently put together an estate plan and learned a lot in the process. I'm still learning.

As I sit here in my thirty-ninth year, I'm like 100 years old in internet years. I play a young person's game. I got my first computer, a secondhand laptop when I was seven, and I've spent most of my life online. While I'm grateful that I've been able to use the internet to make most of my money, I'm excited to do more offline.

I just recently opened my brick-and-mortar bookstore, Clintonville Books. While this is a passion project of mine, I'm excited to learn an entirely new business and build a business that's analog. Reading, writing, collecting, and sharing books with others are some of my favorite things to do, so the bookstore is a natural extension for me. I'm hopeful it will help me grow in ways I've never imagined. I'm also excited to give back to my community and reinvest in where I live. This makes me happy.

I love my family and friends, and I'm making new friends. I get to live between Columbus, Ohio, and Brooklyn, New York, eat the best food, hear great music, travel, and write books. I get to be a dad, a partner, an investor, and a bookseller.

What more could I ask for? I have everything I need.

I wish I could pass this peace back to my twenty-five-year-old self when he needed it. To tell him that the sleepless nights, stress, and uncertainty will all be worth it. That not knowing is a good thing. It means there's something new around the corner. That you're investing in the you you've yet to become. That it's all a process of becoming. That you won't always be seeking. That you're headed to a place where you'll one day arrive. That you're closer to a life you love than you think.

I've accomplished far more in my life than I had imagined, but looking back, it's easy to see I was thinking too small. We tend to see only the top of the ladder that we're on. Maybe deep down, I'm afraid, so I don't take big enough risks. But I can live with that. It's a limit I'm choosing. Not taking on any debt for any of my businesses has inevitably limited their growth, but trading my freedom wouldn't have been worth it. I've never wanted to be a billionaire. I've never wanted to run a big company. I've never wanted to travel to all the countries in the world, climb Mount Everest, or run a marathon. I've never wanted to be a great chef, drummer, or poker player.

I just wanted to be free and find some peace in my life. That was it.

But what I discovered was so much more. I've learned it's even more fulfilling to help others after you have enough. You can unlock only so much joy for yourself. Life is a multiplayer game. Legacy is built beyond us—whether we care about it or not. It's our mark on the universe. It's the impression we leave on others, even if we don't know it. It's the love we have for others and what we care about. We can give others our money, time, and knowledge. I'm starting to give more.

If you've reached the end of this book before you've matured—or even started—as an entrepreneur, the information I shared may seem overwhelming or irrelevant to your life. And, right now, that might be the case. But remember: all you need to be an entrepreneur is something to sell and someone to buy it. It's never been easier to reach people who are looking for exactly what you're offering.

When you're ready to grow, double down on what works. Accelerate the flywheel. Building a business can get hard. It can get messy. Plan for nothing to go as planned. Keep making choices and keep up the momentum. You learn from the doing. Keep going. Adapt. Pivot. Learn. Grow. Breathe. Don't hold on to anything too tightly. Learn to let go of ideas when you need to. There are always new ideas. With some curiosity, creativity, persistence, and self-reflection, you can make money in ways you could have never imagined.

More than half the challenge is not stopping. Of the hundreds of personal finance bloggers who started when I did in 2015, only three of us are left. Often, it's the last one standing who finds success. Expect that going in and adapt. Experience is valuable, but don't let it cloud your judgment. Lean into your beginner's mind. See things with a fresh perspective. Keep a long-term focus to even out the short-term ups and downs. Humans are terrible at predicting the future, so spend most of your time focusing on today, tomorrow, and the next ninety days.

We all live between an irrational level of fear and an illusion of control.

I still have fear when I launch a new business. That's just part of the path and one of the many reasons it feels so rewarding when it works. But sometimes things don't work out for reasons beyond your control. Maybe it wasn't the right time. It happens to all of us. That's why experimenting is so important.

You can always go back to a full-time job or working for someone else if things don't work out. But at least you won't look back with regret on what you wished you had done. I guarantee that no matter what happens on your entrepreneurship journey, you'll learn a lot and grow in ways you never could have imagined. The benefits of the pursuit far outweigh doing nothing. Rewards come to those who take risks.

Remember the 7 Truths:

1. Freedom comes from limits, not unlimited choices.

2. Trust what you feel before what you think.

3. Double down on your strengths instead of fixing your weaknesses.

4. Incentives drive everything.

5. Master one thing, then diversify for resilience.

6. Cooperation is more powerful than competition.

7. Momentum is the most powerful force in business.

I've covered a lot in this book, but take only what you need. You can choose what being an entrepreneur means. What money means to you. There are no right answers to any of this, just the right ones for you. Entrepreneurship can be lonely, but it doesn't have to be. Bring others along on your journey. Give, expecting nothing in return. Help others. Root for them. Return favors. Collaborate. Be open. Be kind. Be honest. Be a giver. Share everything you've learned with others.

There is more than enough for everyone.

You will continue to change, as will your relationship with time and money. The trade-offs you're willing to make today you might not want to make in the future. Don't forget to check in with yourself to see how far you've come and who you've become. Don't compare yourself to others. But learn from them. Define success for yourself. Care. But don't take it all too seriously. Make sure you take advantage of the freedom you already have.

Energy compounds, so surround yourself with people who give you energy, not those who deplete it. Think about why you want more money. Is it worth trading your time? Maybe you've already won the game? Take care of your health. Rest. Spend more time with your family and friends. You'll never regret it.

Everything is a trade-off for something else. Find your limits. Find your space of freedom.

Don't accept the status quo. Don't drift. If you're holding on too tightly, maybe you should be letting go. Do what makes you feel alive. Lean into your story. Keep making decisions. Open to the world expecting nothing. Let go of who you think you are and see what happens.

Everything you seek is already within you. Spend more time going inside. That's where the good stuff is. Time is a created thing. Now, go. Create. Build something.

There is no more important work than this. This is your life.

I wish you much success and peace on your journey.

Reach Me: Email me at grant@grantsabatier.com (yes, that's my actual email).

If you want to dive deeper on any of these topics, accelerate your financial independence journey, or get support, check out https://grantsabatier.com/community.

If you want to support my bookstore, Clintonville Books, you can buy any book you want through us, and have it shipped directly to your house, at https://clintonvillebooks.com.

If you enjoyed this book, the best way to support my work and help it reach others is to leave a review on your favorite platform (Amazon and Goodreads are popular ones).

Thank you for your support.

ACKNOWLEDGMENTS

Writing a book into being is magic; I could not do this alone, nor would I want to. This second time around, I had a baby in the middle of it, and the Avery/Penguin Random House team was generous in giving me extra time. This support meant everything.

Thank you to Caroline Sutton, who acquired this book, but left Penguin during the writing, so Lauren Appleton, with the help of Ashley Alliano, stepped in without missing a beat. I'm grateful to you both for your feedback and believing in this project.

To Brooke Carey for agreeing to write another book with me. I can't imagine writing books without you. Your curiosity, openness, and care make this possible.

To my agent, Faye Atchison, thank you for your kind words, design sense, and support.

To Cody Berman, Jordan Grumet, Rob Phelan, Logan Leckie, and Trevor Seret for your feedback.

To Travis Hornsby, Harry Campbell, Ashley Hamilton, and Julie Berlinger for sharing your stories.

To my MMG crew, Matt and Meghan Bundrick, Andrea and David Tolar. I love building with you.

To Vicki Robin for your continued mentorship, guidance, and friendship.

To my mom and dad, who always supported my creativity and continue to support me on this journey.

To my partner, Erin, thank you for wisdom, heart, and our daughter. I love our family and our life.

Last but not least, I want to thank my readers all over the world. Everything you've shared with me makes life so beautiful.

APPENDIX: FURTHER READING

These are some books that have changed my life or greatly influenced my entrepreneur journey.

ENTREPRENEURSHIP

Blue Ocean Strategy—W. Chan Kim and Renée Mauborgne

The 4-Hour Workweek—Tim Ferriss

Traction—Gino Wickman

12 Months to $1 Million—Ryan Daniel Moran

The Lean Startup—Eric Ries

Company of One—Paul Jarvis

The Minimalist Entrepreneur—Sahil Lavingia

The $100 Startup—Chris Guillebeau

The Personal MBA—Josh Kaufman

Rework—Jason Fried and David Heinemeier Hansson

The E-Myth Revisited—Michael E. Gerber

The Millionaire Fastlane—MJ DeMarco

80/20 Sales and Marketing—Perry Marshall

Competitive Strategy—Michael E. Porter

What It Takes—Stephen A. Schwarzman

Am I Being Too Subtle?—Sam Zell

I Love Capitalism!—Ken Langone

Built to Sell—John Warrillow

Buy Then Build—Walker Deibel

One from Many—Dee Hock
Invest and Wander: The Collected Writings of Jeff Bezos
The Innovator's Dilemma—Clayton M. Christensen
Small Giants—Bo Burlingham
Lost and Founder—Rand Fishkin

INVESTING

The Education of a Value Investor—Guy Spier
The Dhandho Investor—Mohnish Pabrai
Richer, Wiser, Happier—William Green
The Essays of Warren Buffett—Lawrence A. Cunningham, compiler
Poor Charlie's Almanack—Charles T. Munger
The Bogleheads' Guide to Investing—Taylor Larimore, Mel Lindauer, and Michael LeBoeuf
Common Sense on Mutual Funds—John C. Bogle
The Four Pillars of Investing—William Bernstein
The Intelligent Investor—Benjamin Graham
The Only Investment Guide You'll Ever Need—Andrew Tobias

REAL ESTATE INVESTING

The Millionaire Real Estate Investor—Gary Keller with Dave Jenks and Jay Papasan
The Book on Rental Property Investing—Brandon Turner
Retire Early with Real Estate—Chad Carson
What Every Real Estate Investor Needs to Know about Cash Flow—Frank Gallinelli

LIFE

In Love with the World—Yongey Mingyur Rinpoche
The Art of Living—Thich Nhat Hanh
When Breath Becomes Air—Paul Kalanithi
Devatma Shakti (Kundalini) Divine Power—Swami Vishnu Tirtha
Start Where You Are—Pema Chödrön
Going to Pieces without Falling Apart—Mark Epstein
The Scripture of the Golden Eternity—Jack Kerouac
The Top Five Regrets of the Dying—Bronni Ware

The Wisdom of Insecurity—Alan Watts

Man's Search for Meaning—Viktor E. Frankl

PERSONAL FINANCE / FINANCIAL INDEPENDENCE

Your Money or Your Life—Vicki Robin and Joe Dominguez

The Millionaire Next Door—Thomas J. Stanley and William D. Danko

Set for Life—Scott Trench

I Will Teach You to Be Rich—Ramit Sethi

The Automatic Millionaire—David Bach

The Simple Path to Wealth—JL Collins

NOTES

Chapter 1: It's Never Been Easier or More Essential to Become an Entrepreneur

5 **According to Gallup's report:** Gallup, "State of the Global Workplace 2024 Report," https://www.gallup.com/workplace/349484/state-of-the-global -workplace.aspx.

6 **The freedom and flexibility to do what you want:** Obschonka, M., et al., "Job Burnout and Work Engagement in Entrepreneurs: How the Psychological Utility of Entrepreneurship Drives Healthy Engagement," *Journal of Business Venturing* 38, no. 2 (2023): https://doi.org/10.1016/j.jbusvent .2022.106272.

8 **They're normal human beings:** Rigby, Rhymer, "Psychology of Wealth: Do the New Rich Not Care about Losing Money?," *Financial Times*, May 5, 2019, https://www.ft.com/content/9569eaaa-4009-11e9-9499-290979c 9807a.

Chapter 3: Align Your Passions and Skills with a Mission
to Find the Perfect Idea

53 **According to eMarketer and *Business Insider*:** Yuen, Meaghan, "US Retail ECommerce Sales Will See Increasing Growth through 2027," eMarketer, August 8, 2023, https://www.insiderintelligence.com/content/us-retail -ecommerce-sales-growth-2027.

Chapter 5: Share Your Story, Build a Brand, and Leverage Your Platform

103 **The influencer economy is worth $104 billion:** Pop-Andonov, Neda, "Creator Economy Market Size: Key Statistics in 2022," Influencers.club, June 14, 2022, https://influencers.club/2022/06/14/creator-economy-market-size;

Florida, Richard, "The Creator Economy Is the Future of the Economy," *Fast Company*, November 18, 2022, https://www.fastcompany.com/908 12387/the-creator-economy-is-the-future-of-the-economy.

103 **Setting aside the fact that most online creators:** Roughly half earn less than $50,000 a year, and when you consider the time-money trade-off necessary to engage an online fan base, even that equates to less than minimum wage; 60 percent of creators say they engage with followers "all the time" and are "constantly responding to messages and comments," according to: NeoReach, "Creator Earnings Report Breakdown: Where Are We in the Creator Economy?," https://neoreach.com/creator-earnings/#Creators _Earning_Power.

108 **As of this writing, Google is the most popular search engine:** Delouya, Samantha, "Nearly Half of Gen Z Is Using TikTok and Instagram for Search Instead of Google, According to Google's Own Data," *Business Insider*, July 13, 2022, https://www.businessinsider.com/nearly-half-genz-use-tiktok -instagram-over-google-search-2022-7.

Chapter 7: Create Your Community and a Sustainable Customer Base

168 **Beyond friends and family:** Nielson, "Consumer Trust in Online, Social and Mobile Advertising Grows," April 2012, https://www.nielsen.com /insights/2012/consumer-trust-in-online-social-and-mobile-advertising -grows.

Chapter 10: Double Down on What Works to Accelerate Growth

241 **Retaining existing customers is also significantly cheaper:** Reichheld, Fred, "Prescription for Cutting Costs," Bain & Company, https://media.bain .com/Images/BB_Prescription_cutting_costs.pdf; Gallo, Amy, "The Value of Keeping the Right Customers," *Harvard Business Review*, October 29, 2014, https://hbr.org/2014/10/the-value-of-keeping-the-right-customers.

Chapter 12: Set Yourself Up to Sell (Even If You Don't Want to Sell)

289 **Seventy to 90 percent of acquisitions fail:** Kenny, Graham, "Don't Make This Common M&A Mistake," *Harvard Business Review*, March 16, 2020, https://hbr.org/2020/03/dont-make-this-common-ma-mistake.

Chapter 13: Establish a Holding Company to Grow Your Empire

330 **Or real estate development stocks:** Damodaran, Aswath, "PE Ratio by Sector (US)," NYU Stern, January 2024, https://pages.stern.nyu.edu/~adamodar /New_Home_Page/datafile/pedata.html.

331   **Investment in Private Company via Private Equity:** "Private Investment Benchmarks," Cambridge Associates, https://www.cambridgeassociates.com /private-investment-benchmarks.

331   **Residential Real Estate:** Baldridge, Rebecca, "What Is Real Estate Return on Investment (ROI)?," *Forbes*, August 21, 2023, https://www.forbes .com/advisor/investing/roi-on-real-estate-investment.

Chapter 14: How to Identify Acquisition Opportunities

335   **Home Services:** Wilson, John, *Owned and Operated* newsletter, May 16, 2022.

346   **One of the reasons See's Candies:** Mohamed, Theron, "Warren Buffett's Favorite Business Is a Little Chocolate Maker with an 8000% Return. Here Are 5 Reasons Why He Loves See's Candies," *Business Insider*, July 12, 2019, https://markets.businessinsider.com/news/stocks/warren-buffett -berkshire-hathaway-dream-business-is-sees-candies-2019-7-102 9916323#quality-people-4.

354   **according to the *Harvard Business Review*:** Kenny, Graham, "Don't Make This Common M&A Mistake," *Harvard Business Review*, March 16, 2020, https://hbr.org/2020/03/dont-make-this-common-ma-mistake.

INDEX

ABOUT THE AUTHOR

Grant Sabatier is an entrepreneur, investor, and author of the international bestseller *Financial Freedom: A Proven Path to All the Money You Will Ever Need*, which has been translated into fifteen languages. The book is popular around the world and teaches readers how to prioritize time over money, make more money, and make the most of this one life.

He is also the creator of Millennial Money, which was acquired by the Motley Fool and was later reacquired by Grant through his holding company MMG Media Group. As an active investor in over fifty private companies, he's always on the hunt for new acquisitions and opportunities. In addition to his online businesses, Grant is also the owner of Clintonville Books, a new, used, and rare bookshop in Columbus, Ohio.

Grant's story and writing have been featured in over four hundred international media outlets, including the *New York Times*, *Wall Street Journal*, *Washington Post*, BBC, NPR, CNBC, *Sydney Morning Herald*, *Business Insider*, *Marketwatch*, and many others. He's also been a featured guest on *ABC Nightline*, the *Rachael Ray* show, and NPR's *Here and Now*.

To learn more, visit https://grantsabatier.com.